D1031738

# RUSSIA AND THE WORLD

*Also by Leo Cooper*

* POLITICAL ECONOMY OF SOVIET MILITARY POWER

POWER AND POLITICS IN THE SOVIET UNION

* SOVIET REFORMS AND BEYOND

STAKHANOVITES – AND OTHERS: The Story of a Worker in the Soviet Union, 1939–1946

* *From the same publishers*

# Russia and the World

## New State-of-Play on the International Stage

Leo Cooper
*Senior Research Associate*
*Contemporary Europe Research Centre*
*and*
*Centre for Russian and Euro-Asian Studies*
*both at University of Melbourne, Australia*

Foreword by Leslie Holmes

First published in Great Britain 1999 by
**MACMILLAN PRESS LTD**
Houndmills, Basingstoke, Hampshire RG21 6XS and London
Companies and representatives throughout the world

A catalogue record for this book is available from the British Library.

ISBN 0–333–72067–9

---

First published in the United States of America 1999 by
**ST. MARTIN'S PRESS, INC.,**
Scholarly and Reference Division,
175 Fifth Avenue, New York, N.Y. 10010

ISBN 0–312–21569–X

Library of Congress Cataloging-in-Publication Data
Cooper, Leo, 1922–
Russia and the world : new state-of-play on the international
stage / Leo Cooper ; foreword by Leslie Holmes.
p.   cm.
Includes bibliographical references and index.
ISBN 0–312–21569–X (cloth)
1. Russia (Federation)—Foreign relations.   I. Title.
DK510.764.C66   1998
327.47—dc21                                    98–21077
                                               CIP

---

This book is printed on paper suitable for recycling and made from fully managed and
sustained forest sources.

10   9   8   7   6   5   4   3   2   1
08   07   06   05   04   03   02   01   00   99

Printed and bound in Great Britain by
Antony Rowe Ltd, Chippenham, Wiltshire

# Contents

# List of Tables

# Foreword

Between 1989 and 1991, communist power in Central and Eastern Europe and the USSR collapsed; a revolution had taken place. The domestic revolutions were soon followed by revolutions in international relations; with the collapse of the Warsaw Treaty Organisation and the Council for Mutual Economic Assistance, and the ending of the Cold War, an era had closed. Initially, many in both East and West were ecstatic about all these changes, with analysts and politicians alike talking of a 'New World Order' and even 'the end of history'. But the euphoria was short-lived, and soon the talk was of a new world disorder and the clash of civilisations.

Of particular interest in this issue of the collapse of communism and the radical change in international relations is the demise of the USSR and the role played in the 1990s by its most significant successor state, Russia. All post-communist states have the legacy of communist rule to overcome; but most have found this just a little easier than Russia because of the bonding effects in formerly communist states that feel they are now more genuinely sovereign than before, or in formerly federal units that have recently become sovereign states in their own right. In contrast, Russia was the heart of a centuries-old empire, and the home of the first socialist revolution and Leninism. The simultaneous meltdown of communist power and the Soviet empire led to mixed reactions within Russia; while many initially welcomed the former, few were pleased about the latter. These mixed reactions have led to an identity crisis and increasing polarisation in Russia in the 1990s, with groups and individuals blaming each other for the loss of empire. Such recriminations mean that the development of a culture of compromise is proving even more difficult to achieve in Russia than in many other post-communist states. This in turn makes the democratisation process more difficult, and hence increases the possibilities of an extremist coming to power in Russia. Were such a person to become the leader, he – and it would almost certainly be a man – would seek to resurrect at least some of Russia's former glory, as part of the attempt to overcome Russians' current identity problems. Since this might well involve Russian expansionism, the implications for international relations would be profound. Russia has already come close to such a scenario in the 1990s, with the earlier popularity of Vladimir Zhirinovskii, and the strong performance of Gennadii Zyuganov in the 1996 presidential elections. So far, the existence of strong, more democratically inclined and forward-looking politicians such as Boris Yeltsin has helped to prevent such a development. While most reasonably-minded people around the world hope that such politicians will continue to dominate Russian politics, nothing can be taken for granted in the confusion and uncertainty of contemporary Russian politics.

If it is remembered that Russia still possesses a substantial nuclear arsenal, the potential significance of domestic Russian politics for international relations comes even more sharply into focus. It is this significance that makes Leo Cooper's latest book so important and timely. Dr Cooper starts by providing a history of the USSR and its collapse, as a way of setting the scene for the contemporary domestic conflicts. He then considers the all-important role of the military, and the dangers of contemporary Russian military policy. He highlights the problems of the Russian economy, but also the fact that one of the very few issues about which most Russians agree is that they resent excessive interference by outsiders. In this context, of even greater concern to most Russians than what they perceive to be IMF meddling in their internal affairs are the eastward moves of NATO. The unifying and bonding effect of NATO expansion on Russian culture, and its ramifications for global politics, is justifiably one of Dr Cooper's principal foci in this study, as he examines the factors leading to increasing nationalism – the rise of 'the Russian Idea' – in recent years.

Throughout this book, Leo Cooper builds on his earlier work on the Russian military, economy, culture and politics, producing a masterful synthesis that locates what is happening inside today's Russia within the larger international context. As ever, an important part of his approach is the attempt to look at both Russian domestic politics and the world beyond Russia through numerous Russian eyes, while also being very aware of Western interpretations. The comprehensiveness of the approach, the sensitivity to different perspectives, and the importance to us all of the subject matter make this book a significant contribution to the literature, and of relevance to anyone with an interest in the big questions of contemporary world politics.

LESLIE HOLMES
*University of Melbourne*

# 1 The Setting of the Stage: an Introduction

The dramatic changes that have taken place in the former Soviet Union since the collapse of communism and the disintegration of the USSR have created a new geo-political reality not only within the former communist bloc, but a new international environment and a new set of international relations. Internal as well as external factors usually determine the course of foreign policy of any country – in this respect Russia is no exeption – but in Russia, there are also other factors which, in contrast to a Western state, exert strong influence upon Russia's relations with the outside world.

One of the more significant determinants of Russia's foreign policy is the economy. Since the demise of the centralised command economy, Russia has undertaken many steps aimed at transforming her economic system into a market-oriented one. The reforms were justified by the Russian leadership on one major ground – to make the economy more efficient, thereby improving the general standard of living, which has been declining during the Brezhnev era of 'stagnation'. This objective is also to be achieved by the integration of the Russian economy into the world economic system. It was generally conceded that Soviet isolationism resulted in Russia falling behind Western economic progress – consequently leading to an economic decline and falling standard of living.

The end of the Cold War and of the state of confrontation between the two superpowers were seen by most observers as a harbinger of a peaceful world, at least within the area of the former East–West conflict. However, the economic and political reforms in Russia, while promising in the long run an improvement in the country's conditions, have also resulted in an atmosphere of scepticism due to the inability of the Russian government to implement some of the reforms and to the apparent failure to improve the lot of the average citizen. The process of reforms, therefore, while presenting opportunities for economic progress as well as prospects for a durable peace between East and West, also contain some features which have the potential to cause internal instability in Russia and strained relations between Russia and the West.

1

The general euphoria which came as a result of the collapse of communism and the disintegration of the USSR – a former Western objective – has subsided and given way to a more realistic appraisal of the situation in Russia. The economic and political reforms became the subject of closer scrutiny by Western politicians and analysts who began to look at the reforms in the context of Western economies and democratic traditions. Increasingly, Western assistance has become dependent on economic reforms along the lines suggested by the World Bank and the IMF, and on the democratisation of Russia. According to one Russian politician: 'voices have been heard recently in the US, at the Congress in the first place, calling for a rollback of US aid to Russia. The pretexts range from accusations of inefficiency of the assistance programmes to the desire to penalise Russia in this way' (Rybkin, 1995, p. 32).

The international situation has also undergone significant changes. During the Cold War period, the United States and the Soviet Union were the major players on the world stage. They were adversaries due to ideological differences, but today's world politics are said to be determined by non-ideological factors. A number of clashes of an economic nature have already taken place between Russia and the US. The Russian sale of cryogenic missile technologies to India, arms deliveries to China, the sale of a nuclear reactor to Iran and the exclusion of Russia from the nuclear deal with North Korea, are but a few examples of emerging problems between the superpowers.

Furthermore, the kind of democracy which is emerging in Russia can be seen as a blend of democracy and authoritarian rule. Democracy in Russia is still in its infancy despite the freedoms now available to the Russian people. Many political and economic decisions are still being adopted by decrees rather than by consultation between the government and the parliament. The Russian constitution gives the President extensive powers to plan and carry out domestic and foreign policies.

The Russian parliament, however, is gradually increasing its influence, and elements of the former regime who advocate a nationalistic approach to domestic and foreign policies, have become much more vocal. The Duma, in its expression of support for the restoration of the Soviet Union, has been sending ominous signals to the West. Most political blocs in the Duma, while rejecting isolationism, are in favour of Russia retaining its military potential and its position as a world power. They oppose NATO's plans to expand eastward. In the words of the Chairman of the Duma: 'some Western military and political figures are prone to talk lightly, and I would say irresponsibly, about nuclear weapons being deployed close to Russia's borders.' There are voices in Russia that speak of a 'cold peace' (Vasilchuk, 1995).

Political factors are tightly interwoven with the state of the Russian economy. The economic situation in Russia is, therefore, determining not only the stability of the country, but its relations with the West as well. As one Russian observer noted: 'you cannot expand your influence unless you clean up the mess in your own house and put your relations with your neighbours on a partnership footing' (Rybkin, 1995, p. 29).

Despite the reforms aimed at transforming Russia into a market economy, Russia desperately needs Western capital and foreign investment. However, the IMF and the World Bank are reluctant to meet Russia's needs and impose a number of conditions. Foreign investment, on the other hand, is dependent upon Russia's internal stability and on the introduction of appropriate legislation.

The dilemma that the West faces is whether to grant maximum economic aid to Russia regardless of the course of economic and political reforms, thereby running the risk of inefficient use of resources, or to withhold such aid until all the reforms are in place, which in turn may contribute to the worsening of the economic situation and lead to internal instability. Conversely, whoever holds the position of the president of Russia is facing the choice between a continuation of reforms and improved relations with the West, or the adoption of a more nationalistic stance which would certainly lead to Russia's isolation.

There is also an additional factor which has so far attracted little attention in the West. The collapse of communism created an ideological vacuum, which the Russian society desperately tries to fill. It is a search for an ideology that would rally the Russian nation and, according to some Russian political and social commentators, would provide the Russians with a sense of national unity. This is known in Russia as the 'Russian Idea'. The concept of a Russian idea is interpreted by some Russians as patriotism, which often borders on extreme nationalism. Such interpretation of the Russian idea has lately begun to exert its influence on Russia's foreign policy.

It is this latter factor that makes Russia different from a Western country. Russian society is endowed with a higher degree of spirituality than its Western counterparts. This may be defined as a kind of romanticism, which is perhaps an anachronism at the end of the twentieth century, but Russian society still lives to a large extent in the past. It is practically impossible to offer a political analysis of contemporary Russia without reference to her early history and that of the more recent Soviet period. The objective of this study is to analyse the various factors that determine East–West relations. It adopts a composite view that embraces all the facets affecting the present transitional period. It examines the economic policies adopted by the Russian government in its search for the most appropriate way of transforming the economic and political system. It also considers non-economic and non-political factors that determine Russia's relations with the West – that is, her foreign policy. The study adopts an unconventional approach by also considering non-economic and non-political factors that are instrumental in shaping Russia's policies.

One of the non-economic factors is the concept of a national ideology. While the term national ideology bears little, if any, similarity with communist ideas, it, nevertheless, seems to indicate a continuation rather than a break with old traditions. The concept of a national ideology or as it is known – the Russian idea – is taken very seriously in Russia, although it is being interpreted in ways that conform to the political colouring of a particular Russian politician. We shall argue that Russia's attitudes to the outside world cannot be scrutinised by applying exclusively Western criteria.

The study begins with a brief survey of Soviet foreign policy during the post-revolutionary period when the USSR in its quest for economic self-sufficiency became politically isolated on the international arena. It analyses the role of ideology in Soviet foreign policy and examines the about-face of Soviet foreign policy when faced with a new international situation. It then proceeds to an analysis of the Cold War, détente and the 'New Thinking' as a prelude to the emergence of a new Russia. The survey serves as a background to the main subject of the book, which is an analysis of Russia's contemporary policies.

This is followed by an examination of the international scene subsequent to the collapse of the Soviet Union as a state and of communism as a leading ideology in Russia. It emphasises the confusion that arose as a result of the unexpected turn of events, not only in the West but also within Russia itself. The cause of the collapse of the Soviet Union is still the subject of discussions among political scientists, and various theories ranging from the rational to the absurd are being offered. Chapter 3 analyses the factors that led to the disintegration of the USSR and the emergence of Russia as an independent state.

The study then proceeds with an analysis of the factors that determine Russia's relations with the world. It devotes much attention to the role of military power, and Russia's military policy following the end of the Cold War. Closely linked to the military policy is the state of the Russian economy, which must allocate resources for the maintenance of its military power. The study examines the operation and performance of the Russian economy within the context of Russia's attempts at integration into the world economy. An important factor in Russia's economic performance is foreign trade. A question frequently asked by Russian economists is whether Russia is to become the supplier of raw materials to the West and an importer of finished goods, or will Russia be able to produce goods suitable for exporting to the West instead of to its former partners and now neighbours? In this respect, the study analyses the Western perception of Russia as a potential competitor on the world market.

Then follows an analysis of Russia's present-day foreign policy(ies). Russia's relations with specific states and regions is discussed, particularly the question of the sometimes conflicting interests of Russia and the West. An important issue affecting Russia's attitude toward the West is NATO's enlargement. NATO's expansion was met with strong opposition from the Russian government and seems to gain overwhelming support within the Russian population. Despite Russia's apparent acquiescence to the expansion, the relations between Russia and the United States – the main promoter of the expansion – are assuming a potentially dangerous character.

The following chapter deals with the important issue of the 'Russian idea'. It is a search for an ideology that would unite the Russian nation and provide the people with an identity which it had lost during the communist rule – an ideology that would replace the legacy of the past 70 years. The search represents, at the same time, another aspect of the old conflict between Westernisers and Slavophiles. It is closely linked with the general perception of Russia's place on the world stage. We shall argue that this question has serious implications for US–Russia relations and is crucial for the understanding of Russia as a country with a unique past and culture.

The concluding chapter brings together all the various factors which play a role in the determination of Russia's foreign policy. It emphasises the importance of the mutual perceptions of the two major players on the international stage and considers the ramification of such perceptions for global stability.

# 2 From the Russian to the Soviet Empire, 1917–91

Writing about Russia used to be like writing about a 'mystery wrapped in an enigma', but even today, although the enigma has been unwrapped, the mystery still remains. The situation in that country is unclear and complicated. Communism as a state ideology has collapsed together with that state, and Russia appears to be adopting a system of liberal democracy. However, many Russian and Western analysts believe that the kind of democracy that will finally emerge in Russia will be quite unlike the Western system of government. A question which not only Russian academics and political observers but also Western politicians are asking themselves is: where is Russia heading today?

Some analysts offer an answer to this question based on economic factors. They see Russia's present problems as a result of economic mismanagement and her future development closely linked to implementation of economic reforms. A great number of observers, however, probe much deeper and adopt a view which takes into account not only the present situation but includes references to Russia's past. They assert that for a broader understanding of contemporary Russia it is necessary to delve into her origins and into the nature of the Russian Empire from which today's Russia, right through the Soviet period, has emerged (Reshetar, 1974, p. 1).

From an historical perspective it can be seen that Russia's existence as a state has often been determined by major events such as invasions from the east and the west, and due to her geographical location – distance from major sources of world civilisation – Russia found herself on the periphery of Europe. In fact some historians see Russia as a particular civilisation as in the cases of Rome, Byzantium, India or China (Sakharov, 1996).

According to Sakharov, a contemporary Russian historian, Russia, since the middle of the twentieth century, has entered a period of transition from a medieval form of society into modern, civilised forms of existence. Russia is simply undergoing with significant delay, the same evolutionary phases as other developed countries. At present, Russia is moving toward the future through a dramatic collision with old values. A synthesis between Western and Soviet traditions is taking place (loc. cit.). The Russian philosopher Nicolas Berdyaev, saw the Russians as a contradictory people characterised by dualism which had resulted from long historical experience – a conflict between Eastern and Western cultural influence – and the inability of the Russians to identify themselves with either. He defined the Russians as a 'polarised people to the highest degree, a combination of opposites' (Berdyayev, 1946, p. 5). There were attempts by Russia to adopt Western values, but the Russians are not and could not become a Western people, according to Berdyaev. He saw Russian communism as having national roots and regarded Leninism as a peculiar Russian phenomenon (Berdyayev, 1948).

An important factor in shaping the character of the Russian people was the size of the country. 'The Russian people fell victim to the immensity of its territory', and having acquired the world's largest empire, it had to accept a despotic regime in order to retain and organise its vast territorial possessions (Berdyayev, 1946, p. 9). The history of the Russian empire is, therefore, a history of conquest and expansion. A fact rarely mentioned is that the status of Russia as a superpower and its position as equal among the great powers has not just been achieved since the Second World War, but since the beginning of the eighteenth century following a long struggle against foreign invaders (Cooper, 1989, p. 22).

After the Revolution of 1917, the Soviet regime managed to retain most of the vast empire of the tsar, except Poland, Finland, the Baltic states and Bessarabia. Some years later, in September 1939, the USSR regained most of the territories which were the domain of the Russian empire before the Revolution. It annexed western Ukraine and western Belorussia, which had been part of Poland, and in 1940 it succeeded in incorporating the three Baltic states into the Soviet Union. It has also regained part of its Finnish territory after a short and bloody war. In 1945 Russia acquired the northern half of east Prussia, including the German city of Königsberg (renamed Kaliningrad), and the Kuril islands from Japan. The history of Russian expansionism is thus an important factor in the analysis of contemporary Russia. Russia's expansion continued over more than four centuries and was constant in its nature although it suffered certain reversals. No single factor can be attributed to the steady process of expansion, but the search for security has been cited as an important one. Subsequent Soviet foreign policy has been justified on account of state security. Despite the collapse of the Soviet Union and the loss of most of the territories of the former empire, the idea of a new Russian Empire is still alive today as will be indicated in this study.


## RUSSIA AND WORLD REVOLUTION

One of the most important periods in Russian history which is crucial to the understanding of the nature of contemporary Russian politics, is that which spans the revolutionary years and those following immediately after. It was during those years that the economic and political structures of the Soviet state emerged. From its inception, the driving force of the new socialist state was communist ideology and there were attempts at putting ideological doctrines into immediate practical effect. In the area of state power, the Bolsheviks had no previous experience neither could they apply classical Marxist theory which apart from the rather vague concept of 'dictatorship of the proletariat', did not offer any guide to the organisation of a socialist state. Prior to the Revolution, the nature of the state once the Tsar was overthrown, had been seen by the then Social-Democrats as a democratic republic, where large land-holdings would be confiscated and an eight-hour day introduced. Those rather modest aims were necessary in view of Russia's backwardness and the fact that a bourgeois revolution had not yet taken place (*Komunisticheskaya partia*, 1953, p. 324). Even as late as April 1917 the Bolsheviks contemplated a relatively long period of socialisation because '. . . the Russian proletariat acting in one of the most backward countries of Europe, among a mass of small-peasantry, cannot aim for the immediate realisation of socialist transformation' (ibid., p. 351). Another reason was the uncertainty about the degree of support the Bolsheviks could expect. They thought that '. . . it is necessary to proceed with utmost care in order to convince the overwhelming majority of the population of the correctness of the policy' (ibid., p. 352).

On the level of the Party, the question of organisational structure presented fewer difficulties because of a revolutionary tradition, and thanks to Lenin who, already before the Revolution, formulated a blue-print of the party organisation as a vanguard of the proletariat (Lenin, passim.). He also introduced the principle of democratic centralism which, in the long run, contributed to the domination of the Party over the state apparatus and secured the self-perpetuation of its leading role by virtually eliminating the possibility of the emergence of an effective opposition.

From an historical perspective it can be seen that power, that is absolute power, is rooted in Russian psychology. Historically and traditionally, the Russians have always required authority and the power of the state had always been approved by the population. The tsar was accepted as the divine ruler not on account of his special abilities, but of the power he represented. The sources of Soviet totalitarianism lie in Russian history.

A major feature of the pre-revolutionary political culture, was the Byzantine-Russian absolutist heritage, some elements of which could be observed all along Russia's history. It was Russia's cultural and political heritage that made Russia and its society so different from the West. Russia's history, culture and traditions have always contributed, and to some extent still do, to the retention of national peculiarities which even today assume some significance. Former features of Russian character such as apathy, submissiveness to authority and a large degree of conformity are noticeable even today.

The system of domination, which was a feature of tsarist Russia, became also a powerful factor after the victory of the Bolsheviks. The Bolsheviks have grasped the significance of autocratic rule over the population and whether consciously or unconsciously began to apply it in practice. There was no contradiction between ideology and practical policies. The emergence of absolute rule by the Party and subsequently by Stalin, may not have been an historical aberration, but a logical outcome of Russia's cultural heritage.

However, confrontation with reality has immediately created several problems that necessitated the accommodation of ideological theory with practical policies. The way in which the problems were solved had, to some degree, determined the course of future actions and responses to given situations by the Soviet government. The Soviet leaders had to adjust to a reality which did not conform to their earlier expectations. It created a series of conflicts and required accommodation and concessions between pragmatism and ideology (Brzezinski, 1973, p. 161). The Party had to resolve a number of contradictions which arose on the ideological level and which were in conflict with the theory. It involved, in the first place, relations with the outside world within the context of the theory of world revolution.

Despite the 'treachery' of European Social Democracy in supporting fierce nationalism at the outbreak of the First World War, there was a firm belief among the Russian revolutionaries that as a result of the example of the Russian proletariat, the working classes of the major industrialised countries in Europe would overthrow the 'imperialist governments'. It was thought that what happened in Russia '. . . confirms the prediction of the Basle Manifesto of 1912 about the inevitability of proletarian revolution. The Russian revolution is only the first stage of the first of proletarian revolutions' (*Kommunisticheskaya partia*, p. 350). There were, nonetheless, fears that in the absence of a European-wide revolution, the fate of the new regime might be in jeopardy. The Seventh Congress of the Party in March 1918 saw '. . . the best hope of a guarantee . . . [for] the victorious socialist revolution in Russia, only in her transformation into an international workers revolution'. It also saw the '. . . socialist Russian proletariat . . . giving . . . with all its strength and with all means at its disposal, brotherly support to the revolutionary proletariat of all countries' (ibid., p. 405).

One of the first political actions undertaken by the Bolsheviks after they came to power was a call to end the war. The 'Decree on Peace' was passed by the second all-Russian Congress of Workers', Soldiers' and Peasants' deputies in November 1917. The call and the Decree were closely linked to the expectation that a revolutionary movement of the entire European proletariat would rise against their governments and join Russia in the revolutionary struggle. This expectation did not materialise.

## STATE INTEREST AND IDEOLOGY

With the realisation that world revolution was still far away, came the practical problem of the war with Germany and the first test of the ideology at Brest-Litovsk where a peace treaty was signed on 15 October 1917. Among the conditions of the Treaty was an agreement that '. . . the contracting parties will refrain from agitation or propaganda against the government or public and military institutions of the other party . . . Russia is to put an end to all agitation or propaganda against the government or the public institutions of the Ukraine Republic' (Degras, p. 17).

This did not prevent, only a few days later, the People's Commissariat for Foreign Affairs sending an appeal to the 'toiling, oppressed and exhausted peoples of Europe . . .' and assuring them that the Soviet government would '. . . use all the means at its disposal to help the working class in all lands to overthrow the rule of capital and to seize political power' (ibid., p. 19). On 26 December 1917, the Council of Peoples Commissariat issued a decree appropriating two million roubles for the international revolutionary movement. Bukharin proposed a propaganda and revolutionary offensive that would destroy Germany from inside. But it soon became obvious that there would be no revolution in Germany. Attempts at seizing power in Germany in March 1921 and in October 1923 failed, as did attempts in Bulgaria in 1923 and in Estonia during December 1924. They also failed in China in 1927 when Chiang Kai-shek moved to crush the Chinese communist party.

Lenin, when he realised that a revolution was not around the corner, suggested a modified and more realistic interpretation of the revolutionary situation in Europe. He declared that one must not assume that the Russian revolution is a starting point in a general revolution in Europe, and he denied that the Bolsheviks relied on a European revolution breaking out at a definitive date (Lenin, 1965, pp. 289–90). 'It was impossible', according to Lenin, 'to accurately estimate when a revolution is likely to occur, but its coming is beyond doubt, and this certainty has a scientific basis.' Lenin rejected the argument that Brest-Litovsk was an 'imperialist deal' and contrary to the principles of proletarian internationalism. 'We never gave any pledge to start a revolutionary war without taking into account how far it is possible to wage it at any given moment . . .'. (Degras, p. 37).

Another dilemma the Soviets had to face was linked to the economy. Economic difficulties and food shortages, caused by the resistance of the peasants to government measures, forced the leadership to change its approach to economic problems from a purely Marxist to a more pragmatic one. This was the key element of NEP, which in the view of ardent ideologues was equivalent to capitalist restoration. Lenin, on the other hand, defended the new policy on the ground that it was absolutely necessary to do so in order 'that we may retain political power' (Hill, 1972, p. 146).

A number of other problems were solved by taking a pragmatic rather than ideological approach. The granting of concessions to foreign firms was justified by Lenin as a way to get needed means of production. But at the same time '. . . to exploit the contradictions and antagonisms between . . . the system of capitalist states, inciting them one against the other ... but as soon as we are strong enough to fight the whole of capitalism, we shall at once take it by the neck' (Degras, p. 222).

As subsequent events have shown, there was a willingness, forced by circumstances, to compromise and adopt policies that were quite often contrary to ideological principles. The Bolsheviks realised from the outset that strict adherence to ideological tenets would become increasingly difficult and they created a device to circumvent any contradictions that might arise as a result of any future actions by foreign and Soviet governments. The Seventh Congress of the Party in March 1918 decided '... to change the programme of the Party, to revise the theoretical part or to complete it with a more precise definition of the characteristics of imperialism and the just begun period of international revolution ... The change of the political part of our programme must consist of a more accurate determination of the features of the new type of government' (*Kommunisticheskaya partia*, p. 406). By means of revisions of the Party programmes and the interpretation of theoretical principles in the light of a given situation, the Soviet leadership freed itself from theoretical dogma and made it possible to adapt its ideological position to the requirements of the moment. This made ideology much more flexible. The Tenth Party Congress in March 1921 used this principle to justify the introduction of NEP.

> The Party revolutionary Marxism denies the search for the absolute correct forms of party organisation and its methods suitable for all stages of the revolutionary process. On the contrary, forms and methods are fully determined by the nature of the given concrete historical circumstances and such tasks as may directly arise from such circumstances (ibid., p. 517).

It became increasingly evident that Soviet policies, including foreign policy, were dictated by state interests at the expense of ideological principles. Soviet foreign policy consisted of a series of responses to actual situations rather than new initiatives. Such policies appeared to have been an attempt at reconciling the goal of a world revolution with the interests of the state. This became obvious during the period of consolidation of power in the hands of Stalin when an ideological controversy created a sharp conflict between the policies of the Soviet Union and the position of the Communist International.

THE COMINTERN

The Comintern was created in March 1919 'to facilitate the co-ordination of the forces of the working classes in countries of Western Europe in their struggle against capitalism and at the same time to render support to the Russian Revolution'. However, a revolution-ary party of the Bolshevik type did not exist in Europe, and Lenin saw the necessity of creating one on a European and world scale. He thought that 'Europe's greatest misfortune and danger is that it has no revolutionary party' – hence the Communist International, the 'world Party of Revolution' (Lenin, 1965, vol. 28, p. 113). In closing the First Congress of the Comintern Lenin said: 'the vic-tory of the proletarian revolution on a world scale is assured. The founding of an international Soviet republic is on the way' (ibid., p. 476).

The concept of internationalism was expressed in the idea that the USSR as the only socialist country in the world must be de-fended by the whole international proletariat. It brought about an increasing emphasis on the preservation of the achievements of the Russian revolution at the expense of world-wide revolution. This implied that the strengthening and defence of the first socialist state would also strengthen world revolutionary forces.

From its inception, the Comintern had been dominated by members of the Russian Communist party. It was, therefore, the task of that Party to impose its views and shape the policies of the Comintern. It wasn't a particularly difficult task given that the only country where the activities of the Comintern were not subject to any re-strictions was the Soviet Union. This allowed the CPSU to exer-cise complete control over the Comintern. The Communist Party of the Soviet Union actively intervened in the internal affairs of other communist parties – including the German Party – replacing its leadership in 1921, 1923, and 1925. Non-Soviet communist par-ties were also compelled by Stalin to become involved in the So-viet power struggle during the 1920s and those leaders who supported Stalin's opponents were removed. The interests of other parties were subordinated to those of the Soviet regime.

As subsequent events indicate, Soviet foreign policy was on many occasions in direct conflict with the policies promoted by the Comintern. The establishment of diplomatic relations with Musso-lini's Italy, which was the first to recognise *de jure* the Soviet Union but also the first to suppress the local Communist Party, is but one example. The question of the reconciliation of ideological objectives of the Comintern with Soviet foreign policy was finally solved by Stalin. His rise and the application of his ideas removed to a large extent the contradictions between ideology and politics. In foreign affairs it meant a more pragmatic approach dictated by the prevailing international situation, while on the domestic front the emphasis was on building 'socialism in one country'.

The principle of building socialism under conditions of capitalist encirclement and the imperative of its defence, were to become the guiding principles of the Comintern. What began to take place in the Comintern reflected similar events in the Russian Communist Party. As old revolutionaries were being removed from the Bolshevik Party, they were also replaced within the Comintern. Classical revolutionary principles were modified by equating the interest of the Soviet state with the world communist movement. The 'preservation of the first socialist country and the prevention of hostile acts against the USSR are the duties of communists in all countries' (Gruber, 1974, p. 4). Thus, the Comintern succumbed to the domination of the Russian Party and, in fact, became an auxiliary of Soviet foreign policy; the activities of the Comintern were largely subordinated to the requirements of the Soviet state. There is no evidence to suggest that the Comintern had been directly involved in activities that would meet Soviet foreign policy objectives. This was the task of Soviet intelligence, which may have utilised the links between the Comintern and the communist parties in many countries. The main task of the Comintern was to transmit the policy of the Soviet government to the particular parties and to persuade them that it conformed to communist ideology.

In the West, the activities of the Comintern gave rise to fears that the Soviet Union was engaged in subversion against the capitalist world and in fact resulted in communist parties in a number of countries being declared illegal. This forced the communists to act as an underground movement, which in turn reinforced Western suspicions of Soviet intentions. Membership of a communist party became synonymous with the services of a secret agent of the Soviet state.

## A COUNTRY IN ISOLATION

Western suspicions of Soviet intentions on the one side, and Russia's mistrust of the capitalist world on the other, have been the main cause of the Soviet Union's isolation on the world arena. What contributed to this seclusion was the ever existing complex of capitalist encirclement which meant not only a fear of armed intervention but also of economic pressures. It resulted in a quest for economic self-sufficiency whose aim was to avoid dependency on the capitalist world. Ironically, the most important bastion of capitalism, the United States, had been, albeit unwillingly, presented by the Soviet as an example of economic achievement – 'to catch up and overtake in the economic area the leading capitalist countries and the United States' – became a rallying slogan.

The United States was one of the last countries to recognise the Soviet Union. When the US established diplomatic relations with the USSR in 1933, it requested that the Soviet Union curb the activities of the Comintern and cease spreading communist propaganda. The USSR consented in principle, and on the establishment of diplomatic relations with the United States undertook:

> To refrain and restrain all persons or organisations over which the Soviet Union has direct or indirect control . . . from any acts tending to . . . the bringing about by force of a change in the political or social order . . . of the United States. Not to permit the formation or residence on its [Soviet] territory and to prevent the activity . . . of any organisation which has as its aim the subversion of the American political order (Degras, 1971, p. 36).

The above undertaking implicitly included the Comintern. Two years later, when the Americans protested against the intervention of the Comintern Congress in the internal affairs of the United States, the Soviet government declined any responsibility for the activities of the Communist International. In reply to the American protest the Soviet government declared that 'it is certainly not new to the government of the United States that the . . . USSR cannot take upon itself and has not taken upon itself obligations of any kind with regard to the Communist International' (ibid., p. 139).

The apparent conflict between the USSR and the United States regarding the activities of the Comintern was of secondary importance in Soviet foreign policy. Soviet foreign policy of the early 1930s clearly indicates growing concern with the security of the

USSR – a concern imposed by the international situation. The Resolution of the 11th ECCI plenum in April 1931 about the danger of a war of intervention against the USSR reflected Soviet apprehension about the situation in Europe.

> The French bourgeoisie – the chief organisers of the anti-Soviet war – have already established a number of political alliances to encircle the Soviet Union ... French social-democracy is the champion of the most aggressive anti-Soviet policy of French imperialism (Degras, 1971, p. 166).

And a resolution of the 7th Comintern Congress on 20 August 1935 stated that 'German imperialism has found an ally in Europe in fascist Poland, which is also striving to extend its territory at the expense of Czechoslovakia, the Baltic countries and the Soviet Union' (loc. cit).

As late as 1938, Stalin was still promoting the idea of capitalist encirclement. In an Open Letter of 12 February 1938 he quoted Lenin as saying that a socialist state cannot be free of danger as long as capitalist encirclement exists.

> ... we are living not only in a state but in a system of states, and the existence of the Soviet Republic side by side with imperialist states is in the long run unthinkable ... the most terrible clashes between the Soviet republic and bourgeois states are unavoidable' (ibid., p. 273).

## THE SOVIET–GERMAN PACT

For those political analysts who at the time looked upon Soviet foreign policy as representing communist objectives, the Soviet–German Non-aggression Treaty came as a surprise, and a shock to the Communist International. The signing of the treaty created a severe problem of credibility among the European member parties of the Comintern, but soon the Moscow-based propaganda machine was set in motion and the interpretation of the political situation which classified England and France as imperialist warmongers was generally accepted by most communist parties. It was a clear indication of the overriding importance of policies aimed at protecting the interests of the Soviet state over ideological considerations. In terms of power politics, the treaty could indeed be seen as a rational action, as a counterweight in the balance of power against England and France.

As far as can be ascertained, there was no attempt on the part of the Soviets to infiltrate or to subvert the Nazi regime, which had earlier been denounced as a menace to peace. It is true that the possibility of interference was rather remote given the total control that the Nazis exercised over the population, but the absence of anti-Nazi propaganda within the Soviet Union itself at the time, would seem to indicate that Stalin was more concerned with practical matters affecting the Soviet state. There is no evidence to suggest that prior to 1939 Soviet foreign policy was governed by a serious long-range plan. It appears to have responded to problems, threats and possibilities thrown up by the course of events outside the Soviet Union (Rostow, 1967, p. 136). In a speech to the Fourth (extraordinary) Session of the Supreme Soviet on 31 August 1939, Molotov defending the Non-aggression Treaty said 'it is our duty to think of the interests of the Soviet people, the interests of the USSR ... We are convinced that the interests of the USSR coincide with the fundamental interests of the peoples of other countries' (Degras, p. 365). He also defended the Treaty on the ground of the 'Leninist principle of peaceful coexistence' of the Soviet state and capitalist countries. Accordingly, even relations with a 'state of a fascist type' are possible. The attempt at justifying the Treaty on ideological grounds was clearly contradicted by the secret Additional Protocol to the Non-aggression Treaty. It defined respective spheres of interest in Eastern Europe 'in the event of a territorial and political transformation' (ibid., p. 360).

The subsequent occupation of Poland was seen as adding to the security of the Soviet Union in terms of space and population. 'The territories which have passed to the Soviet Union had an area of 196 000 square kilometres and a population of about 13 million', Molotov said (ibid., p. 393). Equally, the incorporation of the Baltic states and Bessarabia into the Soviet Union, and the war against Finland, which shifted the common border away from Leningrad, can be seen in the light of strategic considerations of security – the advance or spread of communism was never mentioned. In the eyes of the world, however, it signified the expansion of the Soviet empire.

## THE GREAT PATRIOTIC WAR

The next dramatic turnaround in Soviet foreign policy came after the German attack against the USSR in June 1941. Whatever still remained of the official communist ideology had been largely replaced by Russian nationalism. There was no longer any mention about the defence of socialism or world revolution, and the all-out effort to defeat the German invaders was in the name of Russian patriotism: 'to defend freedom, honour, the motherland in our patriotic war against German fascism' (Stalin, 1967, p. 9). Stalin correctly assumed that nationalism was still an effective force and that 'the moral strength of the army consists in the fact that it defends the motherland' (ibid., p. 17). His confidence in Russian patriotism did not deceive him and he was ready to recognise it when at a reception in the Kremlin on 24 May 1945 he toasted the Russian people 'as the leading force of the Soviet Union ... also because it has a clear mind, strong character, patience' (ibid., p. 204).

While Stalin appealed to Russian patriotism to gain the support of the people, he attempted to remove any misgivings that the allies may have had regarding his post-war objectives. As early as November 1941 he tried to subdue fears of Soviet expansion by saying 'we do not have and we cannot have such a war-aim as to force our will and our regime on Slavs and other European nations ... we will not interfere in the internal matters of other nations' (ibid., p. 29). The dissolution of the Comintern in 1943 served as additional proof of Stalin's good faith – renouncing the idea of world revolution. At the same time, the International, the official anthem of the Soviet Union, was replaced by a new one which emphasised the greatness of Russia.

The dissolution of the Comintern attracted much criticism from some communists who saw in this act the surrender of an ideal to the pressure of capitalist states and a betrayal of Marxist internationalism. They saw it as being done on Stalin's orders so as to facilitate negotiations with Roosevelt and Churchill in order to partition Europe among the 'Big Three'. There is no official evidence that the allies demanded the abolition of the Comintern, but it is clear that the latter had lost its utility in view of the circumstances of the war.

With the approaching end of the war and the liberation of territories bordering the USSR, the political future of neighbouring countries became an important issue. At the end of 1943 Stalin still claimed to support the principle of granting 'to the liberated peoples of Europe, full rights of freedom to decide for themselves the question of the system of their governments' (Stalin, 1967, p. 125). He nevertheless insisted that the security of the Soviet Union required that it should be surrounded by regimes that are not hostile to it. Regarding Poland, he demanded 'a government which will pursue a friendly policy toward the Soviet Union and not one of a 'cordon sanitaire' against the USSR' (ibid., p. 201). Poland was particularly important to the Soviet Union as the central link in the chain of defences around the Soviet state. Thus it was necessary to secure governments in neighbouring states which would be unconditionally pro-Soviet. Although the Americans wished to preserve United States' economic interests in Eastern Europe, they did accept Soviet special interests in border areas. They perceived the understanding reached in Yalta regarding the organisation of Eastern Europe in terms of governments with Western type democracies and demanded the inclusion of representatives of democratic elements and the holding of free elections.

While the political future of Poland was being debated among the allies, the Polish underground in Poland itself resorted to many acts of hostility toward the advancing Red Army aimed at preventing the installation of a communist-dominated government. In response, Stalin ordered the Soviet army and the security services to take control of the key institutions in the liberated areas and to curtail the activities of the elements unfriendly to the Soviet Union. The exceptions were Austria, Finland and Iran where independent governments were formed, although in the case of Finland, it remained in the Soviet sphere of influence. The establishment of communist governments in Eastern Europe may have been justified in terms of the security of the USSR, but from the Western point of view it meant that Stalin intended to spread Soviet rule over the area under his control. The signals emanating from the Soviet Union indicated a return to the old ideologically justified foreign policy based on the notion that the capitalist world had again become a hostile power determined to destroy the Soviet state.

The nature of the link between politics and ideology was well analysed by Hans Morgentau. 'The true nature of a policy is very often concealed by ideological justification and rationalisation', wrote Morgentau (Morgentau, 1973, p. 88). While all politics is necessarily pursuit of power, ideologies render involvement in that contest for power psychologically and morally acceptable to the actors and their audience. To determine the true character of a foreign policy behind its deliberate or unconscious ideological façade becomes particularly difficult. After the end of the Second World War, both the US and Soviet Russia presented to their people the objective of their foreign policies in ideological terms – the US in the advancement of human rights and Russia in terms of Russian nationalism (ibid., p. 98). The conflicting perceptions of each other's intentions with regard to the organisation of the post-war world, particularly Eastern Europe, was certainly responsible for the advent of the Cold War.

## THE COLD WAR

The end of the Second World War did not bring with it the expected era of world peace. The war-time alliance had been followed by a period of mutual suspicion. The threat of communism spreading over the world, which was the main cause of confrontation between the West and the USSR before the Nazi aggression in Europe, surfaced again. The defeat of the Third Reich was received with mixed reactions. On the one hand there was general euphoria following the victory over Nazism, on the other, the spectre of communism reappeared once more. The perception that the USSR having contributed to the victory of the allies would demand its share of the spoils, which meant spreading its sphere of influence over the countries of Eastern and Central Europe, had no doubt been instrumental in Churchill's Fulton speech in which he proclaimed that 'an iron curtain has descended upon Europe'.

Stalin's reaction to the change in the position of the allies had been predictable. It was marked by a sharp change in Soviet foreign policy. The old perception of capitalist encirclement became again the rallying cry, and hostile statements about imperialism were propagated not only within the USSR but among the communists in Europe and elsewhere. Furthermore, the largest military power in Europe – the Soviet Union – had several million of its troops deployed in Europe.

At the time, the American monopoly of the atom bomb represented a security shield against direct communist aggression in Europe, but the Soviet announcement of the explosion of the first atom bomb in 1948 sent cold shivers down the spines of Western politicians; it was the catalyst of the unprecedented arms race. The

Cold War with all its ramifications began to determine the relationship between the two powers.

The prospect of a nuclear war had forced the Soviet leadership to revise its Marxist approach to the question of war and peace. There can be little doubt that the modified approach to war had been prompted by the prospect of mutual annihilation in a nuclear confrontation. This principle was known in the West as 'nuclear deterrence', but has been subsequently adopted by the Soviets as well. However, the credit for its effectiveness was claimed by the Soviet Union who saw its acquisition of nuclear weapons as the main factor that helped to avoid a new world war. 'Nuclear arms in the hands of socialism is an effective factor of avoiding a world war' (Aboltin, 1968, p. 341). The ensuing period of détente was regarded by Soviet analysts as the result of the Soviet Union's possession of nuclear weapons which forced 'the governments of the bourgeois countries into negotiations and the signing of treaties and agreements in order to safeguard peace' (Lebedev, 1978, p. 74).

## DÉTENTE

Open hostility toward the West predominated until Stalin's death in 1953. Subsequent changes in the distribution of power among the Soviet leadership after Stalin's death were accompanied by changes in policies. The main change – a change that reflected the new composition of the Central Committee of the CPSU, was the process of destalinisation and the end of the cult of personality which was announced by Khrushchev in his famous Secret Speech. Khrushchev performed a brave act by making virtue out of adversity when he said: '... bold and merciless self-criticism in regard to the cult of personality was a new and striking testimony of the strength and solidity of our party and the Soviet socialist order' (Hodnett, 1974, p. 59). There was also a significant change in Soviet military doctrine and in its view on a potential war. Until Khrushchev appeared on the scene, the Soviet idea about a future nuclear war was that 'strategic bombing will not decide the outcome of war, but the soldiers on the battlefield'. But after the announced first flight of the Russian ICBM in August 1957, there was an increased emphasis on nuclear missile forces. Khrushchev announced a reduction in the number of Soviet troops, which he claimed was made possible because the USSR has 'new types of weapons – nuclear missiles – that can strike at any part of the world'. Thus the Soviet Union had accepted the notion of deterrence – a concept that assumed increased significance in Soviet military thinking. The development of the Soviet ICBM and the launching of the sputnik removed the 'invulnerability of the United States to a nuclear response' and 'led to the collapse of imperialist military strategy' (Lebedev, 1978, p. 31). The interpretation of the Cuban missile crisis was based on the above view and was considered as a 'retreat on the part of the United States' (ibid., p. 44).

Khrushchev's innovation reflected a conviction that military policy was meaningless under conditions of a nuclear stalemate (Graebner, 1963, p. xv). It also embodied the Russian idea of a country that was equal among the great powers – an idea that had dominated the consciousness of the Russian people since time immemorial. The acquisition of nuclear weapons and the launching of the Russian sputnik, imbued the Russian people with a real sense of national pride; it signified not only a socialist achievement, but an accomplishment of the Russian intellect. In the economic sphere, Krushchev introduced moderate decentralisation of administrative authority, increased attention to the agricultural sector and a relaxation of coercive labour control. His main impact, however, was in foreign affairs. Destalinisation in this area included a relaxation of tension with the West. The Geneva summit in the summer of 1955 and the conclusion of a Treaty with Austria, reflected the new foreign policy course of the Soviet Union. The attempt to ideologically justify the new policy was based, according to Khrushchev, on the 'Leninist principle of peaceful coexistence among countries with different social systems.'

Certain aspects of communist ideology dealing with foreign relations were modified by Khrushchev in February 1956, when he declared that the Second World War had not been 'fatalistically inevitable'. He explicitly proclaimed the end of the 'capitalist encirclement' of the Soviet Union – a key concept of Stalin's thinking. He explained the end of encirclement which he said was not due to changed Western attitudes, but to the emergence of a world socialist system with its military power and the Soviet Union with its superpower status. Khrushchev's new position regarding international relations included the concept of 'peaceful coexistence'. It was to be based on economic competition between the two systems – a competition in which the Soviet Union was to be the inevitable victor. Khrushchev's new policy, however, also recognised the rights of peoples to wars of liberation (Khrushchev, 1959). In an address delivered on 6 January 1961, Khrushchev said: 'There will be wars of liberation as long as imperialism exists, as long as colonialism exists. These are revolutionary wars. Such wars are not only possible but inevitable' (Pentony, 1962).

Peaceful coexistence, therefore, did not exclude intervention in other states. It was justified on theoretical grounds – a method invariably applied to explain any contradictions in Soviet policies. It was a method of dialectic reasoning based on the notion that there is only one truth which only Marxism-Leninism contains (Kubalkova, 1980, p. 137). According to this reasoning sovereignty of a people is vested in the people – in the nation. It may also sometimes be the state, but state sovereignty in the capitalist system is vested in the bourgeoisie. Only in a socialist (pro-Soviet) state are state and people's sovereignty merged into one. There is no intervention where there is self-determination and self-determination only existed in a pro-Soviet state (ibid., p. 138).

Despite the apparent change in Soviet foreign policy and the acceptance of the principle of peaceful coexistence, it was still based on old dogmas which the Communist party applied to justify the new direction. Soviet foreign policy continued to contain the principle of class warfare between the capitalist world and the Soviet Union. This policy was based on a world view that any relaxation of tension between the superpowers is an illusory state of affairs without any prospect of permanent reconciliation. Capitalism by its very nature makes conflict between the two opposing systems unavoidable. At the same time, the Soviet government justified its position on account of state interest. National interest is said to be the driving force in any state. Every country evaluates its own external moves in one way and interprets actions of foreign governments in another, particularly if it considers them unfriendly. In this context, given the perceived hostile surroundings, the main motivation of Soviet foreign policy was its national interest and security (Kulski, 1973, p. vii).

> Our foreign policy is and will continue to be characterised by resoluteness in defending the state interests of the Soviet people, in safeguarding the inviolability of our land fortress, maritime coasts and air space, and in protecting the dignity of the Soviet flag and the rights and security of Soviet citizens (*Pravda*, 28 June 1968).

In the West, the view on irreconcilability between socialism and capitalism made the Soviet assertion that there was no contradiction between the latter and peaceful coexistence appear rather ambiguous. One view widely held in the West was that during the period of détente, the Soviet Union's foreign policy had been geared to preserve and enhance its security and the areas under its influence. It attempted to persuade the Western Powers – especially the United States – to recognise its various acquisitions and to accept its current borders (Reshetar, 1974).

## FOREIGN POLICY UNDER BREZHNEV

The demise of Khrushchev was seen in the West as a turn for the worse in international relations and even the relaxation of tension did not signify a radical change in the mutual perception of both superpowers. The Soviet leadership while speaking of a new reality and the possibility of accommodation with the West, continued relentlessly to interpret the world situation in Leninist terms. It still maintained the need for vigilance and perceived a danger to its security. The warning of the dangers of détente had been sounded by the well-known Georgi Arbatov who said that 'the ideological struggle, the battle for people's minds, remains one of the principal bridgeheads of the struggle against imperialism ... [it] remains acute in spite of the relaxation of international tension' (Arbatov, 1973, p. 8). As late as 1985, prior to *perestroika*, another Soviet ideologue, Leonid Zamyatin, stated that 'it cannot be otherwise, because the world outlook and class objectives of socialism and capitalism are diametrically opposed and irreconcilable' (Zamyatin, 1985, p. 58).

Similar attitudes could be clearly detected in the writings of prominent Western analysts as well. The mistrust of Soviet intentions was expressed in no uncertain terms, and the danger to Western civilisation was seen in the existence of a state that was determined to subvert the West by any means possible. The perception of attempts to spread world revolution had been reinforced by the so-called Brezhnev Doctrine which, at the time, justified the invasion of Czechoslovakia and the right of interference in the affairs of socialist states.

Laws and norms of law are subordinated to the laws of the class struggle. The class approach to the matter cannot be discarded in the name of legalistic considerations (*Pravda*, 26 September 1968).

The Brezhnev Doctrine held that, once communism is established in a country, it becomes irreversible and the Soviet Union can properly use military intervention to protect that rule. The Doctrine also justified Soviet intervention in 'wars of national liberation'. The Brezhnev Doctrine was seen as particularly disturbing because it was being actively pursued in many parts of the world. It justified the presence of Soviet troops in Afghanistan and explained the intensive Soviet destabilising efforts in the Middle East. The USSR was seen as in a state of permanent war with the West, even 'if it had occasionally agreed to an armistice' (Kampelman, 1985, p. 22).

The USSR justified its support for wars of liberation by referring to article 28 of the new Soviet Constitution (1977) which spoke of 'supporting the struggles of peoples for national liberation and social progress'. But on a more pragmatic level it was a quest for areas of influence – a world-wide competition with the United States. It certainly conflicted with the spirit of détente. The Soviet policy of support for liberation movement had not been without ambiguity. While the Soviet Union had supported directly and sometimes by proxy, Marxist revolutionaries, it had also shown apparent sympathy, or rendered assistance, to regimes which it would be difficult to describe as revolutionary let alone socialist. In many of these countries communist parties were illegal and some of their members severely persecuted and jailed. This did not prevent the Soviet Union from defining these regimes as 'progressive forces'. Generally, the 'progressiveness' of a regime or movement was usually gauged by its attitude toward the USSR; the more it supported Soviet policies and the more it resisted American influence, the more progressive it was.

An analysis of how the Soviet Union had perceived capitalism in the context of the given world situation, sheds some light on the question of Russia's foreign policy and its relations with the world. Although the perception of the world may be found in speeches of former Soviet leaders and in official or Party-approved commentaries, their connection or relevance to actual policies can only be ascertained by surveying actual events and actions by former Soviet governments. This, however, is not as simple as it may appear to be, for sometimes Soviet foreign policy could be interpreted in ideological terms while at others it ran counter to communist principles. What can be said with a degree of certainty is that the official Soviet view of a Marxist analysis of international relations which must take into account 'objective' conditions, seemed to have indicated a realistic approach to foreign policy when it clashed with theory. The theoretical element in the official Soviet view of world capitalism was based on the traditional concept of inherent danger of war due to the existence of the Soviet Republic side by side with imperialist states.

> Everything confirms that in contemporary conditions imperialists have not given up the hope of using war as a means to attain their political and strategic aims . . . not only in relation to the Soviet Union but to strangle the national liberation struggle of peoples and revolutionary movements in capitalist countries in order to establish their undivided rule over the world (*Kommunist*, no. 11, July 1979, p. 27).

At the same time, the Soviet Union recognised that under contemporary conditions, war, although possible, was not inevitable and it saw the possibility of preserving capitalism in certain areas of the world (ibid., p. 26). While these interpretations of a given situation represented a change in the theoretical approach to capitalism, references were usually made to the writings of Lenin or Marx which would prove the correctness of the Soviet position. The classical theory of capitalist development with its inherent contradictions, was reconciled with the possibility of a peaceful transition to socialism.

In the final analysis it was not communist ideology that determined Soviet foreign policy, but the interests of the USSR and in particular its perceived security. Communist ideology had been used as an apology and a justification of policies for its own citizens and supporters in other countries. When reality forced a change of Soviet policy and the ideological tenets could no longer be sustained, a new policy was adopted. It can safely be assumed that Soviet foreign policy was determined by national interest or rather by state interest because the USSR had been a multinational state. It acted in a way that was not dissimilar to pre-revolutionary policies of the tsarist government. Geopolitical and strategic factors appeared to explain a certain resemblance between tsarist Russia and Soviet foreign policies. The striking similarity between tsarist Russia and the Soviet state structure and policies were often underlined by Western political analysts, but were only recently pointed out by

Russian commentators. Aleksei Arbatov, a Russian historian and director of the Centre for Geopolitical and Military Forecasting, drew attention to the fact that the Russian and Soviet states had four major common features (Arbatov, 1994, pp. 5–6).

First – a centralised and government-controlled economy, whose main function was to support the state's military potential. Second – a strict hierarchical and totalitarian political system and a kind of messianic ideology which was applied in the management of the state's economy and the vast military establishment. Third – imperial ambitions, constant territorial and political expansion restricted only by geography and by the resistance of other nations. Fourth – due to the continual expansion, Russia as well as the Soviet Union were both doomed to constant confrontation with the outside world.

## SOVIET–US RELATIONS IN THE POST-BREZHNEV PERIOD

This latter similarity was certainly confirmed by US–Soviet relations. Until Gorbachev appeared on the scene, American politicians continued to express deep mistrust in Soviet foreign policy announcements and demanded significant concessions as proof of change. Before his inauguration in 1981, President Reagan stated: 'The Soviet Empire should know that there will be no further concessions unless there is a concession in return' (*Time*, 5 January 1981). However, despite his confrontational assertion about the 'Evil Empire', Reagan modified his position by stating: 'Neither we nor the Soviet Union can wish away the differences between our two societies and our philosophies, but we should always remember that we do have common interests' (*New York Times*, 17 January 1984). In this he followed the practice of former presidents who for pragmatic reasons modified their views regarding the USSR. President Kennedy when he came to power, appeared ready to confront the USSR whenever he considered it necessary. He claimed that this confrontation was ... 'in order to assure the survival and success of liberty' (Kennedy, 1969). But following the Cuban Missile crisis he changed his position. A similar change in attitude could be observed with each US president since the end of the Second World War (Caldwell, 1985, p. 6).

Ronald Reagan is known to have been a zealous anti-communist. On numerous occasions he made no attempt to hide his views regarding the 'war with the most dangerous enemy known to man'. Soon after he came to power, he openly declared that 'the only morality they recognise is what will further their cause, meaning they reserve unto themselves the right to commit any crime, to lie, to cheat . . .' (*Los Angeles Times*, 30 January 1981). Reagan also introduced a second factor – linkage – negotiations on arms control would be dependent upon acceptable Soviet behaviour (Gwertzman, 1980). Another important principle introduced by Reagan was competition with the Soviet Union. However, this was not meant to be a peaceful challenge – it was, rather, confrontational. It was believed at the time that the United States could literally drive the Soviet Union into the ground in an all-out economic and military competition. Some political analysts believed that economic sanctions against the USSR would force Soviet leaders to reform the Soviet economic system (Pipes, 1981).

Following the invasion of Afghanistan, President Carter imposed a grain embargo against the Soviet Union, but this was cancelled in April 1981 by President Reagan. In November 1982, he also cancelled sanctions on US and foreign companies selling pipeline equipment to the Soviet Union imposed earlier after the declaration of martial law in Poland. The removal of some sanctions were not due to a change of heart, but because of objections raised by European allies to American contradictory policies. While the US pressurised its allies not to sell pipeline equipment, it was selling grain to the Soviet Union.

Max Kampelman, a former chief US delegate to the Madrid Conference on European Security, expressed his misgivings about Soviet policies, and his reservations on a possible US–Soviet agreement, in an article published in March 1985, shortly before Gorbachev's accession to power (Kampelman, 1985). The Soviet Union, said Kampelman, is governed by a political and military elite which has been engaged in a deliberate programme to intimidate and frighten the world half to death. It is an elite which does not have the legitimacy of consent and seeks to provide legitimacy through use of an omnipresent state police and extraordinary military power. It is an elite committed to an ideology in which violence plays a central role. Max Kampelman's views on the Soviet Union were representative of the general perception of the USSR as a threat to Western democracy. The opinion expressed by him was significant at a time when communism as a theoretical model of a future society had already lost its attraction due to the economic and technological advances of capitalist economies and the failures of the command system. It had been recognised that the 'correlation of forces' – a term often used by the Soviets – had moved against the Soviet Union. The advances in technology and particularly communication made it practically impossible for the Soviet leaders to isolate their people from Western ideas.

While the economic conditions in the Soviet Union remained precarious during the 1980s, many American politicians were against providing the Soviet Union with industrial assistance as this would 'significantly help its military effort, even if indirectly'. Much of Western sales and credits to the Soviet Union were for 'dual use' technology which it was thought could have been applied to both civilian and military purposes. Western aid for the development of Soviet energy resources has had the effect of providing the USSR with hard currency which its own economy could not generate. This, according to some Western commentators, confirmed Lenin's prediction that the capitalist world would sell them (on credit) the rope they would use to hang the capitalists.

## GORBACHEV AND THE NEW THINKING

On·8 March 1985, came the announcement of the death of the Secretary General of the CPSU Chernenko followed by the nomination on 11 March of Mikhail Gorbachev as the new General Secretary. The relatively young age of the new leader signalled the emergence of a new generation of Soviet leadership. In anticipation of a new direction in Soviet foreign and domestic policies, the appointment of the new Secretary had been received in the West with the usual caution.

The first indication of the views of the new leader came during the plenum of the Central Committee of the CPSU held on the day of his appointment in a speech at the Plenum (assembly) of the Central Committee of the CPSU (*Pravda*, 12 March 1985). It was Gorbachev's first public statement on the Soviet Union's future policy. Basically it did not differ from any previous positions adopted by the communist party. The central theme of his speech was the threat of a war imposed on the USSR by the capitalist world – the United States. He also perceived a danger to the Soviet Union coming from contamination by Western ideas. The Party, he said, 'will take decisive measures to further introduce order and cleanse our life from foreign manifestations'. Regarding relations with the capitalist world, Gorbachev declared that he would pursue the Leninist path of peace and peaceful coexistence. But, he said, 'everyone should know that the Soviet Union will never yield anything that is against the interests of the USSR and its allies'. He referred to the détente achieved in the 1970s, but made it conditional upon the disarmament process – particularly the end of the nuclear arms race. He warned the potential aggressor that any encroachment upon the security of the country and its allies will be met by a 'devastating response'. The armed forces of the Soviet Union will continue to have everything it needs at its disposal. At the same time, he said, 'we must strengthen fraternal friendship with our closest brothers in arms and allies – with the great community of socialist countries'. Gorbachev declared his willingness to improve relations with China. His position regarding wars of liberation had not changed and he said that the Soviet Union would always support the struggle of the peoples for liberation from colonialist repression. 'Our sympathy is on the side of the countries of Asia, Africa and Latin America.'

In contrast to his predecessors, Gorbachev adopted the practice of public appearance as a means of strengthening his popularity within the country. His interview by the editor of *Pravda* on 8 April 1985 was widely publicised in the press and radio. Speaking about Soviet–American relations, Gorbachev appeared to have shifted slightly his position. The interview took place shortly after the beginning of the Geneva Soviet–American nuclear and space-arms negotiations. Gorbachev was still accusing the United States of relying on force, which he said the Americans were not even trying to conceal. He reiterated that international imperialism was responsible for creating tensions, and again attacked the ruling circles of the United States. As a countermeasure, Gorbachev asserted the necessity of close cooperation between socialist countries. The Warsaw Pact Bloc would function as long as NATO existed. It wasn't clear at the time whether he contemplated the dissolution of the Warsaw Pact if NATO did likewise. A few days later on 26 April, the Warsaw Pact treaty was renewed by member nations for another 20 years.

The improvement in Soviet–US relations began in 1985 with the first Reagan–Gorbachev summit. During Gorbachev's first few months as General Secretary there were clear indications of the Soviet leader's determination to improve relations with the United States.

Three years of intense negotiations and four superpower summits, resulted in substantial progress toward the conclusion of a new strategic arms reduction (START) agreement, and in December 1987, the signing of the treaty eliminating intermediate-range nuclear forces.

An indication of the radical change in the Soviet world view came with the launching of the New Thinking by Gorbachev in mid-1988. The ideas expressed in Gorbachev's book *Perestroika and New Thinking* had been in the making for quite some time. It is not certain whether the other members of the Politburo had been consulted or if it was a scheme devised by Gorbachev to catch the other members of the CC and the public by surprise. In his book Gorbachev analysed the process of reform and its relevance to the USSR's relations with the West. At first, Gorbachev noted, most of the Western media had been rather sceptical about the changes which were proclaimed by the Party in April 1985. The Western media considered that one team had been replaced by another – one programme by a new one. 'The Russians are an emotional people and they are used to new leaders blaming the previous one for all the shortcomings, but basically everything remains the same' (Gorbachev, 1988, p. 126). Gorbachev made special reference to the principle of non-interference in the affairs of other countries. In this way he tried to allay suspicions about Soviet subversive activities through the communist movement. Non-interference, said Gorbachev, is an acknowledgment that each nation has the right to choose its own path of social development, it is the rejection of interference in the affairs of other countries, it is respect for others while taking into account an objective and self-critical view of its own society. People have the right to choose between capitalism and socialism. Countries should not form alliances with either the US or the USSR. This means separating political positions from ideological intolerance (ibid., p. 146).

In the same context he analysed the relations between the USSR and the satellites. The basis of political cooperation between socialist countries remained the interaction of the ruling communist parties, but much emphasis in the New Thinking was on the integration of the CMEA – Council of Mutual Economic Assistance. Gorbachev failed to admit that the Soviet system had been imposed upon the countries of eastern and central Europe through the presence of Soviet armed forces in these countries. He still retained the illusion of 'fraternal' relations within the socialist camp and blamed wrong political and economic policies for the failure in economic progress. He also accused the West of attempting to undermine the development of these countries.

An important feature of the new foreign policy approach within the New Thinking was that the USSR is part of Europe. It was Christianity that united Russia with Europe, Gorbachev said, Europe is our 'common house' – it is Europe from the Atlantic to the Urals' (ibid., p. 207). It was a weak echo of the nineteenth-century westernising trend in tsarist Russia. Gorbachev tried to establish Russia's place on the European continent as a major player. He also attempted to exploit the differences of view between the major European countries like France and Germany, in order to prevent the US from having a decisive voice in East–West relations. When Gorbachev spoke of a 'common European home' he certainly excluded the United States. As for Eastern Europe, Gorbachev implied that the Soviet model may not be one to be emulated by its neighbours. 'We have become convinced that unity does not mean identity and uniformity. We have also become convinced that there is no 'model' of socialism to be emulated by everyone . . .' (Gorbachev, 1987, p. 28).

Criticising American policy, Gorbachev noted that it was based on two fallacies. The first one – a belief that the Soviet economic system is about to collapse and that *perestroika* will fail. The second – the belief in the superiority of the West in technology and, in the final account, in the military area. 'Such illusions feed the striving for the exhaustion of socialism through an arms race, in order to be able to dictate certain conditions to the USSR' (Gorbachev, 1988, p. 232). Gorbachev repeated the old motto of Soviet self-sufficiency. The USSR, said Gorbachev, can live without the United States and also America could exist without the Soviet Union. Mutual trading relations are minimal not only with the US but also with the rest of the world. This, according to Gorbachev, was because the international partners are not always reliable. They are not averse to using trade as an instrument of political blackmail and pressure on the USSR. He nevertheless admitted 'it is quite possible that trade depends also on us. Perhaps we do not know how to trade, perhaps we do not make a strong enough effort because we can manage without it' (ibid., p. 236).

Earlier, in February 1986, during the 27th Congress, Gorbachev started to convey an unusually complex appreciation of what constituted national security. He began to promote the idea that national security cannot be divorced from mutual security. That meant the security of one country cannot be assured at the expense of the security of another. 'To think otherwise', he said in August 1986, 'is to live in a world of illusions, in a world of self-deception' (Dallin, 1995, p. 423). At the 27th Party Congress in 1986, he introduced the notion of 'reasonable sufficiency'. Moscow's new thinking was aimed at demonstrating that what drives the correlation of forces is not military or economic power but also the power of ideas. His new thinking was not based on an abandonment of socialism as a final objective, but its improvement.

Despite the classical interpretation of the international situation and criticism of the West as responsible for past confrontations, US–Soviet relations began to improve. What had contributed to this improvement, was a series of face-to-face meetings between the leaders of the two superpowers. The first of such summit meetings between President Reagan and Gorbachev took place in Geneva from 19–21 November 1985. Nothing concrete had eventuated, but the communiqué issued after the meeting spoke of 'frank and useful' talks. The summit established 'personal diplomacy', which would come to characterise future summits and meetings with American heads of state.

Referring to the Geneva conference Gorbachev said that 'there were early indications that the United States is reluctant to reach an agreement with the Soviet Union'. The West was quite familiar with this kind of statement, but the Soviet Union's declaration of a moratorium on redeployment of medium-range missiles, took the West by surprise. This, Gorbachev said, is not the only step taken by the Soviet Union. Since 1982, the Soviet Union undertook unilaterally not to be the first to use nuclear weapons, and in 1993 it announced a unilateral moratorium on launching nuclear weapons into space.

The most significant summit meeting between the two leaders took place in Washington in December 1987 when Reagan and Gorbachev signed the Intermediate-Range Nuclear Forces (INF) Treaty. One Soviet observer described the summit as unprecedented and of historical significance. For the first time, both superpowers reached an agreement not only on the limitation of the nuclear arms race but also on its actual curtailment (Aeab-Ogly, 1988, p. 51). The statement by President Reagan issued after the meeting was significant in that it expressed an opinion that ran counter to the views of many members on both sides of the House:

I assume that some people are against the agreement and even refuse to accept the idea of the possibility of reaching mutual understanding at any time. These people ... base their opposition on the view that a war is inevitable, that a war between the two superpowers must erupt (ibid., p. 52).

Reagan and Gorbachev met again in Moscow from 30 May–2 June 1988. It was their fourth summit. The Americans stressed human rights and the Soviets emphasised 'new realism' in US–Soviet relations. After US President Ronald Reagan returned from Moscow, relations between the US and the USSR entered a relatively inert phase; America was busy choosing President Reagan's successor. The pause in the superpower leadership meetings continued during the first several months of 1989, while the new administration, led by George Bush, began a comprehensive review of America's national security policy, including a fresh look at Soviet–American relations (*The Washington Post*, 9 February 1989).

On 12 May 1989, President Bush, in a public address, reaffirmed the US desire for the success of *perestroika* and stated that the US sought the integration of the Soviet Union into the community of nations. He asserted that it was the US that prevailed in the struggle between 'democracy and freedom' and 'tyranny and conflict' (*The New York Times*, 13 May 1989). His statement was received in Moscow with a degree of scepticism. One Soviet commentator accused Bush of persisting in 'old clichés' and 'stereotypes' (*Pravda*, 14 May 1989). Nevertheless, relations between the superpowers seemed to have taken a turn for the better. The review of American policy had no doubt been prompted by the events in Moscow.

On 25 May 1989, the Congress of People's Deputies, chosen on the basis of competitive elections the previous March, convened in Moscow. Open and frank discussions on major issues characterised the first sessions. The gathering selected the membership of the new bicameral Supreme Soviet from its own ranks, and elected Mikhail Gorbachev President of the Soviet Union. The West faced a new ruler of Soviet Russia.

Secretary Baker and Soviet Foreign Minister Shevardnadze met in Wyoming in September 1989. Following that meeting, the Soviet Union announced that it would no longer insist on an agreement on defence and space as a precondition for a strategic arms reduction (START) treaty and that it was prepared to eliminate the Krasnoyarsk radar, a violation of the Anti-Ballistic (ABM) Treaty.

A further improvement came as a result of Soviet change in its position regarding Eastern Europe. On 6 March 1989, speaking on Hungarian television, Soviet Foreign Ministry spokesman Gennadii Gerasimov said that every East European country's future 'is in its own hands', thereby renouncing the Brezhnev Doctrine. A few months later, on 27 October 1989 – the Warsaw Pact nations issued a statement endorsing the right of each member-country to seek its own political doctrine, followed by a statement on 28 October by Yevgenii Primakov that member states are free to leave the alliance.

Concerning NATO, Gorbachev had clearly similar plans. When in December 1988 he announced the decision of a unilateral cut in troops, he expected a weakening of NATO's military efforts and cohesion. Gorbachev had argued for the retention of existing institutions such as the Warsaw Pact and NATO, but the final result was the disintegration of the Warsaw Pact security structure while NATO remained unimpaired. Nevertheless, Moscow and Washington talked a similar language concerning the transformation of their alliances from military organisations to 'political' ones. Again the course of events changed the perception on both sides, and after the dissolution of the Warsaw Pact, NATO remained a military rather than a political institution.

By the time the Malta summit of December 1989 had taken place, most East European communist regimes had already collapsed. It was the first summit between President Bush and Gorbachev. It was described by the US administration as a 'get-to-know-each-other' meeting. Both leaders discussed the new structure of international relations following the collapse of East European communist regimes. The next meeting between Bush and Gorbachev on 31 May–3 June 1990 in Washington, focussed on German reunification. The US had long been committed to the idea of German unity provided it was according to the 'free self-determination of peoples and states' and 'freedom of choice' in Eastern Europe. Gorbachev on the other hand, clearly hoped that the East Germans would choose to remain a separate state. The Soviets pledged 'to defend the GDR' against outside interference with its right to choose a separate sovereign existence. But Gorbachev emphasised the 'existing realities' of the two German states and as he said he preferred to leave it to 'history' to decide. History had clearly decided an outcome that was not favourable to Gorbachev's ideas and even contrary to the US official position at the time. The US view was that German unification must be in accord with the 1975 Helsinki agreements, which stipulated that the post-war boundaries of Europe be fixed and only changeable by 'peaceful negotiations'. Reunification of both Germanies was peaceful indeed, but it did not come as a result of negotiations.

Having reluctantly accepted the idea of German reunification, Gorbachev voiced his firm opposition to the inclusion of a united Germany into the system of West European security. He reiterated his position on 6 March 1990 when he said that NATO membership for a united Germany was 'absolutely out of the question'. In retrospect this seems a hollow statement devoid of any reality, but at the time Soviet troops were still deployed in East Germany. A few months later, on 16 July 1990, faced with a desperate domestic economic situation and pressure from NATO countries, the USSR dropped its objection to united Germany's membership in NATO. In exchange the Soviets were to receive economic assistance from West Germany and assurances from the NATO allies that a united Germany's military would be subject to certain limitations. On the domestic front, Gorbachev attempted to retain his position of power and succeeded in being overwhelmingly re-elected general secretary at the Twenty-Eighth CPSU Congress in July 1990. At that time there were already ominous signs of problems within the Party. At the end of the Congress, Boris Yeltsin resigned from the Party and on 20 December 1990 Eduard Shevardnadze announced his resignation, warning of an 'impending dictatorship'.

While the economic situation in the Soviet Union appeared to be worsening, a movement calling for increased autonomy, or even secession, complicated the difficult task of reform. There were various forces on the right that offered apparent solutions and familiar instruments to deal with their own anxieties and those of the society at large. According to one American analyst, Gorbachev turned to the right to preserve his credibility as a leader and to preserve the Union. In September 1990, Gorbachev rejected Shatalin's 500-days Plan and repudiated the reformers. He retained Ryzhkov as his prime minister, affirming his intention not to abandon the existing governmental structure. In October, Gorbachev secured adoption of a more vaguely worded compromise economic reform programme, and in December, he acquired vast new presidential powers to implement this programme. The same month he made key personnel changes at the Interior and Justice Ministries, and secured stronger enforcement powers for the KGB and military to act internally. By the end of the year, almost all of Gorbachev's *perestroika* team had departed. Finally, in January 1991, the Soviet leadership opted for intimidation in the Baltics, which became an arena for a show of force and then violence.

It could be argued that the turn to the right had been forced upon Gorbachev by the deteriorating economic situation. The transition from a state-controlled to a market economy proved to be much more difficult than at first thought. Even Western economists were busy formulating a theory of transition from a socialist to a market economy without reaching a conclusion. Gorbachev certainly did not act according to a theory but rather on pragmatic grounds.

The change in Soviet foreign policy has been ascribed to the preoccupation of the leadership with domestic economic problems. The most ardent advocate of the primacy of domestic policy was the Soviet foreign minister, Eduard Shevardnadze. He saw the urgent necessity to repair the economic and social damage to a society subjected to decades of Stalinist and neo-Stalinist rules, and placed internal considerations above foreign affairs. He perceived the more favourable international atmosphere as a positive factor for the introduction of domestic reforms in the Soviet Union. Invoking foreign threat could no longer be of use to the Soviet leadership and could no longer serve as a rallying call for further sacrifices.

The introduction of the reforms brought about a debate as to how, or indeed whether the United States should assist Gorbachev. The new direction in Soviet domestic policy implied that it would be in the West's interest to endorse Gorbachev's domestic programme and to cooperate with this new political thinking. The discussions were mainly concentrated on the question of whether the new apparent radical change in the thinking of the Soviet leadership was of a permanent nature or whether it was only a temporary stage of a long-term plan for improving the system. The state of uncertainty ended with the disintegration of the Soviet Union and the emergence of independent Russia as the main international actor replacing the former Soviet Union.

# 3 Period of Uncertainty – 1985–91

The launching of *glasnost* and *perestroika* in the former Soviet Union by Mikhail Gorbachev, came as a surprise to the West. Although there were already some indications of a forthcoming change in Soviet policies, the extent of the reforms and the new thinking about foreign policy, had certainly been unexpected. The question asked at the time was what was one to make of this new thinking? Was Soviet domestic and foreign policy undergoing radical modification, or was the new policy merely a more sophisticated mask concealing the old political thinking? It was not only a question about the nature of the changes but also of how the West should respond to the new situation. For a short period between 1985 and 1991 – the year when the Soviet Union finally disintegrated – there was much confusion and uncertainty in the West.

In the Soviet Union, the situation was similar; there was a great deal of bewilderment as Gorbachev initiated a series of reforms and pronouncements of a kind never previously heard. Many Russian commentators, especially Party ideologues, began to analyse the new situation applying traditional Marxist tenets. They saw new thinking as a normal process of development of a socialist society. Others, who were more pragmatic, rejected the Marxist interpretation and taking advantage of the new freedoms began to see the new situation in a different light.

The debate among Russian intellectuals regarding the merits of the reforms and the possibility of their implementation provided a wide field of analysis for Western observers. However, in contrast with the past when everything that was written in the Soviet press had been taken as the expression of official policy, the plethora of views and opinions appearing under *glasnost*, made the task of rational analysis of the situation in Russia more difficult. Before Gorbachev came to power, the discussions about the internal situation in the Soviet Union and its implications for Soviet policies, focused on the question whether the Soviet Union was subject to change and if it was, what were the factors that would bring about that change. Most Western analysis of East–West relations, or to be more precise, Soviet–American relations, were based on the fundamental differences between the two societies. Such differences were perceived as being caused by the contrasting ideologies, which in turn determined their political structures. In the words of Richard Pipes 'these differences affect relations between the two societies because of the close and direct relationship that exists between a country's internal condition and its external conduct: foreign policy, after all, is driven mainly by domestic interest and shaped by a society's political culture' (Pipes, 1984, p. 48).

Pipes asserted that totalitarian regimes are by definition incapable of evolution from within and impervious to change from without (ibid., p. 49). But he found the Soviet Union to be 'in the throes of a serious systemic crisis which sooner or later will require action of a decisive kind – action which will exert the most profound influence on Soviet external policy.' Economic difficulties were the catalyst to change, according to Pipes. 'Changes for the better that one can expect in the nature of the Soviet government and in its conduct of foreign relations would come about only from failures, instabilities, and fears of collapse and not from growing confidence and sense of security' (ibid., p. 56). Pipes was, therefore, against détente asserting that the notion 'that the more confident and secure the Soviet elite feels, the more restrained its conduct will be' was wrong. Instead, Pipes suggested a policy that would 'deny the Soviet bloc various forms of economic aid, which would help to intensify the formidable pressures exerted on their creaky economies'. This, he said, will push them in the direction of general liberalisation as well as accommodation with the West.

His predictions may have come true in the sense that Russia adopted the path of liberalisation, but the debate whether the collapse of communism and of the Soviet empire was due to internal or external pressures, or if there were other forces at work, is still going on. Furthermore, the question of how to respond to the changes in Russia, has still to be resolved.

## THE END OF THE COLD WAR

The forces that constrained and ultimately changed Soviet international behaviour were seen in the breakdown of the Soviet system. The collapse had hampered Moscow's ability to achieve its stated objectives at home and abroad (Lynch, 1990, p. 21). Thus, the West was seen as the beneficiary of the diminished Soviet power. The only concern was the likelihood of Gorbachev being removed from his position and a possible reversal of his policies.

An extreme view was that 'the system cannot be restructured or reformed, but can only stagnate or be dismantled and replaced by market institutions over a long period of time . . . In this case any aid the West may render to the Soviet state to save or improve the existing system would be futile: . . . Gorbachev is beyond Western help' ('Z', 1990, p. 338). Such a view was based on the assumption that Gorbachev aimed at improving the system rather than drastically changing it. The consensus of opinion was that genuine reforms would put an end to the communist party's leading role and could even spell the end of communism, something Gorbachev did not intend to bring about. Western sceptics, asserted that the new Soviet leader was prepared to offer any concessions the West would demand in order to leave him a free hand in his attempts to improve the operation of the Soviet system. They thought that what Gorbachev was aiming at, and hoping to succeed in, was an improvement in the country's economic situation and that once this was achieved, he would be able to turn his attention again to international affairs and regain the position the Soviet Union was prepared to relinquish temporarily. It was also generally assumed that Gorbachev hoped that *perestroika* would spread to Eastern Europe where similar reforms would be introduced thereby 'renewing socialism'. But his image of a new socialist alliance had already been upset by events in Poland and elsewhere.

Tadeusz Mazowiecki, a Catholic intellectual, became the prime minister of a Solidarity-dominated government in Poland. A month later, in September 1989, thousands of East Germans were fleeing the German Democratic Republic through Hungary and Czechoslovakia, and pro-democracy demonstrations were taking place in the major cities of East Germany. The collapse of communist domination of Eastern Europe made a crucial difference. It provided tangible evidence of a change in the policies of the USSR that could not be explained as a temporary tactical retreat after which the Soviet Union would resume its old ways.

It is generally accepted that the 40-year-long conflict between the US and the Soviet Union came to a close at the end of the 1980s. The meetings between President Reagan and Gorbachev established a personal relationship between the leaders of the two countries. Later, at the Malta summit between President George

Bush and Gorbachev, the convergence of American and Soviet positions on most agenda items was as much unprecedented as it was unexpected. There appeared to be a genuine desire on both sides to reach a compromise and to find solutions to military and political difficulties which prevailed throughout the period of the Cold War. As a result there was a significant shift in America's foreign policy. The administration came to the conclusion that it was in America's interest to support Gorbachev's reforms and to render Moscow technical assistance in restructuring its economy. The United States foreign policy towards the Soviet Union became in a way dependent on the success of *perestroika* and on Gorbachev's survival. America was vitally interested to see *perestroika* succeed in the belief that it would bring about a Soviet Union more inclined to satisfy the needs of its people and less so in propagating aggressive policies abroad (Backgrounder, 1990).

The apparent end of the Cold War presented the US as well as the USSR with new challenges. The old method of containing the conflict between the two superpowers had suddenly become outdated. Neither Moscow nor Washington could see what would replace the cold-war system (Horelick, 1990). On the Soviet side the new international situation was expressed in terms of an end to a bipolar world – a world in which international politics were determined by the East–West conflict. Gorbachev in his extended review of new Soviet policies clearly indicated that with the approaching end of the bipolar world system, the USSR placed increasing emphasis on the role of the United Nations in solving conflicts. This was seen in the West as an attempt to prevent the US from dictating its rules to the world through the United Nations where, Gorbachev hoped, the Soviet Union would still maintain its role as one of the superpowers (Gorbachev, 1988, p. 142). The Americans faced problems of a different kind. With the disappearance of an enemy, the existence of which imposed the adoption of certain military strategies and fuelled the arms-race, a new set of play on the international arena called for a revision of America's posture and for a new ideology that would be acceptable to the American public. It sparked a lively debate among political analysts about the American policy toward the Soviet Union. There was, nonetheless, general recognition that the change in Soviet leadership heralded a new era in Soviet–US relations.

THE WEST IN CONFUSION

Following the change in Soviet leadership in 1985 and the subsequent introduction of reforms, Western analysts began debating whether Gorbachev genuinely intended to radically reform the Soviet system, whether Gorbachev's reforms heralded a new era in Soviet history or a continuation of the class war by other means (Dallin, 1995, p. 419). There was also a great deal of uncertainty among Western analysts and policy-makers concerning the fundamental intentions of the new leadership with respect to Soviet foreign and defence policy. Initially, opinions in the West were divided as to the possibility of the Soviet Union becoming part of the 'civilised world', which meant in effect the acceptance by the Soviet Union of Western values and of the Western democratic system. It was, therefore, understandable that Gorbachev's new policy was met in the West with much suspicion. The suspicions as to the true intentions of the Communist party, of which Gorbachev was the Secretary General, had been reinforced by the militant declarations by a number of Soviet officials and the military.

Public opinion in the United States, unlike the Soviet Union, was not restricted by any form of censorship, and was free to comment and even sharply criticise American foreign policy in relation to the USSR. American observers initiated a debate as to how the United States should react to the latest twist in Soviet policy. However, after a few years of Gorbachev's rule, it had been generally agreed that Gorbachev was sincere in his desire for domestic reforms and that there was a fundamentally new trend in Soviet foreign policy. The question on which there were differences of opinion was how should the West respond?

There were basically two alternative views. One was to maintain Western positions until the changes in the Soviet Union were substantial and became irreversible. Partisans of this view dismissed Gorbachev's programme as another attempt at improving socialism. His foreign policy ideas were seen as merely trying to restrain the West while the Soviets caught up. The United States should continue to exploit the economic weaknesses of the Soviet Union by further undermining its influence in the world and by forcing it to waste resources in the arms race. At the other end of the spectrum were people like John Kenneth Galbraith, who faithful to his theory of convergence, advocated prompt and generous assistance to countries in the process of liberalisation by suspending debt service.

The International Monetary Fund, Kenneth Galbraith asserted, should cease lecturing these countries on austerity. 'The affirmative help in grants and loans should not be confined to capital goods; it must extend generously to food and consumer goods, the area of most serious past socialist failure and those in present need' (Galbraith, 1990). A further argument put forward by Galbraith was that as the military threat diminishes, it also reduces claims on public resources in the West. These should be used to ease the transition to a more secure world.

By contrast, most members of the American administration held the view that concessions in favour of the Soviet Union were not conducive to a change in Soviet policy. The opinion among some Western political observers was that 'Soviet military leaders are nostalgic for the Stalinist concept of Fortress Russia and are concerned that the thaw in US–Soviet relations may weaken their grip on the economy's resources' (Ploss, 1986, p. 57). There was, nevertheless, general agreement that the reforms could have major repercussions for Soviet foreign relations. The emphasis on improving Soviet living standards would be translated into increasing trade relations with the West, and this in turn would be conducive to a more peaceful international atmosphere. The confusion and lack of a decisive policy within the US Administration was clearly evident during the crisis in the Baltic states. Soviet policy at the time was to retain its control over the area at any price. Attempts in Lithuania to break its links with the Soviet Union were met with little enthusiasm in the West. A Soviet analyst quoted the British Foreign Minister as saying: 'A disintegration of the Soviet Union is not in our interest', and President Bush attempted to follow a careful path between the historical policy of non-recognition of the incorporation of Lithuania into the USSR and a desire not to create additional difficulties for President Gorbachev (*Krasnaya zvezda*, 8 April 1990). There was strong pressure in the Congress from adherents of a harder line towards the Soviet Union and for more support for Lithuanian demands for independence. Generally, however, there was fear in the US that the Baltic crisis may undermine efforts to reach agreement in the area of arms limitations and a reduction in the American military budget.

An extreme opinion was expressed in the anti-Soviet journal *Commentary* in November 1988 (Codevilla, 1988). It was the voice of those in the United States who were suspicious of Soviet intentions and promoted a position of mistrust of the Soviets. According to this view the case for the proposition that 'peace is breaking out all over' rested, at best, on American hopes attached to Soviet actions' (Ploss, p. 23). The case also rested on American interpretations of the general Soviet situation, especially the economic situation, which it was believed, would force profound changes in the area of disarmament and peace. The case to the contrary – that the Soviet Union posed as much of a threat as ever, maybe an even greater one – was based on a different set of assessments, according to the journal: Soviet military power relative to that of the United States continued to grow, while Soviet efforts to cushion the consequences of military spending by acquiring Western capital and technology were more successful than they had been for many years.

Opponents of a softer line asserted that 'the military balance is continuing its long term shift in the Soviet Union's favour, and that recent American cutbacks are accelerating that trend' (Codevilla, 1988, p. 24). Contrary to a widespread belief, the US has not become militarily stronger over the past decade relative to the Soviet Union. Given the alleged superiority of the USSR, the arms-control agreement which Mikhail Gorbachev proposed at the Reykjavik summit in 1986 – a 50 per cent reduction in each side's long-range nuclear warheads – would further increase the ratio of Soviet warheads to American strategic targets. The conclusion was that arms control is not a solution. It was part of the problem, for there were more Russian divisions in East Germany than in the entire active US Army, and more divisions in Czechoslovakia than there were US divisions in all of Europe. Under Gorbachev, not one of these divisions was eliminated or even reduced.

The ideological factor which had been an apparent justification for Soviet past policies, has also been fostered by Western analysts. 'The ongoing need to counter the Soviet Union has served to remind us that the United States of America is not just another nation among nations but a beacon and a help to free men everywhere' (ibid., p. 23). This meant opposition to what was called at the time 'shared leadership in a world of powerful friends'. American foreign policy must aim at US world sole leadership – in other words at a unipolar world.

A more benign view was adopted by a number of Western analysts who saw the new international situation as evidence of the decline in the ability of the Soviet/Russian state to influence international politics and that Russia's position on the international arena became weaker than at any time since the mid-eighteenth century.

'Its borders have receded far back to the east and were on the periphery to the pre-Russian Empire period' (Lynch, 1990).

In early 1986, the debate concentrated more on tangible evidence of the change of Soviet policy rather than theoretical discussion about the likelihood of a significant change. Some saw the possibility of reforms as being dependent on Gorbachev's consolidation of power. There was also strong emphasis on the personality of Gorbachev. He was identified with the group of people within the Politburo who held more reformist views. Since the old guard such as Brezhnev, Andropov and Chernenko died, and Romanov and Tikhonov, both old hardliners, were removed from the Politburo, Gorbachev became the natural successor. He had been considered as more open to the ideas of the experts. But while the Western world was lavish in its praise of Gorbachev's statesmanship and diplomacy, in the Soviet Union it was a period that saw the steady erosion of Gorbachev's popularity as *perestroika* continued to fail.

During the last year of Reagan's second term, the debate over how to deal with Gorbachev's Soviet Union was at its peak. There was still strong opposition in some circles to any relaxation of pressure on the USSR. Such pressure was seen as a means of compelling Moscow into a global retreat and of forcing it to abandon communism. Another group in the State Department saw Gorbachev's preoccupation with domestic reform as an opportunity to reach arms control and regional agreements on favourable terms. Some European allies were urging Washington to respond more effectively to Gorbachev's initiatives, if only because they were attentive to European public opinion.

By the time George Bush took office in January 1989, the latter opinion prevailed. At first President Bush and his team also had doubts about Gorbachev's intentions. There was much scepticism about his chances of survival and the chances of succeeding with *perestroika*. Brent Scowcroft, the US national security adviser, suggested that Gorbachev's real intention was to drive a wedge between the United States and its European allies. He saw Gorbachev's concessions as a means of splitting the Western alliance. President Bush, however, in his speech in May 1989 in New London, Connecticut, declared that it was time to 'move beyond containment' and to integrate the USSR into the 'community of nations'. Apparently, the administration came to the conclusion that it was in America's interest to support Gorbachev's reforms and to render Moscow technical assistance in restructuring its economy. At the same time, Secretary of Defense Dick Cheney and Deputy National Adviser Robert Gate in particular, publicly stated that the prospects for both Gorbachev and *perestroika* were poor and suggested caution (ibid., p. 57).

According to one official American assessment at the time, the USSR had demonstrated in a series of foreign policy moves its willingness to create a more stable international atmosphere, especially in Europe, and to accept solutions of conflicts not based on the victory of 'progressive forces'. Moves such as strict adherence to the agreement on reduction of medium- and short-range missiles and readiness to make further reductions, the withdrawal from Afghanistan, reduction in its activities among the 'class related' regimes in the Third World and its reluctance to intervene in the affairs of Eastern Europe, were seen as a confirmation of this appraisal. This allowed President Bush to draw the conclusion that the changes in Soviet foreign policy were of a radical nature and deserved American support (Trofimenko, 1990).

An American official review of US–Soviet relations published in April 1990, some five years after Gorbachev introduced his new policy, noted that 'since the 1917 Revolution, the US–Soviet relationship has evolved through several phases, including a period of minimal contact, a wartime alliance, an intense cold war, hopes for détente, and disappointment'. But relations with the Soviet Union have improved considerably since 1985 when Mikhail Gorbachev launched significant changes in the policies and practices of the Soviet government. 'Moscow has allowed greater freedoms at home in the context of *perestroika* and *glasnost* and shown greater restraint and a less threatening military posture abroad' (Backgrounder, 1990). In a fluid situation, the review noted, the United States must be prudent but not stand back from engaging with the Soviets. The US approach to the Soviet Union was based on a realistic view of the nature of the USSR and of the differences of history, geography, ideology, and national experiences. These differences set America apart and, at the same time, ensure that some aspects of relationship will remain competitive. America must maintain the ability to protect US security and that of its allies and friends with the necessary strength – military, economic, technological, and political – to counter threats of the use of force. It was a position that mirrored Soviet accusations of the use of military power by the United States.

A review of American foreign policy published one year later in April 1991, shortly before the disintegration of the USSR, indicates that the US perception of the Soviet Union, which had undergone a radical change under President Bush in 1990, has shown signs of reversion to the past. Robert Zoelick, counsellor for the State Department, said 'I think we are in for a difficult period' in US–Soviet relations (Backgrounder, 1991). The US, he said, must probe the 'new thinking' in Soviet foreign policy, seeking to shape and, where possible, to alter Soviet policy calculations so that the Soviets may face up to the contradictions between the new thinking and old habits. There was little evidence, he said, to show that past American attempts at altering Soviet thinking had been effective.

## THE CONFUSION IN RUSSIA

Gorbachev's New Thinking and subsequent changes in Soviet foreign policy, brought about a mixed reaction not only in the United States but also within Russia itself. Conflicting and quite often contradictory comments in the Russian press indicated a reluctance by some Russian political analysts and Russian political figures, particularly the military, to accept the new direction in Soviet foreign policy. Two years after the beginning of *glasnost*, in February 1987, Gorbachev addressed the Soviet mass media, instructing journalists and propagandists on goals and limits of *glasnost*. As late as October 1989, in a closed meeting with Soviet editors and cultural personalities, Gorbachev criticised the mass media for exploiting *glasnost* and allowing publicity harmful to the goals of *perestroika* and to national morale. The chief editor of the popular journal *Argumenty i fakty*, Vladislav Starkov, was singled out and pressured to resign. However, despite a virtual ultimatum from Gorbachev, Starkov, with the support of his staff, refused to go. It had taken quite some time for an independent press to emerge in Russia, and for opinions at variance with official government policies to be printed. It took another four years for the freedom of the press to be officially recognised. On 12 June 1990, the USSR Supreme Soviet passed a Law on the Press, which forbade state censorship.

At first, the new direction in Soviet thinking took a subtle turn by revising the old principle of the inevitability of war between the USSR and the capitalist world. Gorbachev clearly stated his intention to improve relations with the West, particularly with the United States. There was, however, some internal resistance against Gorbachev's first steps towards a reconciliation with the West. The former Chief of General Staff, Marshal Nikolai Ogarkov, in a booklet published in April 1985, said that the current international situation 'to a certain degree reminds one of the years which preceded the Second World War' (Ogarkov, 1985). This was flatly contradicted by Gorbachev who in a speech held at the 40th V-E Day rally (May 1985) said that 'the present world is absolutely unlike that of the nineteen thirties'.

Gorbachev's November 1985 summit in Geneva, Switzerland, with President Ronald Reagan, aroused further hostility from the Soviet military. One hard-liner, General Aleksei Epishev, who often expressed a tough view, severely criticised the 'political naivety' that led some to think that 'the potential aggressor' could be stopped by 'concessions and acts of good will' (loc. cit.).

In the 1980s most Russian comments on foreign policy were limited to the question of the military balance between the United States and the Soviet Union. The arms limitation agreements between the two superpowers were met with diverse reactions. Some Russians welcomed the new development, while many saw in them a sign of Russia's weakness and a surrender to Western pressures. But most Russian observers looked at the new foreign policy from a purely national security point of view. They were particularly concerned with the question of a military balance. Some observers accused Western officials of continuing to fabricate confrontational aspects of the process of *perestroika* and of seeing the reduction of military confrontation through the prism of achieving military superiority. The Chief of Staff of NATO, George Galvin, was quoted as asserting that the Soviet Union was ahead of the US in production of military equipment including armoured vehicles and had not reduced the supply of modern weapon-systems to its armed forces. He emphasised the necessity for NATO to possess sufficient nuclear forces by stressing the manifold superiority of the USSR in these kinds of weapons (Orlov, 1990). To refute this allegation, one Soviet commentator claimed that the USSR had reduced its military budget by 8.2 per cent, and had reduced its purchases of military equipment and technology by 4.8 per cent. Expenditure on R & D was also to be reduced by 15 per cent. Furthermore, he asserted, while the USSR projected to reduce its military budget by more than 14 per cent within the next two years, the American Administration was planning to reduce its budget by only 1.3 per cent. The basic feature of the American military budget, according to another Soviet source, was the programme of rapid accumulation of its war potential through the acquisition of new weapon-systems and war technology. Expenditure on SDI was to be increased by 1 billion dollars. It is understandable, according to the Soviet view, that while assuming the role of a guarantor of freedom and democracy, and in order to find support for its projected military plans, the Administration needed the myth about the 'Soviet military threat' (ibid.).

A TASS statement published in February 1986 in Washington was assumed to represent Soviet government foreign policy at the time. It was at variance with the spirit of *perestroika* and was a clear indication of the disorientation among Soviet political circles. The main concern seemed to have been with the ongoing arms race. The statement accused Washington of openly declaring its intention to pursue its militaristic course, while the XXVII Congress of the CPSU appealed 'to reason and to the conscience of the world to stop the arms race and eradicate the hanging threat of nuclear destruction' (*Pravda*, 28 February 1986). TASS asserted that most Western politicians claimed the necessity for the United States to aim for superiority despite Soviet unilateral steps. President Reagan himself stated that his administration would not allow any slowing down in the pace of growth of the current military budget nor in the future. Boasting about the results of the modernisation of the American armed forces, Reagan claimed credit for the creation of new generations of weapons such as MX missiles, the Trident system of submarines, B-1B and 'stealth' bombers and 'Pershing-2' missiles stationed in Western Europe. According to TASS, Reagan justified his military policy as necessary for the successful outcome of negotiations with the Soviet Union. 'Preparation for war is one of the most effective means of securing peace', the President was quoted as saying, 'sitting now at the negotiating table with the USSR we should not deprive ourselves of a trump card'. He again proclaimed the militarisation of outer space and insisted on a speedy realisation of the programme of 'Star Wars'. The President clearly indicated that the administration would not limit itself to research only in the area of SDI, but was already planning the immediate creation of a real system of outer space weapons. TASS commented that in order to justify the course toward military superiority, the President again turned to confrontational rhetorics against the Soviet Union. TASS also objected to Reagan's claim that 'soon there will be an end to the long list of governments which were under Soviet domination'.

The Soviet government was clearly concerned by Reagan's call for the continuation of support for its allies in strategic regions of the world and with his praise for the 'enemies' of the peoples of Afghanistan, Kampuchea, Laos, Nicaragua and Ethiopia to whom the administration was sending armaments and money in order to realise the 'American imperialist doctrine of neo-globism'. A similar position was adopted by some Soviet commentators with links with the CPSU. The Communist party remained for a number of years the sole proponent of the old thinking and has never accepted the new rules introduced by Gorbachev.

A *Pravda* commentator, Gennadii Vasiliev, in an article published in *Pravda* (9 September 1990, p. 4), while speaking of domestic problems, the economy and ethnic unrest, pointed out that foreign policy questions were preoccupying Soviet citizens more than ever before. According to *Pravda*, the unilateral reduction of Soviet military forces elicited the question in some people's minds whether such a step on the part of the Soviet government would not weaken the defences of the USSR and endanger its national security. *Pravda*'s article referred to the official announcement that the Soviet Union would reduce the number of troops by 500 000, tanks by 10 000, pieces of artillery by 8500 and combat aircraft by 800. Defence expenditure would also be reduced by almost 30 billion rubles relative to the adopted Five-Year Plan. Was this going too far?, asked *Pravda*. In answering this question *Pravda* took a somewhat ambiguous position. It claimed that even after the adoption of the above-mentioned measures, the security of the USSR would still be maintained. On the other hand it criticised the policy of the Soviet government, which was to mirror the military efforts of the West. For every new Western missile the response was another missile, for every tank – two tanks. The policy of the government, *Pravda* said, was a transition from superarmament to reasonable and reliable sufficiency for defence. But, *Pravda* concluded, the reaction of the United States and other NATO countries could not be considered adequate. Washington's new step had been judged by the Soviet commentator as non-constructive. 'It would be wrong for the West to rely on the principle of acting from a position of strength in order to "squeeze" out more of the socialist countries.'

Similar views could be found in the army newspaper *Krasnaya zvezda* (28 March 1990). The same Gennadii Vasiliev, an army colonel, expressed the position of the army in comparable terms. Noting the end of the Cold War and the new Soviet military doctrine linked

to the new thinking, Vasiliev drew attention to the fact that the
United States was still maintaining their earlier programmes of
qualitative improvement of their armed forces. 'The US was planning
the creation of basically new weapon-systems whose destructive capabilities will be comparable to the means of mass destruction.' This,
according to the author, had been particularly relevant to the military naval forces. As the American Secretary for Defense said: 'we
continue to strive to emphasise the importance of navy superiority
and the control over the oceans'. To support this assertion, the
Americans claimed that the US is a great sea power and the role
of the navy is strictly defensive. Vasiliev refuted this assertion. The
naval forces of the US were vastly exceeding their defence needs
and were vastly exceeding the Soviet naval forces. He followed his
argument by a detailed analysis of the size and composition of the
American navy. What was most menacing from the Soviet point of
view, concluded Vasiliev, was that the American navy exercises had
been taking place close to Soviet territorial waters. The number,
scale and composition of the participants in these dangerous
manoeuvres was increasing – '. . . one cannot extend one's soft
hand while clenching the other into a fist' (loc. cit.).

   A different approach to US–Soviet relations was adopted by many
Russian intellectuals. While in the past they usually followed the
party line, they became more independent and objective in their
analysis after the introduction of *glasnost*. Increasingly they reflected
the true spirit of Gorbachev's New Thinking. On the theoretical
level, they still adopted a dialectical, but not necessarily Marxist,
approach in an attempt to formulate a theory of contemporary East–
West relations. An article by Oleg Bykov, deputy director of the
MEIMO Institute of the Academy of Science of the USSR, dealt
with the relevant questions in a fashion peculiar to Soviet political
theorists whereby political, economic or social processes must be
justified by an appropriate theory. Such a kind of dialectic invariably contained a great deal of revisionism and alternative interpretations of Leninist principles (Bykov, 1990). Bykov spoke of 'a real
breakthrough in the theoretical approach to the problems of peaceful
coexistence' – from a rigid framework of intergovernmental relations of socialist and capitalist structures to a wider horizon of human
civilisation parameters. The main aspect of his approach was the
rejection of the theory of the inevitable split of the world into two
systems and the class confrontation on the world arena, which would
lead to a transformation of the capitalist system into a socialist

economic structure. The contradiction between peaceful coexistence and world revolution was at the core of Soviet foreign policy.
It goes back to the Revolution when it was thought that capitalism
was about to crumble. From such a perspective it was difficult to
consider long-term relations with bourgeois governments. It led to
a course geared to the destruction of capitalism through the 'export of revolution' including provoking 'revolutionary wars'. It was
the stabilisation of Western capitalism that brought with it the need
to create conditions for the existence of the sole socialist country
in foreign surroundings (ibid.).

According to the author it was Lenin, who first understood the
situation. In his analysis Lenin tried to avoid the class approach
but to understand the dialectic of a world historical process which
would include not only confrontation but common interests of states
with different systems. It was not a question of breathing-space or
cease-fire, but of a lengthy period of coexistence of a socialist state
with other non-socialist states. Yet, Bykov said, the simple view of
capitalism as parasitic and dying out persisted. In addition, the
emergence of a peculiar type of socialism, of the Stalinist totalitarian kind, complicated the relations between the USSR and the rest
of the world. However, history proved that countries with differing
systems can not only coexist but cooperate as was the case during
the Second World War. The aftermath of the war and the emergence of nuclear weapons brought about the Cold War, for which,
says the author, both superpowers bear equal responsibility.

During the post-Second World War years, peaceful coexistence
was exploited by the Soviet Union as a tactical means of removing
the threat of war through the destruction of imperialism. Despite
new realities, the dogmatic concept of the inevitability of war between capitalist countries for the benefit of socialism persisted. The
inconsequential approach to the question of peace persisted even
in the post-Stalin era. Krushchev still claimed 'that we will bury'
capitalism, and after the XX Congress of the CPSU, the view persisted that a nuclear war would spell the end of capitalism. Although, says the author, the US has contributed to the state of
confrontation between the superpowers, it is undeniable that the
Soviet Union has responded in a mirror-like fashion. The achievement of strategic parity in Europe, its actions in Eastern Europe,
and especially in Afghanistan were proof of it.

It was only with the initiation of *perestroika* that the potentials
of peaceful coexistence were realised. Despite the old dogma of

the inevitability of war among capitalist states, the new principle corresponded to the essence and character of the intergovernmental relations of contemporary capitalism. The author concludes that humanity can no longer secure its future in the conditions of the permanent confrontation of the two systems, but destabilising trends are still active and would probably remain so for a long time. The latter appraisal of the situation proved to have been quite correct for despite the collapse of communism, an antagonism of a different kind between Russia and the United States began slowly to emerge, as will be indicated in the following chapters of this study.

Ponomarev, a reviewer of the army newspaper *Krasnaya zvezda*, (8 April 1990) saw a softening of the US position toward the Soviet Union, but insisted that the new 'soft line' of Western governments has not been met with general approval and support. An enemy no longer existed, but the chief of the Pentagon kept insisting that it would be dangerous to establish a policy based on the assumption that the Soviet Union would never again become a real military threat. All this must put an imprint on Soviet–American relations, said the author, and it did not augur well for the intention declared by both sides of reducing their strategic offensive weapons by 50 per cent.

A radically different view that placed the responsibility for the confrontation mainly on the Soviet Union was presented by Genrikh Trofimenko of the Institute of the US and Canada of the Academy of Sciences of the USSR (Trofimenko, 1990). According to the author, the USSR had finally begun conducting itself on the world scene in a 'civilised' manner. It accepted the priority of values common to mankind, it realised the disastrous effects of 'peaceful coexistence' based on class struggle and accepted the United Nations as an instrument for solving conflicts – an institution created by the former allies but transformed into a propaganda platform. The author notes that American foreign policy has always been determined by its attitude to the Soviet Union. Washington understood that the USSR today is quite different from what it had been during the Cold War. But what kind of a Soviet Union will the US face in the future 'is not clear to them just as it is not clear to us'. For the US to establish a new strategy it must be sure of what kind of political and economic structures will prevail in the USSR. Therefore, US foreign policy is, for the time being, more or less improvised without a clear future perspective (ibid.).

It must be noted, said the author, that after Bush came to power his Administration rapidly evaluated the international situation and took appropriate action. As a result, Bush proposed to meet Gorbachev in Malta. By doing this, Bush demonstrated a more positive attitude to Gorbachev's domestic and foreign policy than did Reagan, and because it was usual for American analysts to personify politics, it was thought that the new policy of the USSR was Gorbachev's personal policy rather than that of the Soviet Union. It was for this reason that it was considered in the interest of the US to support Gorbachev since internal democratisation and *glasnost* as well as Gorbachev's foreign policy met American long-term objectives.

The new relationship between the two states did not mean that there were no disagreements. The Soviet Union realised that even after signing agreements on arms reduction, the arms race might still continue. For the USSR, according to the author, the only way to limit the extent of the arms race, was to continue on the path of new thinking, that is not to provide the other side with reasons for increased fears. However, the psychology of the Cold War still persists in the US today. One of its by-products is the reluctance by the US to grant or to guarantee large credits to the Soviet Union, the argument being that it would be useless to assist the Soviet Union at the expense of American finances while Soviet military spending remained at a high level. 'Pluralism of views' within the Soviet Union – that is contradictory statements by politicians and the military – had not been helpful either, according to the author. The military spending was officially estimated at 4.4 per cent of GDP, while in the committees of the Supreme Soviet the figure of 25 per cent had been circulated (ibid.).

The problem of Eastern Europe was also a sore point in Soviet–American relations. The Soviet Union, said the author, must realise that with all its readiness to widen and strengthen the system of cooperation and security in Europe, the US can hardly be expected to accept it as a replacement for NATO. The US needs the latter not so much as a countervailing factor to the 'threat', as for retaining its influence on the policies of West European countries. NATO will still occupy itself with military planning and military activities, including preparations for a hypothetical 'Soviet invasion'. This last comment is particularly significant in view of the subsequent developments regarding NATO's role in Europe. We shall come back to this question in Chapter 9.

## THE END OF CONFUSION

In retrospect it can be seen that the apparent division of opinions among Soviet and American commentators and politicians resulted from the general confusion regarding the real situation within the Soviet Union and the intentions of the new leadership. The confusion ended with the emergence of Russia as an independent state replacing the USSR. The collapse of the Union had been expected by some Western analysts but not its timing. Events following the failure of the attempted coup placed the United States in a situation that called for a revision of America's posture and for a new ideology that would be acceptable to the American public. With the disappearance of an enemy, the US had to adopt a position that would be in accordance with Western values, and at the same time would assure the world of its continued leadership.

With the imminent collapse of the Warsaw Pact alliance, the United States was faced with the task of determining the role of NATO in Europe. Initially it was thought that with the dissolution of the USSR, European security no longer required a military alliance, and this perception of security was reinforced by the disbanding of the Warsaw Pact. The United States' decision to retain NATO as a military organisation signalled the end of the earlier confusion and uncertainty regarding a policy toward Russia, but created a new situation of potential conflict between the East (Russia) and the West (United States).

In Russia, the signals emanating from the West regarding NATO's future, have also spelled the end of the uncertainty regarding its relations with the West. In addition, Boris Yeltsin had to face a domestic economic situation that demanded a quick solution. In the search for a solution Yeltsin had to confront not only the reluctance by Western financial institutions to grant Russia assistance, but also internal resistance from former communists and Russian nationalists who have gained a combined majority in the Duma. Thus, simultaneously with the search for a solution to Russia's economic difficulties, there also arose a need to formulate a new foreign policy that would be acceptable for those political circles who demanded a proper place for Russia in the international arena, especially a policy that would counter the retention of NATO as a military alliance.

At the same time, many Russian intellectuals and political figures of all colours, began an inquiry into the causes of the collapse of the Soviet Union. Such investigation was thought to be not only of historical interest, but also of great importance for the Russian government because of the question of nationalities, which is considered to be a major cause of the collapse of the Soviet Union. The Russian Federation with its relatively large number of ethnic minorities faces similar problems. The war in Chechnya was the first violent encounter between Moscow and the periphery which demanded self-determination. The danger, as perceived by the Kremlin, is that, not unlike the Soviet Union, it may lead to the disintegration of the Russian Federation. It is for this reason that the analysis of the causes of the collapse of the Soviet Union assumes political significance for the Russian government today.

# 4 The Fall of an Empire

Historically, the fall of an empire has always been accompanied by bloody upheavals, but what occurred in the Soviet Union was a unique event in recent history. The Soviet Union has been considered by many as an imperial state, but according to most Russian analysts, the Soviet Union was not an empire under the classical definition. The Russian Federation, the largest within the Union, never claimed to be a metropolis ruling over the other republics – it was the Union that in a way transcended all of its constituent parts. For over seventy years the Moscow party–government centre with all its power structure held in subordination the peoples of all the republics including the Russian Federation. This mighty power structure collapsed without an armed struggle and without military intervention.

From a historical perspective it can be seen that both imperial Russia and the USSR have managed to exist thanks to four main, interrelated pillars of power. The first – a centralised, state-controlled economy whose main task was to support a huge military machine. The second – a strictly hierarchical, authoritarian or totalitarian political system combined with a messianic ideology, which was used to manage an economy based on military power. The third – territorial and political expansion limited only by geography and resistance by other nations. By its very nature, such a country was condemned to permanent confrontations with the outside world and this confrontation was the fourth pillar on which the system relied – it was a justification of the regime with all its peculiarities (Arbatov, 1994, p. 6).

It was practically impossible to eliminate one of the four pillars of power without undermining all the others. In 1985, Mikhail Gorbachev began to destroy one of the pillars through the 'new political thinking' which signified a more benign image of the outside world. As a result of the elimination of the siege mentality, the colossal fortress crumbled within a few years. The Soviet Union officially collapsed on 21 December 1991. Eleven former Union republics declared its dissolution. Four other republics – the Baltic states and Georgia – actually supported this historical act. A great power ruling over a vast Eurasian space, over 320 million people and over a military-strategic and economic potential equal to that of the United States, has virtually disappeared from the world political map. This may have largely removed the internal and external confusion that arose after the introduction of *perestroika*, but it has created a new set of play on the international arena, the concluding act of which is still to be staged.

Although the precise date of the collapse of the Soviet Union has been put at 21 December 1991, there were already ominous signs of its impending disintegration, but the suddenness of the collapse shook the entire world and many politicians and political analysts began the task of probing into its causes. The reasons for the collapse of the Soviet Union are very complex. Some analysts emphasise the economic factor, while others disagree. Economic conditions in the USSR since the Revolution have always been difficult and the standard of living very low compared to the West, nevertheless, there were no visible signs of general discontent among the population. The population at large saw the economic problems reflected in the shortages of goods to which it had been used for decades. The exact nature of the economic problems facing the former USSR was known only to the leadership of the country. Yet, an awareness that problems did exist could be seen in the many attempts at reforming the economy. The domestic factor assumed importance only after the introduction of political and economic reforms by Gorbachev. The reforms and the subsequent collapse came from above not from below as had been expected (Maksimova, 1992). It should be noted that the dissolution of the Union took place despite the expressed will of the peoples who clearly stated their decision during the referendum in April 1991 when they voted for the retention of the Union. The dissolution of the Union had been declared without any constitutional procedure.

## THE NATIONALITIES QUESTION

One hypothesis is that the main cause of the disintegration of the former Soviet Union was the problem of relations between the various Soviet nationalities, which were considered for a long time as non-conflicting – as almost totally harmonious. Any analysis of conflicting trends in this area were forbidden territory. The XXII Congress of the CPSU devoted its attention for the first time to the problem of nationalities, but it considered the question in a rather simplistic way – 'the prosperity of nationalities leads to their drawing together, and their drawing together leads to prosperity'. The writings of Soviet social scientists expressed only the ideas about the drawing together of nationalities and cultures. What was absent was an objective evaluation of national trends toward retention and development of their cultures and languages. The nationalities conflict was therefore just under the surface and erupted when the conditions became opportune.

A major factor in the inter-ethnic conflict was the demography of various republics. It was the historical fact of the dispersion of more than 150 nationalities over the territory of the former Soviet Union that did not always coincide with the administrative division of the country. Over 60 million people – almost one-fifth of the total population of the former USSR – lived outside their national republic. Out of 150 million Russians, 25 million live outside the Federation – 11 million in Ukraine (20 per cent of the population) and over 6 million in Kazahkstan (38 per cent of the population). The same applied to other nationalities. Overall, national minorities numbered about 70 million or almost 25 per cent of the population of the former Soviet Union. All republics, except Armenia, have between 20 per cent (Azerbaidjan, Lithuania) and 60 per cent (Kazakhstan) of non-indigenous people. Another factor was the problem of internal borders and territorial disputes. About 85 per cent of inter-republican borders in the former USSR were not marked. During the years of Soviet rule, borders were often arbitrarily changed and entire populations were deported. All this became a source of potential conflict.

In the majority of republics the movement towards sovereignty acquired nationalistic features. If in the beginning the national forces of liberation demanded increased freedom in decision-making, in the end, when they came to power, they demanded full state independence and secession from the Union. The first to put forward such demands were the parliaments of the Baltic states. They were followed by Moldova, Georgia, Armenia and Ukraine. Attempts by the leadership of the USSR to stop this process by means of military force ended in failure.

In Kazakhstan, where the Russian population at one stage exceeded that of native Kazakhs, the trend reversed at the end of the 1980s when Kazakhs exceeded the number of Russians in the republic (Carrère, 1990, p. 67). Evidence of ethnic conflict appeared for the first time on 17 December 1986 in Alma Ata during the violence which erupted between Kazakh demonstrators and the forces of law and order.

Karabakh, a mountainous region of Caucasia, was for a long time the subject of conflict between Armenians and Azerbaidjanis who demanded possession of it. When in December of 1920, Armenia lost its independence, it was implicitly understood that Karabakh with a 95 per cent majority of Armenians would be part of the republic of Armenia, but being an enclave within the republic of Aizerbaidjan, it became an autonomous region of the latter. The conflict between the two nations has been brewing ever since.

The national antagonism between the Azerbaidjanis and the Armenians came to the surface on 18 February 1988, when large demonstrations took place in Erevan and Stepanakert. They were not directed against the USSR or the system – it was rather a call for self-determination. During subsequent disorders two Azerbaidjanis were killed. The response of the latter was violent. A pogrom erupted in Sumgait, a suburb of Baku, during which 31 people were killed and 300 wounded. It led to an exodus of Armenians from Azerbaidjan and of Azerbaidjanis from Armenia.

The reaction of the central authorities in Moscow was one of vacillation between the two adversaries. Both first secretaries of the Communist party of Armenia and Azerbaidjan, Demirchian and Baghirov were sacked. But to no avail. On 15 June, the Supreme Soviet of Armenia unanimously voted for the annexation of Karabakh to the Armenian republic, while two days later Azerbaidjan adopted a similar resolution. Gorbachev declared himself against any territorial change. After the March 1989 election to the Supreme Soviet of the USSR, the Armenian deputies suggested a referendum in Karabakh which would decide the fate of the region. Gorbachev rejected this solution. At the same time, a religious factor came into play whereby the Azerbaidjanis saw the link between Christian Armenia and Russia. From then on the conflict acquired a religious connotation – the Muslims against the infidels. In Tadjikistan, Kirgizia, Uzbekistan and Turkmenistan the national problem took a somewhat similar form. In June 1986 a few thousand Tadjiks in Dushanbe, the capital of Tadjikistan, attacked anyone who looked foreign. In October, disorders took place in Frunze the capital of Kirgizia where Kirgiz students attacked anyone who was not Kirgizian, and in December 1988 and April 1989, bloody battles aimed against foreigners erupted in Tashkent – the capital of Uzbekistan. In May 1989, Ashkhabad, the capital of Turkmenistan, and Nebit-Dag, were the theatre of violent demonstrations. Here the disorders had an economic background; they were directed against the cooperatives and speculators.

Another arena of inter-ethnic clashes was Georgia. Sunday 9 April 1989 saw a bloody confrontation in Tbilisi where a peaceful demonstration was dispersed by the army resulting in over twenty dead and hundreds of wounded. The demonstration had at its origin the conflict between the Georgians and the Abkhazians. The Georgian Soviet republic included in its territory the Autonomous Republic of Abkhazia. The latter constituted a relatively small minority in Georgia (93 213 Abkhazians against 3 789 385 Georgians). They were also a minority in the republic of Abkhazia itself (90 213 against 242 304 Georgians). In fact, Georgia being a kind of mini-federation included other small minorities such as Adjaria and Ossetia. Three separate movements confronting each other and putting forward different demands paralysed Georgia in 1989. One was composed of Georgians of the Autonomous Republic of Abkhazia against Abkhazians, the second, Abkhazians against the Georgians, and the third, the entire population of Georgia against the Soviet Union. The movements were suppressed by force resulting in 16 to 18 dead according to the authorities and hundreds of dead according to the Popular Front.

In the Baltic states the movement towards liberation from Soviet rule took a decisive turn in 1988. In less than four months – June to October 1988 – popular fronts emerged in the three Baltic republics annexed by Stalin in 1940, but the memory of their independent existence and of the system of government which allowed a multi-party regime was still retained. It was for this reason that the Baltic states were the first to attempt to draw tangible benefit from *perestroika* and *glasnost* that would meet their national aspirations.

The first national front to emerge was that of Lithuania under the name of Saiudis established on 3 June 1988. It immediately began to assert its national character and since its inception it distanced itself from the Gorbachev concept of *perestroika*. The same principle guided the creation of the Popular Front of Estonia, established on 1 October 1988 in Tallinn, and that of Latvia in Riga on 8 October 1988. From the very beginning, the three fronts have established a close link. In May 1989, representatives of the three fronts, assembled in Estonia created a Council of Baltic Popular Fronts whose function was to coordinate their activities.

In an attempt to defuse the situation, the Soviet Parliament passed a law on 27 July 1989 which recognised the economic autonomy of the three republics. In order to make the transition towards independence orderly, the parliament passed a law on secession on 3 April 1990. But the law made it almost impossible for a republic to secede. A two-thirds majority in a referendum was required before the question of secession could be considered, and it gave the minorities in the autonomous republics and regions the right to vote separately in a referendum. If a referendum failed it could not be initiated again for ten years. It took less than one year – from November 1988 to July 1989 – for the Baltic states to assert their independence. All three declared their economic and political independence through the adoption of relevant laws. In Estonia, where there was a sizeable Russian minority, the law has limited the voting rights for non-Estonians.

In October 1988, a Belorussian National Front was created in Minsk, but was immediately confronted by a hostile reaction from the local Communist Party. The first demonstration by the Front on 30 October was violently dispersed by the forces of law and order. The excuse was the defence of the minorities in the Belorussian republics (1 341 000 Russian, 290 000 Ukrainians, 418 000 Poles and 188 000 Jews).

In the Ukraine it took longer for a front to emerge. The Ukraine was the second largest republic in the Union with 51.5 million inhabitants, including 11 million Russians. A large part of Soviet industry was located in the Ukraine, as were coal mines, and a number of nuclear power stations. The idea of independence from Moscow was also adopted by Moldova. Detached since the end of the Second World War from Rumania, Moldova had been a multi-ethnic republic.

The deterioration in inter-ethnic relations in the Soviet Union had become the most pressing question by the end of 1990. Under the influence of nationalistic trends, there was a widespread conviction that a separation from the Union would solve all political and economic problems.

OTHER CAUSES OF THE COLLAPSE

Another cause of the collapse of the USSR, according to a Russian analyst, was the failure of the Soviet elite to control the situation

(Shapoval, 1996). In most countries, notes the commentator, the leadership consists of a so-called elite. In Russia such an elite was the Party nomenklatura; this elite had crumbled. Its weakness and the sense of doom had not arisen because of the capitalist spirit of the elite – the elite had become corrupted and had sunk deeply into the struggle for privileges and material benefits. It was only through the force of inertia that the system had continued to retain its hold, and it had collapsed when Gorbachev with his *perestroika* and especially his policy of *glasnost*, disturbed this inertia. Even Brezhnev with his apparent low intellect, instinctively felt that it would be dangerous for the system to touch a single stone, for fear that the whole edifice would collapse. Gorbachev lacked such intuition (Mirskii, 1996).

The loss of the ability of the elite, of which Gorbachev and his team were members, to manage the country, led to a search for new forms of management. All this took place against the background of the collapse of the Party. A key moment was the November 1990 and April 1991 plenum of the Central Committee of the CPSU. The plenum decided to call an extraordinary Congress of the CPSU on 3 September 1991 followed by a Congress of People's Deputies of the USSR with one question on the agenda: the replacement of the general secretary of the party and the re-election of a president of the USSR. A new formula of power had been decided upon – the post of president was to be retained, the Congress of People's Deputies was to be abolished, and a government of the renewed Union and a new Supreme Soviet was to be established. Subsequently, the so-called Union Treaty was initialled, and was to be signed on 21 August 1991. It was never signed because of the attempted coup that took place two days earlier.

It had been self-evident that the nucleus of the Soviet government was the CPSU. The government – neither of the Union nor Republican – did not adopt a single resolution without the confirmation of the relevant party organ. The major battle for power unfolded within the CPSU. The turning point in this struggle was the establishment of the Russian Communist Party. Ivan Polozkov and Gennadii Zyuganov hit the last nail into the coffin of the machine called CPSU – the machine that managed the country. The process of the collapse of the CPSU became irreversible after the Putsch. Gorbachev resigned from his post of secretary general and by 1 November 1991, out of 15 republican communist parties, not one remained except the Communist Party of the Russian Federation. With the collapse of the CPSU all mechanisms of management became paralysed.

Another plausible contributing factor to the collapse was the struggle for power between Boris Yeltsin and Gorbachev which came to the surface after the attempted coup of August 1991. But the struggle between the two began much earlier. On 21 October 1987, Boris Yeltsin in one of his first attacks against Gorbachev, criticised him at the Central Committee Plenum of the CPSU for the slow pace of reform, and threatened to resign. As a result of that speech, Boris Yeltsin was dismissed as first secretary of the Moscow City Party Committee. He was accused of non-adherence to democratic centralism in Party affairs. Yeltsin's speech at the XIX all-Union conference of the CPSU in July 1988 (*Izvestia*, 2 July, 1988) may be considered as a watershed in the history of the CPSU. For the first time, the conference deviated from the former practice of unanimity in the course of Party congresses and conferences. The daring opposition to the Party line and the criticism of communist democracy expressed by Yeltsin was unprecedented in the history of the Soviet Union.

A further step toward the disintegration of the Union and the Communist party was the repeal by the national Congress of People's Deputies in March 1990 of Article 6 of the Constitution of the Soviet Union which previously guaranteed the monopoly of power of the CPSU. In an apparent attempt to retain political power, Gorbachev was sworn in as the new president of the Soviet Union (after running unopposed and being elected by a secret ballot).

A few months later, on 16 May, the first Congress of People's Deputies of the Russian Federation opened. On 29 May, after three rounds of balloting, Boris Yeltsin was elected Chairman of the RSFSR Supreme Soviet – the closest position to that of a president of Russia. On 8 June 1990, the Russian republic declared sovereignty over its territory and resources, challenging the authority of the centre, and on 12 June it declared its political sovereignty. This was followed by the declaration of sovereignty by Uzbekistan, Moldova, Ukraine, Belorussia, Armenia, Turkmenistan, Tadjikistan and Kazakhstan.

In the meantime, at the twenty-eighth CPSU Congress in July 1990, Gorbachev was overwhelmingly re-elected general secretary and during the closing days of the Congress, Boris Yeltsin resigned from the Party. From this moment on, Gorbachev's sole political objective was to salvage the Union. But while the Soviet parliament was debating the question of the retention of the Union, three political events took place which seemed to conflict with each other and which put the idea of a new Union in jeopardy.

A draft of a Constitution of the Russian Federation prepared by a Constitutional Commission headed by Boris Yeltsin was published on 22 November 1990. Two days later, on 24 November, a Draft of a new Union Treaty was publicised and presented by Gorbachev. In response, the extraordinary Congress of People's Deputies of the RSFSR, became the scene of heated debate on the question of whether the draft of the Union Treaty should be included in the order of the day of the Congress. It was clear that the long-brewing dispute between Yeltsin and Gorbachev came to a head. Both had in mind quite different and directly conflicting aims. While Gorbachev aimed at the preservation of the Union, every step of Yeltsin's was geared toward reducing Gorbachev's powers through the assertion of Russian independence (Pugachev, 1990). Neither draft contained any reference to ideology. In this respect it can be seen that Gorbachev, although officially the Secretary General of the CPSU, took a pragmatic approach in distancing himself from the Party dogma. As far as Yeltsin was concerned, he had already waged an anti-communist campaign for quite some time, and the new Constitution was a formal break with the ideological overtones that in the past permeated political ideas in the Soviet Union (ibid.).

A few months later, on 19 February 1991, Yeltsin publicly renewed his attack on Gorbachev during an appearance on the national television when he called for Gorbachev to resign. It was one more sign of the impending disintegration of the Communist Party of the Soviet Union and of the Union itself. The failed August coup was the last bomb, which when exploded, had finally destroyed the Soviet empire. However, the general euphoria which pervaded the country after the failure of the attempted coup, soon gave way to a feeling of uncertainty among the population. Millions of people became witnesses to a process beyond their comprehension, to an agony of a great but powerless country.

While the disintegration had been taking place, the four-million-strong army was still in place, the state security apparatus was still functioning as before, and the military-industrial complex still played the role of a 'government within a government' (Maksimova, 1992, p. 11). The vast army of clerks of the command-administrative system was still busy producing mountains of documents, and the Supreme Soviet continued to issue laws which no one obeyed. Everything remained in place as before, except that there was no central power to administer and enforce the application of the laws.

The coup was an opportunity for Yeltsin to assume power in Russia rather than over the Soviet Union which he probably saw disintegrating anyway. Yeltsin's victory on the barricades in front of the White House, became a signal for decisive action in other republics. One after another they began to proclaim their independence. The previously adopted law of orderly secession from the centre became a useless piece of paper. Legally, state power was still in the hands of the Centre, but *de facto* it was the republics that held real power.

A question which is still being asked in the Russian and foreign press, is whether Mikhail Gorbachev, who was endowed with practically unlimited powers (President of the country who received special powers from the Supreme Soviet, General Secretary of the CC of the CPSU, Supreme Commander of the Armed Forces) was able to control the situation and to establish new relations between the Centre and the republics? There is little doubt that such a possibility existed, but the first to challenge Gorbachev and to demand a radical turnaround of *perestroika* and reforms, was Boris Yeltsin. The continuing conflict between the two leaders that took place over the following four years, was an indication not only of a struggle for power, but of an internal conflict which Gorbachev faced. The problem Gorbachev confronted was that as President of the Soviet Union he also retained his position as General Secretary of the Party. This limited his power to act according to his ideas. He was forced to justify his every step, including questions of Party cadres, and to conform with the Politburo, which was composed of representatives of the conservative government hierarchy. In a sense he became hostage to the state apparatus (ibid., p. 9). During this critical moment Gorbachev placed himself on the side of those who in secret had been plotting a return to the old order; he in fact headed the same team which prepared and undertook the attempted coup.

Gorbachev saw that his support for the right had met with negative reaction in the republics. He therefore attempted to save the collapsing Union by calling the Novo-Ogarev negotiations and a round-table meeting with all six leaders of the republics. He then committed one more mistake by adopting the formula, 'strong republics – strong centre'. It was categorically rejected by almost all participants. The final version of the Novo-Ogarev agreement was signed only by Russia, Belorussia and five Central-Asian republics.

Nevertheless, even this agreement, limited though it was in scope, had been considered as a step towards the restoration of the totalitarian powers of the Union. Those who plotted the August coup understood that should the new agreement come into force, it would spell the end of the Soviet Union. It was no coincidence that the coup took place on 19 August – two days before the signing of the agreement.

The final outcome of Gorbachev's New Thinking may be partly due to the mistakes he had committed. When he proclaimed *perestroika* and declared the necessity for New Thinking, he triggered off and brought to life new political forces. In the final analysis it can be seen that neither Gorbachev nor his team did completely repudiate the old system. What Gorbachev wanted to do was not to break with the past but to repair it or renew it. This was expressed in the unrealistic slogan of 'socialist choice', a combination of a planned economy with a market, but a market without private property.

## THE AFTERMATH OF THE COLLAPSE

Having dissolved the Soviet Union, the former republics established the Commonwealth of Independent States, declaring at the same time that the new entity would not be a national state. The aim of the CIS was to make the transition of the former republics into a new structure easier. Its basic function was to be the coordination of the policies of its members in areas of common interest. But while the dissolution of the Union had been effected by a formal act, it left a number of unresolved questions – questions of Union assets, debts, and so on. The economic disintegration of the Union also involved the creation of separate finance-money systems which would further complicate the economic situation. It created a problem of convertibility of a number of currencies (Potapov, 1990, p. 3). There was also another important issue. The dispersion of industry over the entire territory of the Union – energy and natural resources, machinery and equipment producing enterprises in Russia, steel, consumer goods and the food industry in Ukraine, cotton and energy in the Central Asian republics – has been a powerful integrational factor. Mutual dependence of the former Soviet republics on the exchange of goods was much stronger than their links with foreign countries (Gizatov, 1989, p. 14). The disintegration led to the collapse of traditional links between the economies of the former republics.

Under these circumstances, Russia suffered much less, thanks to its relative strength and diversification of its economy and its economic potential. Russia's 'liberation' from the republics that were less prepared for a market economy, made Russia's transition somewhat easier. No longer was Russia forced to subsidise the other republics. Of all the Soviet republics it was Kazakhstan that was the main beneficiary of the transfer of resources from Russia. Russia is said to have contributed about 50 per cent to Kazakhstan's revenue. The relatively populated republic had been considered as an economic burden to the USSR as a whole (Tezisy, 1996).

An attempt had been made to solve these problems through bilateral agreements between the republics, but these proved ineffective. This was the main reason that forced the leaders of the 11 republics to create the Commonwealth of Independent States. In this way, simultaneously with the process of disintegration, there were also forces of integration and unification at work (Gizatov, 1989, p. 12). The CIS could not solve all the emerging problems. After its creation, the leaders of the newly independent states immediately began to diverge from their previously adopted positions. Disagreements which at first were concealed from the public, soon acquired features of an open conflict. Immediately after the declaration of their sovereignty, some republics began to introduce rules limiting the movement of goods across republican boundaries. But while some republics considered themselves endowed with sufficient resources for their economic independence, other outlying republics found themselves in a difficult situation. Thus, the war of laws has been transformed into an economic war. Some republics and regions experienced shortages of consumer goods and fuel. According to the opinion prevalent in some smaller republics – mainly in the Baltic – political independence did not necessarily imply a break in economic links. It was for this reason that a number of republics began to negotiate and some concluded agreements on economic cooperation (Potapov, 1990).

A major cause of sharp disagreements within the CIS, especially between Russia and Ukraine, was the question of the division of the army and the navy. The Central Asian republics were in favour of retaining unified armed forces under a single command, while Ukraine, Moldova, Azerbaidjan and Belarus, claimed national control over the armed forces deployed on their territories. Thanks to an agreement between Russia, Ukraine, Belarus and Kazahkstan, a solution was found to the question of control over strategic nuclear weapons. The pressure exercised by the West played an important role in this respect (Gizatov, 1989, p. 16).

## WHO DESTROYED THE SOVIET UNION?

A 'round-table' conference in which the main participant was the creator of *perestroika* Mikhail Gorbachev, took place on 16 December 1996. Gorbachev's presence aroused a lively discussion about some of the mistakes committed by the main architect of the reform process in Russia. In that sense, the debate can be considered as an historical testimony, a document of the present time. The main question under discussion was 'who destroyed the Soviet Union: history, the West, Yeltsin or Gorbachev?' (*Nezavisimaya gazeta*, 16 January 1997).

The view that the USSR had collapsed in the same way as other empires had, that nothing could have prevented it, that the Soviet empire had attained its peak and through a natural historical process went into decline as had been the fate of other empires, was disputed by Gorbachev. 'For if this were true', Gorbachev said, 'then one should not speak about mistakes' (ibid.). Gorbachev asserted that there was a possibility of saving the USSR from collapse. The major cause of the collapse, according to Gorbachev, was Yeltsin's policy when he came to power in the summer of 1990 and adopted a policy of undermining the Union by declaring a war of laws, which in turn became the beginning of the sovereignty movements. 'No one could prove that the Russian Federation needed its independence from the Union, which actually meant independence from itself.' According to another participant, Georgii Shakhnazarov, the Union collapsed because it had fallen behind Western developed countries, and during the period of stagnation (Brezhnev) the USSR lost all the advantages provided by the socialist system.

Another explanation of the causes of the disintegration was the American CIA plot. Years later, rumours have arisen about the secret strategy of the American Administration which is said to have led to the collapse of the Union. It was disclosed in a book by the American, Peter Schweitzer, who asserted that it was the secret strategy of the American Administration that caused the collapse.

There is no evidence to support this assertion (Mirskii, 1996).

The so-called CIA plot theory was analysed by Sergei Shakhrai. According to Shakhrai, the USSR could not have been destroyed either militarily or by means of an economic blockade. The Soviet Union had the ability to sustain a blockade, because the capacity to mobilise resources was always very strong. However, there was a vulnerable spot: ideology and information. Years of ideological campaigns against the USSR had not been successful because of resistance within the Union. In 1987–88 there was a massive rush of information, which began to penetrate Russian society. This did not mean, according to Shakhrai, that it was initiated by the CIA, but an information explosion did occur. The world is ruled by information, said Shakhrai, information ignores borders and could not be stopped by customs.

There is a trend among some Russian intellectuals to find the causes of collapse in outside factors and conspiracies. They comfort themselves with the thought that the blame lies with Gorbachev and Yeltsin who sold out to the Americans and contributed to the success of the CIA plan for destroying the USSR. Their opinion has been reinforced by the apparent opposition of the US Congress to the reintegration of the former Soviet republics. Earlier, in 1992, President Bush addressed the Ukrainian parliament. In his speech he asked whether Ukraine needs independence, whether she would not be better off to remain in the Union. This seems to contradict the theory of a CIA plot, but at the same time, the US was offering 200–300 million dollars to independent republics on the condition that they didn't unite with Russia, and a US Congress resolution spoke of applying any means to prevent the integration of Russia with former republics.

The perception of foreign interference in Russian affairs, has found some credence not only among the right-wing politicians but also among government circles especially after the announcement of NATO's expansion. The consensus of opinion regarding NATO's expansion to the East is that it is against Russian national interest and is also seen as an international plot to undermine Russia's prestige and authority on the world scene.

For a number of years after the collapse of the Soviet Union, Russia's foreign policy remained in a kind of a limbo – that is, it lacked direction – until it was provided with a new orientation by the US policy aimed at maintaining a military posture in Europe in the form of NATO. Despite the assurances that NATO is not a military alliance, it is seen by the Russian government and indeed by most Russian analysts, as a revival of the old confrontation between the East and the West. On the Russian side this confrontation is expressed mainly in the opposition to NATO's enlargement. NATO's enlargement is also exploited by the Russian military who are critical of Russia's response. Their criticism is aimed primarily at the government's military policy, which they wish to change. The quest for a new military policy entails, in the first place, a modification of the former military doctrine and the creation of a new one that would meet Russia's national security interests. Several variants of the doctrine have already been published in the Russian press. They all contain two main objectives: the determination of who is Russia's potential enemy, and what kind of defence measures Russia should undertake.

# 5 A New Military Policy

## MILITARY POWER IN RUSSIAN HISTORY

Military power has always played an important role in Russia and it has a long tradition in Russian history. A fact rarely mentioned is that the status of a superpower and the position of an equal among the great world powers, has not just been achieved by the Soviet Union since the end of the Second World War, but by Imperial Russia at the beginning of the eighteenth century (Cooper 1989, p. 22). Russia's geographical location which made her the object of constant invasions, coupled with constant expansion and colonisation essential for her survival, was a powerful factor in establishing a powerful military organisation. Russia's military tradition is, therefore, as ancient as her history. In the historical context it can be seen that the role of the military and generally the impact of wars, was incomparably stronger in Russia than in the West. Military power and wars were important factors in shaping Russia's society and politics of the Empire. From the early days, following invasions from the East, Russia has adopted a system of government and administration suitable for a large and expanding state, especially in the essential area of military affairs (Szamuely, 1974, p. 20).

The Russian system of government and social structure have evolved mainly through the organisation of the nation's defence which became the justification and legitimation of the all-powerful state. There is, however one aspect of the role of the military, which remained constant under the tsars and Soviet rulers – never in the history of Russia have the military challenged the authority of the tsar or Soviet power. Neither under the tsar nor under Soviet rule, have the military attempted to seize power and they have never intervened independently in internal affairs. During the Soviet rule the question of the military's role in government policies had to do with their relationship with the Party rather than government – a relationship peculiar to the Soviet Union. This was due to the fact that the role of the armed forces within the structure of the USSR had always remained under the exclusive control of the Party. After the death of Stalin the Party pursued its traditional dominating

73

role over the military. Strict control and enforcement of Party discipline was exercised through the primary Party organisations within the military units, and ideological indoctrination was conducted under the supervision of the Main Political Administration of the Soviet armed forces. The Administration was in fact a department of the Central Committee of the Party and as such has been exercising full control over the military. The degree of influence of the military on the foreign policy of the USSR was always dependent upon the party leadership rather than the military. Military policies in particular have been as a rule determined by the Politburo in conjunction with the military, but in determining foreign policy it was the authority of the Party that usually prevailed.

Under the Communist rule, the ever present complex of capitalist encirclement, which the Soviets have incorporated into their military doctrine, was the main justification for the maintenance of large armed forces. Military policy and military doctrine conformed to Soviet foreign policy, which relied mainly on the status of the Soviet Union as a superpower. Soviet militarism was characterised by foreign policy based exclusively on military power, by the subservience of the needs of society to army requirements, and by the Party's effort to promote the armed forces as the guardians of the achievements of the Revolution. The rationale for the existence and maintenance of a high military power profile was the claim of an irreconcilable conflict between the imperialist West and the Socialist world community.

## GORBACHEV AND THE NEW MILITARY DOCTRINE

A radical change in the Soviet military doctrine coincided with the change in the leadership in 1985. Although the announcement of *glasnost* and *perestroika* came following the accession of Gorbachev to power, there was no immediate evidence about the impending new direction of Soviet military policies. But as early as 1986, after the XXVII Party Congress in February of that year, there were some references by Soviet spokesmen about the introduction of a new military doctrine. The term 'reasonable sufficiency' was coined in that period and it was to mean that the Soviet Union would renounce an offensive war strategy and would replace it with a doctrine that would feature defence only. At a Warsaw Pact meeting in May 1987, the Soviets disclosed a new military doctrine which they defined as one of 'reasonable sufficiency', and at a Soviet Foreign Ministry press conference in June, the deputy Chief of the General Staff, General Gareev, confirmed once more that the basic method of operation of the Soviet Armed Forces in case of foreign aggression would be defensive (*Krasnaya zvezda*, 23 June 1987, p. 3).

Mikhail Gorbachev in his book *Perestroika and New Thinking*, expressed the idea of reasonable sufficiency in the following terms:

We consider that armaments should be reduced to a level of reasonable sufficiency, that is to a level necessary to meet defensive objectives only. The time has come for the introduction of indispensable corrections in the strategic concepts of both military alliances geared toward defence. (Gorbachev, 1988, p. 214).

The main thrust of the new military doctrine was a shift from traditional Soviet emphasis on offensive operations to 'non-offensive defence'. This was considered by some Western analysts as heralding the prospect of unilateral reduction in Soviet military forces and the possibility of negotiating significant cuts in some areas of the Warsaw Pact and NATO military forces (Patersen, 1988, pp. 9–10).

What was new in the doctrine of 'reasonable sufficiency' was not only its defensive concept, which 'presupposes the need for strictly defensive military doctrines on both sides' (*New Times*, No. 40. p. 14), but also its analytical treatment by Soviet commentators who began applying the same criteria to both sides – the US and USSR – rather than the classical Marxist-Leninist approach which always took as its point of departure the hostility of capitalism versus the peaceful intentions of the Soviet Union.

The announcement of the new principle of 'reasonable sufficiency' had not been considered sufficient to change America's attitude toward the USSR. Earlier attempts at establishing better relations with the United States, were met with extreme caution by the Carter Administration. It was for this reason that Moscow initially considered a Republican president a more reliable partner for détente, but Reagan's subsequent hardened position placed the Soviet leadership in a quandary. The announced Strategic Defense Initiative in March 1983, forced the Kremlin to revise the relationship between Soviet military power and security considerations. The Soviet leadership then had to question the value of the former principle of responding by equal measures to the US weapons programme and increased military budget. 'SDI suggested to Soviet leaders that the traditional quantitative approach to the arms race and arms

control was at an end' (Lynch, 1990, p. 24). The relationship between parity and strategic stability began to be questioned. Subsequently, the Soviets were forced to publicly admit that the balance
of nuclear forces consists of the principle of deterrent rather than
on number of missiles. They implicitly accepted that MAD (mutually
assured destruction) was a more appropriate military doctrine than an
economically ruinous path towards meeting the American challenge.

On the American side, the announced SDI programme had been
intended to create an impression of an effective protection against
a nuclear missile attack by the Soviets thereby making nuclear
weapons obsolete. It is doubtful whether the Reagan administration really believed in the possibility of building such a shield and
whether it was possible to allocate huge funds within the United
States' budget. The intention may have been to force the Soviets
into further redirection of resources into the military field at the
expense of consumer satisfaction. It was thought that internal forces
would compel the Kremlin to abandon the competition. Whether
this announcement coincided with the change in Soviet thinking
on matters of war and peace is a mute question, but its impact was
rather dramatic. 'It is hard to imagine that the Reagan Administration could have envisaged the traumatic impact SDI would have
on Soviet leaders, or the role it would play as a catalyst for the
rethinking of security interests and strategic concepts that many in
Moscow had already begun' (loc. cit.).

The American deployment of intermediate-range nuclear missiles in Europe had a similar effect. It undermined the Soviet belief
in the value of military means of achieving security. The cumula-
tive effect of these policies, including the rhetorical and budgetary
commitment to high levels of military spending, coincided with a
kind of latter-day 'scissors crisis' in Soviet foreign security policy.
The agreement on intermediate-range nuclear forces in Europe may
have appeared as a capitulation or a tactical concession from the
Soviets, but the reduction in the Soviet armed forces transformed
the American debate on US–Soviet relations and confirmed the
belief that détente was the only viable policy for the foreseeable
future. At the same time, Gorbachev's tacit acceptance of the disintegration of communism in Eastern Europe reflected his understanding of the nature of concessions. The Stockholm Conference
on Disarmament in Europe, held in 1986, which elaborated a series
of military confidence-building measures in Europe confirms this
point.

## THE MILITARY AND THE PARTY UNDER GORBACHEV

An analysis of the events that have taken place in the former Soviet Union throws some light on the causes of the radical changes in Soviet military thinking. After the advent of *perestroika*, the question of authority in military matters became increasingly important because of the significant changes in the relationship between the government and the Party. From the early days of *perestroika*, there was a quite noticeable attempt by Gorbachev to eliminate the influence of the Party in general and over the determination of Soviet foreign policies in particular. In contrast to previous practices when the course of Soviet foreign and military policies was determined by the Party, it has now become the task of the government to formulate such policies. The initially subtle reforms, had in fact signified the diminishing role of the military in the formulation of foreign policy. One of the factors which contributed to the demise of the Soviet military was the New Thinking introduced by Gorbachev as soon as he came to power. Previously, the role of the military was determined by their relations within the Party–state apparatus, that is, between the party leadership and the high command. The New Thinking overturned the basic principles which in the past allowed the military to retain their importance. Gorbachev shifted the emphasis from military confrontation to cooperation and peaceful resolution of conflicts. There was to be less emphasis on foreign threats to Soviet security and on ideology in international affairs and national security. The New Thinking clearly downgraded the importance of military forces and had subsequently led to the drastic change of the old military doctrine into one of reasonable sufficiency.

However by far the greatest impact on the diminishing role of the military was the public debate that emerged as a result of the policy of *glasnost*. In contrast to previous practices, Gorbachev allowed military matters to become the subject of public debate, especially in the Supreme Soviet. As a result, the military were subjected to wide-ranging criticism in the press. The criticism was connected in the first place to the secrecy surrounding defence expenditure. Unprecedented criticism of the army and increasingly open discussions concerning military matters began to appear in the Soviet press.

Anticipating a reaction from the military, Gorbachev embarked upon a course of replacing potential adversaries from the ranks of the armed forces. He replaced all four commanders in chief of the Soviet Union's Main Theatre of Military Operations. This course reached its climax in April 1989 when a number of older army officers, including Marshal Nikolai Ogarkov and the former defence minister Marshal Sergei Sokolov, were dropped from the CPSU Central Committee. The Mathias Rust affair – that is, the daring young pilot who, avoiding detection, managed to land his light plane right in the middle of Moscow's Red Square – provided a pretext in May 1987 to replace the minister for defence by General Dmitri Yazov. However, despite the significantly reduced prestige of the armed forces, the military did not appear to oppose Gorbachev. Although harsh criticism of government foreign policy had been voiced by high military officials, they did not seem to suggest a change in government leadership, only in its policies.

Persistent rumours of an impending military coup proved groundless, but discussions of such a possibility surfaced openly in June 1988 during the debate on the formation of the Supreme Soviet's committee on defence and state security. A number of delegates argued that the committee should be composed exclusively of civilians 'to ensure that there will never be any kind of coup d'etat by the military or the KGB' (Kramer, 1989, p. 340).

The organisational changes and the replacement of army personnel were clearly aimed at asserting governmental control over the armed forces away from the authority of the CPSU. The government attempted to establish a status for the army not dissimilar to that of the West, while the Party, because of its widespread membership within the armed forces and itself feeling threatened by the new trends in government policies, made every possible effort to retain its position.

Another serious threat to the Party's influence within the armed forces was the widely discussed plan of de-politicisation of the army. This was to be effected by eliminating the monopoly of the CPSU and by allowing other parties to function within the armed forces. With the emergence of various political movements in the Soviet Union, the Party and the army both felt that their former relationship and leading position in Soviet society was being undermined. A new situation had therefore arisen when the military had to take into account the policy of the government which was no longer under the sole authority of the Party, while at the same time, due to its traditional position of being part of the party structure, it also had to consider the party's views. The declining influence of the military could also be seen in the central decision-making apparatus. The failure to promote Yazov to full voting member of the Politburo at the September 1989 CPSU Central Committee Plenum was another step in downgrading the importance of the military. In addition, the Supreme Soviet assumed the responsibility for the appointment of the minister for defence, as well as the power to approve the defence budget. When Yazov was nominated by Gorbachev for the post of Minister for Defence, he had to seek approval by the Supreme Soviet which confirmed his nomination on 3 July 1989.

The endeavour by the Party to maintain its decisive role within the army, placed President Gorbachev in a difficult position. As the First Secretary of the CPSU, the head of the country, and the commander in chief of the armed forces, he seemed at times to have adopted an ambiguous stand. His programme of *perestroika*, which included the separation of government powers between the legislative and the executive and by implication the removal of the Party's authority, had at the same time to reconcile the activities of the Party within the armed forces. Gorbachev attempted to make such a reconciliation in his closing speech to the all-Army conference (TASS, 1991). 'The Party conference', said Gorbachev, 'concluded its works on the process of separation of the functions of military-political organs and party organisations which will acquire full independence in the future. Party activities within the armed forces would be an essential element of democratisation of the army – it would allow to openly present and debate various questions.' The question of democratisation was in clear conflict with the principle of democratic centralism adopted by the all-Army conference, but Gorbachev gave it a different interpretation. 'Political struggle as a kind of competition if it is waged within constitutional rules', he said, 'is a normal occurrence.' But while he announced his opposition to the de-politicisation of the armed forces, he appeared to have in mind the presence of several parties rather than the CPSU alone. In retrospect it can be seen that Gorbachev aimed at establishing the relationship between the armed forces and the government on a Western model – a model that would prevent the military from becoming an independent power within the state structure.

The question of the role of the military within the state structure had finally been resolved by the attempted coup, during which the military adopted a neutral position, by the collapse of the CPSU, and by the dissolution of the Soviet Union. The latter event brought the military under the control of the Russian Federation as the successor of the Soviet Union.

## THE NEW RUSSIA AND THE ARMED FORCES

The presidential decree on the 'Creation of the Armed Forces of the Russian Federation' issued on 7 May 1992 contained a specific recommendation for the Ministry for Defence to 'submit proposals for military reforms of the army and the navy'. Subsequently, the General Staff presented detailed recommendations on the qualitative improvement of the army and its further development up to the year 2000. This document was approved by the President and became the basis for the programme of development of the armed forces for the period 1993–95. The plan has failed, mainly due to the crisis in the Russian economy. The armed forces were placed in a situation in which they had to reform themselves without adequate financial and material government support (*Nezavisimaya gazeta*, 7 May 1997).

Russian observers generally approved the actions of the heads of the Ministry for Defence and the General Staff who continued to adopt measures for improvements in the structure of the army. A new strategic territorial unit – the Kaliningrad special region – was created. There were structural changes in the Black Sea navy and Caspian Sea fleet. Russia had also concluded agreements with Georgia and Armenia to build military bases and deploy Russian troops on their territory.

During the first few years following President Yeltsin's signing of the decree 'On the creation of the armed forces of the Russian Federation', Russia's military policy has concentrated on the withdrawal of military forces from Eastern Europe and cutbacks in their total numerical strength. Between 1992–96, the Russian armed forces were reduced from 2.8 million to 1.7 million personnel, and according to official data, between 1992 and 1994, over 300 000 military personnel were relocated onto Russian territory. When members of their families are included, the number was estimated at 1.2 million. The completion of this operation was hailed by Boris Yeltsin as 'a major success' (ibid.).

His opinion was not shared by Russian politicians and representatives of political movements. Some considered the troop withdrawal from the near- and far-abroad as a 'foolish flight' from regions where Russia previously had geopolitical and strategic supremacy. In addition, Russia having allocated enormous resources to transportation, had abandoned the previously created excellent army infrastructure, and had just dumped the relocated personnel without further plans of rehabilitation into civilian or military life. According to some Russian analysts, if Russia had not withdrawn the army from Europe, the question of NATO's expansion would not have created the subsequent problems in Russia–US relations (ibid.)

## COLLECTIVE SECURITY – THE CIS

The dissolution of the Union imposed upon the Russian government an important task. In order to conform to the disarmament treaties concluded earlier by the Soviet Union, Russia had to assume complete control over its nuclear arsenal. Since a significant number of nuclear weapons were deployed on the territory of the former Union republics, Russia was forced to normalise its relations with those republics regarding military matters. But for Russia, the role of its armed forces assumed additional importance due to perceived Western hostility and the subsequent plans for NATO's enlargement. In the words of Igor Korotchenko, a Russian commentator:

> Four years have passed since the collapse of the Soviet Union and a decade since the end of confrontation between the two social and political systems. The world, however, has not become more stable. On the contrary, recent events indicate the opposite. Many regions are the theatre of local wars and armed conflicts. The question of expansion of the North Atlantic alliance and its proximity to the borders of CIS are on the agenda. It is for this reason that the formation of a system of collective security will acquire additional urgency in 1996' (Korotchenko, 1996).

Realising the significance of collective defence, the heads of the CIS countries decided on 15 May 1992 to create a defensive alliance and have signed A Treaty of Collective Security. Between 1992–94 there was a search for acceptable forms of cooperation in the military area and for suitable documentation that would regulate the functioning of the alliance. Since the autumn of 1994, integration processes in the military area began to assume a practical form. On 21 October 1994, the heads of the governments of the CIS signed a Memorandum of the Council of heads of governments of the Commonwealth entitled 'Basic directions of the integration developments of CIS', and on 10 February 1995, all CIS governments (with the exception of Azerbaidjan) signed 'The Concept of collective security of countries – participants in the Treaty on collective security.' Two working groups of the Council of ministries for defence have drafted a number of versions of documents that were to establish and regulate the functioning of the system of collective security. A united system of air defence was devised in 1995. A warning system against missile attacks has been established with systems deployed on the territories of Azerbaidjan, Belarus, Latvia and Ukraine (ibid.). The means of warning against missile attacks that were to be deployed on the territories of Belarus and Latvia, had the status of the military forces of the Russian Federation, but on the territory of Ukraine – they were considered as national military forces of that republic. The status of the anti-missile defence deployed on the territory of Azerbaidjan, has not yet been determined. The servicing and the use of these installations is to be effected by the Russian army. The process of integration entered an active phase in 1995. Since then, negotiations are taking place regarding military and technological cooperation and also regarding production and maintenance of armament.

Russia's new military policy speaks of an 'attempt to create a system of collective security for the common military and strategic space of the CIS based on the Pact of Collective Security signed on 15 May 1992 and other bilateral agreements with CIS countries' (*Nezavisimaya gazeta*, 23 May 1996).

RUSSIA'S NEW MILITARY POLICY

In May 1996, the Russian government officially announced its national security policy under the title 'National security policy of the Russian Federation for the period 1996–2000', which included the guidelines for the structure of the armed forces. In its wording and even in its substance, the document bears a striking similarity to earlier Communist Party-inspired statements. Although it differs from previous documents by the absence of communist ideological overtones, it expresses in no uncertain terms a Russian nationalistic approach to matters of state security and of the armed forces as a symbol of Russia's power and international prestige. It is an amalgam of former reliance on military forces for the attainment of political objectives and a modified position appropriate to current circumstances. The document clearly defines Russia's concerns about a potential danger of war not dissimilar to the former communist position. Although Russia's view on security matters is that 'military policy determines Russia's basic objectives in attaining its interests by military means', which in fact means that armed forces may be used to attain political objectives, the document softens its position by stating that 'military forces should not exceed the level that is sufficient for meeting existing or anticipated military security threats to Russia' (ibid.).

A new and important element in Russian military policy was that Russia renounced the principle of strategic parity with the United States as it had been understood before. Russia now adheres to the principle of deterrence based on the recognition of the existence of a military threat. Deterrence may be considered as Russia's acceptance of the principle of means of preventing a nuclear war, which was never admitted by the communists. 'Equilibrium in nuclear armaments can be secured by the capability of preventing a nuclear attack through assured unacceptable damage and the maintenance of a nuclear balance on an appropriate low level in order to prevent a nuclear attack' (ibid). It is for this reason that Russia declared its intention to retain for the above-mentioned period its status of a nuclear power. In addition to preventing a nuclear attack, or a large-scale aggression with conventional weapons against her allies, it was also meant to offer them nuclear protection. At the same time, Russia declared its readiness to continue the reduction of the nuclear arsenal according to a mutual agreement with the US, while maintaining a balance of forces at a level that will meet the requirements for strategic stability. Russia will adhere to the principle of 'reasonable sufficiency'.

Finally, the document assures that Russia's new military policy is becoming increasingly pragmatic, and it does not signify an anti-Western trend. Russia considers as a real threat to its national interests any action directed toward undermining her territorial integrity and sovereignty, as well as actions whose objective is to reduce Russia's influence in the solution of global, international, and regional problems, and to weaken her position in world politics and economies (ibid.). This last point appears to be a reference to NATO's expansion to the East and an expression of Russia's concern of retaining her place in international affairs.

## RUSSIA'S NAVAL FORCES

The publication of Russia's military policy in May 1996 was closely followed by a presidential decree 'On the special Federal programme of World Oceans'. This can be attributed to the fact that with the collapse of the Soviet Union, Russia lost access to ports on the Black and Baltic seas. In order to secure Russia's national interests on the world oceans, the Russian President issued a decree, which approved a special Federal programme called 'World Oceans' (*Rossiiskaya gazeta*, 28 January 1997). The decree, dated 17 January 1997, speaks of creating a 'World Ocean' programme whose objective is the reinforcement of national security through the exploitation and study of the resources and potentials of World Oceans.

According to one Russian commentator, since the mid-1980s the military and political leadership of the US persistently maintains that Russia (USSR) is a continental and regional power, that she has no enemies at present, consequently she does not need a navy. Such views about 'continental thinking' found support among some Russian academics, politicians and are also being spread by the Russian press. They affirm that Russia does not need an ocean-going navy and that the main task of the Russian navy, in accordance with its defence attributes which are determined by the Russian military doctrine, is the direct protection and defence of her 'markedly diminished' sea frontiers. 'It is clear that the Russian navy was and remains one of the most effective instruments of government policy' (Aleksin, 1996).

Russia has always been among the six great sea powers, and maritime transport has always played an important role in Russia's foreign trade relations (the volume of maritime transportation of goods in 1995 was 81.6 million tonnes, including 26.2 million tonnes by oil tankers). However, with the collapse of the Soviet Union, Russia lost its major sea ports in the Black and Baltic seas, which made access to important sea routes more difficult. Accordingly, the 'World Ocean' programme aims at safeguarding Russia's national interests (*Rossiiskaya gazeta*, 28 January 1997).

With the loss of the climatically suitable, and well-equipped sea ports on the Black and Baltic Seas, Russia's foreign trade became increasingly dependent on the servicing of ships by port authorities located on the territories of former Soviet republics. In 1995, about 33 per cent of the total maritime transport went through these ports. According to Russia's perception, a situation has arisen in which the Baltic states and particularly Ukraine, realising Russia's vital interests in using their sea ports, are attempting to exert economic pressure. The decree speaks of the weakening of Russia's economic and political position, which prompted a number of states to try to force Russia out of world markets of goods and services, and to make it more difficult for Russia to service ships navigating in international waters and through the sea ports of these countries. 'They have introduced stricter rules for visiting Russian ships, particularly the movement of Russian oil tankers through the Black Sea straits' (ibid.).

Besides the economic implications of the loss of sea ports, Russia's military and strategic interests in the World Ocean have also been affected. The navy has always been one of Russia's major factors of national security and national interests in the world oceans area. It has also been a contributing factor in the attainment of state objectives, in the maintenance of military and political stability on the seas and oceans, as well as a major player in Russia's security arrangements and international prestige. An additional objective of Russia's military navy is the protection of Russia's influence and of economic activities on the world oceans. The navy, as part of Russia's overall military power, is seen by the government as a 'restraining factor for the prevention of aggression'. According to a survey conducted by military authorities, the Russian navy is gradually losing its capability of defending Russia's political and economic interests as well as the capability of fully protecting Russia's maritime borders.

The decree attempts to pacify world opinion by stating that the above programme is purely defensive and is meant only to protect Russia's vital national interests. On the other hand, the decree states that the development of Russia's naval forces is also aimed at preserving the necessary combat potential, primarily, its naval strategic nuclear forces – the most effective deterrent. Therefore, the maintenance of the naval nuclear deterrent at a level which will guarantee reasonable defence sufficiency is most important. 'The navy must be capable of repulsing aggression coming from the sea' (ibid.). In its conclusion the decree speaks of the necessity to formulate a military doctrine which will take into account the importance of the navy for the resolution of military problems and for the economic security of the country.

## THE NEW MILITARY DOCTRINE

The concept of a military doctrine had been a basic principle that shaped the former Soviet Union's military policy. Military doctrine in the Soviet understanding had a very wide scope; it embraced all aspects of military power in war as well as in peacetime. It reflected the essence of the Soviet political and economic system that subordinated all facets of activities of the Soviet society to national security objectives. A doctrine, according to the former Soviet definition, was understood to mean a philosophical and scientific theory – a system of guiding principles. It represented the officially adopted views on the character of war, on the method of warfare and on the preparation of the country and the army for war. In that sense, one could say that the doctrine was war oriented; it attempted to foresee the circumstances which might lead to war and the appropriate policy to be adopted prior to the actual outbreak of hostilities (Cooper, 1989, p. 38).

The basic principle of the Soviet military doctrine was based on Lenin's definition of war (borrowed from Clausewitz) as being a continuation of policy by other, namely, violent means. The source and origin of wars were viewed as the result of the existence of antagonistic class societies and war was, therefore, inevitable. This was later modified to allow for the view that war is not inevitable and leading to the term of 'peaceful coexistence – a continuation of the conflict employing peaceful means without war' (Sokolovskii, 1963, p. 171).

A further change in the Soviet military doctrine occurred in the 1980s. The old Clausewitzian principle of war as a continuation of policies by other means ceased to be part of the doctrine, and the Marxist interpretation of the class origin of war and of the victory of socialism as the main factor in preventing war had also been modified. As a corollary to the above, the question of deterrence acquired increased significance. The notion of deterrence began to be propagated by the Soviet military within a new military doctrine. Ogarkov, the chief of staff of the Soviet military forces said that '. . . the most important component of the army and the navy under contemporary circumstances are the strategic nuclear forces, which are the main factor of deterring an aggressor and have the capability of striking an enemy object anywhere in world' (Ogarkov, 1981, p. 87).

*Perestroika* and *glasnost* introduced a new element in the Soviet government approach to military matters, but the question of a new doctrine did not arise until the army came under the control of the Russian government as a successor to the former Soviet Union. A need arose once more for a doctrine that would determine Russia's military policy. The military doctrine, approved in November 1993, legalised the use of military power in internal conflicts, advanced a more aggressive stance on the question of applying conventional and nuclear forces against the former Soviet republics and NATO countries. Under the influence of the electoral success of the nationalist Zhirinovsky, who received wide support from the army, the Russian leadership began to play openly on the mood of the conservative military circles and the military-industrial complex (Arbatov, 1994, p. 8).

According to Vadim Soloviev, a Russian analyst, that doctrine was saturated with phraseology, which did not offer the military personnel any clear directives as to government policy and left them confused. The reason for this state of affairs was the question: 'who is the enemy and how to destroy him?' Army officers felt that any tangible problems linked to the raising of Russia's defence capabilities were sacrificed in favour of political expediency – the military doctrine was on the skid (Soloviev, 1996).

The presidential decree on the formulation of the second Russian military doctrine has been discussed at a meeting of the Defence Council of the Russian Federation in November 1996. The Council noted that over the past three years there was a change in Russia's geopolitical position. There arose a trend among a number of governments to reduce Russia's influence in the Caucasus and Central Asia, while NATO declared its intention to expand to the East, which generated new security problems for Moscow. While the military danger for Russia has increased, there appears to be signs of reduced military preparedness of the Russian armed forces linked mainly to insufficient financing, according to the Defence Council (ibid.). Due no doubt to the economic imperative, the Russian government has put forward various plans for military reforms, and on 16 July 1997, Boris Yeltsin signed a number of decrees affecting the Russian armed forces. Among the measures included in the decrees, was the reorganisation of the Russian armed forces and a reduction in the number of troops by 500 000 (Rodionov, 1997).

Military reform is meeting significant opposition not only from among the military but from various political movements. Opposition to the reform is based mainly on the perception of Russia's military weakness resulting from the reforms. Constant purges of military personnel and cutbacks have reduced the number of troops from 2.8 million in 1991 to 1.7 million in 1997, and a further reduction to 1.2 million is envisaged (Petrov, 1997). Russia's defeat in the war with Chechnya is quoted as evidence of military deficiency. As a result of the resistance to the reforms by the top military leadership, Yeltsin had on several occasions replaced his ministers of defence by individuals who he thought would be willing to follow his ideas.

Among the critics of Russia's military policy is Igor Rodionov, former Minister of Defence. He criticises the government for relegating Russia's national security to second-rate status. Russia is becoming defenceless against foreign enemies, according to Rodionov. The main enemy remains the United States whose leader declared that many former Soviet republics and regions are within the area of US vital interests. The US helps Ukraine to revise its borders with Russia, while Russia makes one territorial concession after another. The US is also applying an arsenal of 'velvet' weapons of struggle against Russia such as economic, information, diplomatic and psychological means (Rodionov, 1997) – an echo of the propaganda and psychological war during communist rule. Such instruments of policy are all based on military power, but entire geopolitical objectives are being attained by 'peaceful' means, according to Rodionov. The collapse of the USSR is cited as an example of attaining geopolitical objectives by other than military means.

Igor Sergeev, the new minister of defence, looks at the military reforms from a point of view that conforms with Yeltsin's position. Military reform ought to be based exclusively on the perception of Russia's security. A systemic analysis of development of the military, political and socio-economic situation, permits of the conclusion that in the short term, up to the year 2005, the probability of direct military threat to Russia is not being envisaged, according to Sergeev. In any case, Russia's strategic nuclear forces and their state of preparedness are enough to counter any emerging threats (Sergeev, 1997). Efficiency, cost and real possibilities are the main criteria in evaluating military reform. Russia's armed forces should become highly professional, highly mobile, well-equipped and, above all, the reorganisation of the Russian armed forces should be within the capacity of the economy (ibid.)

The economic part of the doctrine calls for a close interconnection between the needs of the army and military industry with the real capabilities of the reformed Russian economy. The Ministry for the Economy estimates that by the year 2000 it will be possible to allocate 5.5 per cent of GDP (in 1996 it was only 3.7 per cent) for defence. During the next two years it is hoped to increase defence spending and to hold it subsequently at 4 per cent of GDP (Soloviev, 1996). The new military doctrine includes the old Soviet principle of close relationship between the needs of the army and the potentials of the economy. It envisages, beginning with 1997, an improvement in the mobilisation capacity of the military industry. It also underlines the importance of determining priorities and imposing upon defence enterprises, which are at present producing non-essential civilian goods, in order to conserve their military production potential based on producing goods of dual utility. The 1997 budget envisages, for the first time, a special allocation of 2.5 billion roubles for the conversion of the military-industrial complex aiming at conserving its production potential.

## THE NUCLEAR FACTOR

A significant element in Russia's military policy is the nuclear weapons factor. An article by Dmitrii Evstafiev and Vladimir Krivokhizha entitled 'The rules of use of nuclear weapons' discusses the question of the role of nuclear weapons within Russia's national security (Evstafiev, 1996). Although the authority and qualification of the authors is not known, the publication of their views could be seen as an ominous sign of the emergence of a Cold War atmosphere with its nuclear weapons implications. According to the authors, the doctrinal and military-technological orientation of the Russian nuclear potential to secure mutual nuclear deterrence within the parameters of the imaginary bipolarity, leads Russia toward the use of nuclear weapons in an obviously hypothetical situation. In this way, nuclear weapons are in fact excluded as one of the flexible instruments necessary in the new geopolitical circumstances to solve important military and political problems. Russian nuclear strategy in the post-bipolar period, according to the authors, should be determined by the geopolitical situation and by the kind of threats to Russia's security that could be neutralised through the possible use in one form or another of Russia's nuclear potential. Despite the popular notion in the early 1990s about strategic parity between Russia and the West, the objective of nuclear deterrence still retains its validity. The creation of a nuclear potential is especially important because it would deprive new nuclear countries of any possibility of using the nuclear factor as an instrument of direct or indirect pressure on Russia (ibid.). The area of use of nuclear weapons on a regional scale will soon become much wider than on the global scale. This is the essential difference between the contemporary situation and the Cold War period. It may well be that NATO's process of expansion to the East, begins to acquire a nuclear dimension. A special role in this respect is played by US attempts to legitimise the creation of an operative anti-ballistic missile system, which in fact creates conditions that would allow the realisation of a limited nuclear war scenario in the European war theatre (ibid.).

Russian observers are greatly concerned by the new American plans for a conceptual programme of application of nuclear weapons – in particular, the planning by a group of advisers who are integrated into a group of planners of strategic objectives under the leadership of the former American Secretary of Defense, Thomas Reed. The group has already proposed to create a renewed 'Integrated Plan of Inflicting Strikes' which includes five methods of using nuclear weapons, four of which correspond to the notion of a limited nuclear war. Statements appeared in the US which speak of building a new generation of low-powered nuclear weapons suitable for use in a local conflict.

The basis of Russia's strategic nuclear forces is a realistic understanding of Russia's security interests and a rational evaluation of the economic potential of the country. The question of ratification of START-2 is linked to a large degree to the fact that the Treaty has become the subject of a political struggle in Russia within the concept of strategic partnership with the US (ibid.). In the case of the Americans withdrawing from the Anti-Ballistic Missile Defence Treaty and subsequent development of a programme of space-based ballistic missile defence (variation of 'Star War') Russia will become increasingly vulnerable. Russian experts suggest that Russia create a small number, say 150 units, of air-based ballistic missiles placed on military transport aircrafts. At present this type of weapon is prohibited by the START-2 Treaty, but if the US withdraws from the Anti-Ballistic Missile Defence Treaty, this restriction would no longer be valid (ibid.).

FOREIGN POLICY AND THE ARMED FORCES

'The army is no longer the favoured child of the state', such is the conclusion reached by Russian analysts after five years of existence of the Russian armed forces (*Nezavisimaya gazeta*, 7 May 1997). This was confirmed during a briefing at the Russian Ministry of Defence in January 1997. It revealed the extent of the general, particularly financial, crisis in the Russian armed forces. The government owes over 5 trillion roubles in unpaid salaries, and as a result of budget policy, the Ministry of Defence owes to army suppliers over 29 trillion roubles (Georgiev, 1997). According to the press-service of the Ministry, the expenditure allocated in the 1997 budget to national security will amount to 104.3 trillion roubles, as well as 47.1 trillion roubles for the maintenance of the armed forces. This is considered insufficient for the minimum requirements of the army and navy. For the officially approved salaries of army personnel and the payments of overdue salaries alone, about 45 trillion roubles is needed. Defence expenditure of 104.3 trillion roubles, constitutes 3.82 per cent of Russia's GDP and 19.69 per cent of total Federal budget expenditure. Such expenditure is, according to the Ministry spokesman, 'civilised' when compared with the defence expenditure of leading Western countries (ibid.).

No less serious is the failure to keep the army at full numerical strength. According to the Ministry of Defence, as of 1 January 1997, the army was only about 85 per cent of its planned strength. In addition, the quality of army recruits is deteriorating. A recent survey of army recruits revealed that over 5 per cent had a criminal record (up from 3.5 per cent in 1992), 12 per cent were regular users of drugs and alcohol, over 39 per cent had never worked or studied (up from 4 per cent in 1985 and 10 per cent in 1990), and 20 per cent were from broken homes. In the autumn of 1996, more than 31 000 men evaded military service (*Nezavisimaya gazeta*, 7 May 1997). In the words of the then Minister of Defence, Igor Rodionov, 'military reform should become part of the reform of Russian society, and one of the objectives of government policies'. The reform, Rodionov said, should instil in society a moral and psychological attitude within the concept of defence of Russia. In an interview with the newspaper *Krasnaya zvezda*, Boris Yeltsin expressed his regrets regarding the slow process of military reforms. He said that 'today's huge military organisation is beyond Russia's [economic] capabilities'. He declared his support for the idea of a professional army, but underlined the fact that the army had been infiltrated by corruption, bribery and theft.

The future of the Russian armed forces, their defence capabilities, and an appropriate military policy, are the subjects of intense discussions among Russian specialists in this area. The statement by the Council for Foreign and Defence Policy (a non-governmental research organisation) published in February 1997 ought to be seen in the context of the ongoing debate (*Nezavisimaya gazeta*, 14 February 1997). The published document begins with a recognition that 'the catastrophic situation in the Russian armed forces is acquiring the feature of a national catastrophe'. The deep crisis within the army is evidence of a crisis in society, government and in Russia generally. It is also evidence of the government's loss of authority and of its political will and ability to carry out its decisions. The statement draws attention to the fact that Russia does not possess adequate means to carry out any serious military reform because it lacks resources for the restructuring of its armed forces. Any attempt at reforms without adequate financial and economic support will end in failure and will only precipitate the collapse of the army. Official and non-official data regarding numbers of troops, quantity and quality of armaments and ability to mobilise economic resources in case of a military conflict ought to be viewed with a degree of doubt. 'This has been proven by the events in Chechnya, but an appropriate conclusion has not been drawn. The war in Chechnya did not reveal all the failures by the government – it was only the tip of the iceberg' (ibid.).

The Council noted that in the present circumstances Russia is not able to adequately finance its armed forces. In fact, the army does not function on account of the military budget, but on account of its reserves of armaments and equipment, and thanks to the support of local authorities, and to the legal and illegal commercial activities of army personnel. The Council saw some serious dangers for Russia emanating from this situation. It foresaw a possible total disintegration of the armed forces, an army revolt against the government, and finally, a military putsch, which may lead to a dictatorship or a civil war. The Council did not offer any specific recommendations to alleviate the situation, but suggested the formation of an independent commission that would investigate the real situation in the armed forces. Such a commission must not include any member of the administration or branch of the government.

## NATIONAL SECURITY AND THE ECONOMY

The link between the armed forces and Russia's economic potential has always figured prominently in the formulation of former Soviet military policies. A major principle which determined such policies was that regardless of the economic situation, the army must be given priority in the allocation of resources. Such a state of affairs prevailed until the advent of Gorbachev and his New Thinking. His approach to the question of military policy included a realistic appraisal of the international political environment and of the requirements of the armed forces given the constraints caused by the economic situation in the country.

The official announcement of the formation of the Russian armed forces, brought out once more the question of the role of the Russian armed forces in the context of national security. The new Russian military doctrine, not unlike the previous Soviet one, notes the link between national security and the economy. The doctrine underlines that 'the defence potential of Russia is determined by the economic, scientific, technological and demographic resources of the country'.

The national security policy of the Russian Federation (1996–2000) announced in May 1996, speaks of the problems linked to the diversion of scarce resources to the Russian armed forces. 'Under the conditions of economic difficulties in Russia today, it is necessary to concentrate the limited resources for the purpose of supporting the combat readiness of her military forces, which must be equipped with the most efficient models of armament and military technology, while maintaining an appropriate military-industrial potential' (*Nezavisimaya gazeta*, 23 May 1996).

The new national security policy emphasises the importance of intellectual potential as the source of all other resources of Russian society and government. According to the authors of the new policy, Russia continues to retain its unique scientific, technological and industrial potential. 'Russia is a developed country and its productive forces are quite unlike the productive forces of the third world; they are in principle not much different from the productive forces of the developed countries. Russia has the same type of specialists as well as the same kind of machinery and equipment' (ibid.).

The underlying premise appears to be that Russia must preserve its production capability for the needs of the army, and that the Russian economy must operate in a way as to be easily mobilisable in case of necessity. The spectre of outside aggression still haunts Russia today, and such a perception has significant political and military implications. Should East–West relations deteriorate, and this appears to be the case caused by the enlargement of NATO, then the question of meeting Russia's national security needs could assume potentially serious proportions and could lead to a renewal of the Cold War and perhaps a new arms race. This brings us to the old question: how realistic is Russia's present approach to the problem of its defence capabilities, and what are the resources available to meet the objectives of Russia's national security policy? The answer to this question can only be found by analysing the present economic situation in Russia and its future potential development.

# 6 An Economy in Transition

Looking back to the period of the Cold War and before, one can see that it was characterised not only by political tension and by the arms race, but was also reflected in the economic relations between East and West. Trade relations between Russia and the West were always conditioned by the reluctance of the Soviet Union to entertain closer commercial links with the West, particularly with the United States. It was one of the factors that motivated Stalin to accelerate the process of industrialisation. This also had military significance in allowing the USSR to develop its arsenal of weaponry and consequently to strengthen its defence capabilities. It was a major reason for Russia's quest for self-sufficiency and economic independence, sometimes bordering on autarky. Under Stalin's rule the economic objective of industrialisation was to be achieved as far as possible without dependence on Western economies. Any economic interdependence with the West was regarded as an attempt by the capitalist world to achieve political and economic domination. The Marshall Plan which at first received a favourable reaction from Poland and Czechoslovakia, was perceived by the Soviet Union as an attempt to detach some of the East European states from the Soviet sphere of influence. It was denounced as trying '... to restore the power of imperialism in the countries of the new democracy and force them to abandon their close economic and military collaboration with the Soviet Union ... to form a bloc of states linked to the United States' (Claudin, 1975, p. 469).

The creation of Comecon was a response to the Marshall Plan and was used as a means of diverting the foreign commerce of the satellite states from the West. The aim of this policy was not only to strengthen economic bonds, but to establish political institutional ties. The formation of the Council of Mutual Economic Assistance (CMEA) which had as its prime objective increased production specialisation and economic interdependence within the bloc, was also seen as a security against separatism.

It was only after Stalin's death that the Soviet Union emerged from its economic isolationism and began to trade increasingly with the West. The Soviet leadership apparently came to the conclusion that exchange of goods with ideologically compatible, but economically weak partners was not always a sound economic proposition (Pisar, 1970, p. 20). It had also realised that without access to Western technology, and in view of the inability to transform its own industrial base, the technological gap between the Soviet Union and the West would only widen, and this in turn would affect economic growth.

The new approach to economic problems can be seen in the expansion of trade between the USSR and the capitalist countries which in 1969 reached 35 per cent of the Soviet Union's global turnover (ibid., p. 15). Trade was mainly concentrated in the acquisition of western know-how, but there were also motives of economic rationality. According to the 'Directives' of the 23rd Congress, the USSR should diversify its imports to include 'such types of materials, commodities and finished goods that involve higher costs and capital investments when produced within the country' (*Izvestia*, 10 April 1996). What also contributed to the expansion of trade between the USSR and the West was the more favourable political atmosphere. However, despite the significant increase in Soviet foreign trade with the West, the political implications were never ignored by the Soviet leadership. The USSR still preferred not to depend on the capitalist world and was mainly interested in the transfer of technology.

The Soviets had faced a dilemma on the question of economic and commercial relations with the West. Economic rationality would suggest benefits from trading with the capitalists, but political and security considerations concerning the capitalist world resulted in an attitude of suspicion. This was based on the perception of the capitalist world as being inherently hostile to the Soviet Union. Capitalist economic policies in relation to the USSR were seen as geared to achieving political rather than economic goals. Discrimination in economic, scientific and technical relations with the USSR, restrictions on imports, tariff differentiation and the refusal to grant most-favoured nation status, were viewed as being motivated by political reasons.

By the late 1970s comments by Soviet economic analysts were becoming more pragmatic and more objective. There was a discernible shift in their perception of capitalism, and the fact that this trend was allowed to develop was also an indication of the political and ideological shift among the Soviet leadership.

The recognition of potential benefits that may accrue from economic cooperation led to increased trade between the Soviet Union and the West. Soviet gas started flowing to Bavaria in October 1973, to Finland and Italy in 1974 and to France in 1975. There was also an interlocking of production through specialisation, co-production and subcontracting, as well as 'new forms of economic ties . . . compensation agreements between Western firms and the Soviet Union . . . Wholly Soviet-owned enterprises were set up in cooperation with foreign firms, which provided credits, equipment and licences' (Lebedev, 1978, p. 136).

However, the same dilemma the Soviet Union had faced in trading with the West, also applied to the Western developed countries including the United States. On the one hand there was an eagerness on the part of the Western economies to exploit the opportunities of the East European markets, on the other there was a fear that closer economic ties would provide the Soviet Union with means of controlling Western Europe. A report by the Institute of Conflict Study spoke of the possibility that 'increasing West European dependence on areas under Soviet control for essential raw materials . . . would give the Soviet government a much more effective hold over the economy of Western Europe than Western Europe could exercise over the Soviet economy even if they could operate together' (Pinder, 1976, p. 270). The American administration was particularly concerned and sought to restrain the Europeans in their trading with the Soviets. 'The United States would like to bring economic relations with the Soviets in line with political and security objectives' (*The Age*, 20 July 1981).

NEP – NEW STYLE?

The announcement by Gorbachev of reforms known as *perestroika* and its formal adoption by the Twenty-seventh CPSU Congress in February 1986, sent a clear message to the world that things in the Soviet Union were going to change drastically not only in the political sphere but in the economic area as well. Many Western and Russian analysts saw in the new economic policy a similarity to NEP. They saw *perestroika* as being forced upon the government by the state of the economy and there was uncertainty whether the reforms were of a temporary or permanent nature. It would appear that even Gorbachev himself was unable to formulate a long-term economic policy, and his first measures indicated a degree of indecision. Subsequent events, however, overtook Gorbachev's initial initiatives and like a train whose brakes had failed, the country took an unexpected and unforeseen route – especially after the dissolution of the Soviet Union and the emergence of Russia as an independent state. The Russian economy, as the successor of the Soviet Union, began its rapid descent toward a state of permanent crisis. After a period of experimentation and *ad hoc* presidential decrees aimed at preventing a total collapse rather than restructuring the economy, the Russian government finally abandoned the concept of a socialist economy and chose the path of development of a 'civilised' capitalist society. According to the authors of the reforms, the former socialist system could not function effectively and could not improve the standard of living of the population (Gundarov, 1996). The reforms were aimed at restructuring the economy through radical liberalisation of prices, widespread privatisation of state property, removal of restrictions on individual wealth, and the introduction of a self-regulating market within a framework of a legitimate democratic regime.

The beginning of economic reforms in Russia are put by Russian economists at 3 December 1991, the date of the decree by President Boris Yeltsin, but after more than six years of reforms, the economic situation in Russia is still confused, to say the least. There has been a dramatic decline in production over the past years. The indicator of industrial production for January 1994, for example, was only 51 per cent of the 1991 level – a fall of 49 per cent, and as a result, the standard of living of the Russian population has drastically declined. According to the Ministry of Labour, over 24 million Russians, or 16.4 per cent of the population, are classified as living below the poverty line. About 63 per cent of the population receive incomes below the national average (the average per capita income at the end of the first quarter of 1995 was 281 200 roubles) and real wages in January 1995 were about 25 per cent lower than in January 1994. According to these official statistics the Russian economy should have collapsed long ago. On the other hand, economic data published by Roskomstat (Russian Statistical Committee) at the end of 1995 indicated some stabilisation of the Russian economy. There was a significant slowdown in the rate of decline in industrial production in mid-1994, and during the last quarter of 1994 it remained at a constant level. In contrast with the sharp fall of GDP in previous years, GDP for the January–February 1995 period was only 4 per cent lower than for the corresponding period in 1994. The process of stabilisation of the economy took place against the background of a steady decline in the rate of inflation. In 1994, inflation in Russia was 204 per cent compared with 800 per cent in 1993 and 1353 per cent in 1992. Preliminary data show the rate of inflation for the month of May 1995 at 7.9 per cent.

Another positive element in the Russian economy is foreign trade. For the past few years Russia has had a favourable balance of trade. In 1994 Russia had a 19.8 billion dollars trade surplus compared with 12 billion dollars in 1993. During the period January–April 1995, Russia's foreign trade amounted to 35.6 billion dollars, or 13 per cent more than in January–April 1994. The trade surplus was mainly due to the increase in Russia's export of mineral resources and a sharp fall in imports, especially grain. Fuel-energy resources accounted for 50 per cent of Russia's exports.

Due to the conflicting reports, the real state of the Russian economy is rather obscure. The difficulty in solving this riddle lies in the fact that it is practically impossible to determine the actual level of production. Official statistics do not reflect the real situation because most industrial and agricultural enterprises deliberately conceal the actual volume of sales by the widely used practice of 'black' bookkeeping. Some economic analysts point to the volume of electricity generated by Russian power stations as a more reliable economic indicator. Generation of electric power cannot be concealed or stored for later use. Consequently, the volume of electricity produced is by definition equal to its consumption. As industry uses the bulk of electricity, the fall in industrial production should be reflected in the volume of electricity produced. However, if one compares the 48.15 per cent fall in industrial production between 1991 and 1994 with the 13.3 per cent decrease in electricity generated during the same period, one can only assume that the decline in industrial production cannot be as large as statistics seem to indicate unless part of the output is not reported. Some estimates put this volume of 'black' production at 35–40 per cent. In contrast to the communist period when there was a trend to always embellish economic achievements, there is now a tendency to report results as being worse than they actually are. State enterprises, which still rely on government subsidies, are reporting their financial situation in a way as to obtain maximum subsidies.

The path towards a market economy proved to be laden with economic and political problems. Part of the political problem was and still is the composition of the Russian parliament – the Duma – after the victory of former communists and their allies in the 1993 election. Their fierce resistance to Yeltsin's economic reforms, forces the Russian President to use his veto powers and to rule by decree, which limits the effectiveness of the law. However, the real cause of economic difficulties is the fundamental issue of transition from a centralised state system to a capitalist market economy. The difficulties are also caused by problems directly arising from the collapse of the Soviet Union as a political and economic entity.

## THE RUSSIAN ECONOMY AND THE CIS

The collapse of the Soviet Union and the breakdown of economic links between the former Soviet republics created enormous problems that demanded urgent solutions. As each newly independent republic attempted to establish its own sovereign economy, it found itself relying on supplies of essential goods and resources from other republics. The former economic interdependence between them became a serious obstacle for full political and economic sovereignty. In 1992 and at the beginning of 1993, during the first stage of the newly acquired independence, an organisational structure of cooperation was created. It consisted of a Council of Heads of States, a Council of Heads of Governments, and the Inter-parliamentarian Assembly of the CIS, whose objective was the integration of its members into one economic space in which there would be a free flow of goods, services and finance. An Executive Secretariat – a kind of headquarters of the Commonwealth – has operated in Minsk since 1993 (Rybakov, 1996). An important milestone in relations between the CIS countries was the signing in 1993 of an Agreement to create an Economic Union – an agreement that determines the objectives of integration such as the creation of a common market of goods, services, capital and labour (ibid.).

An intensive attempt at the formation of a legal framework of interaction between the CIS countries began in mid-1993. Hundreds of multilateral and bilateral agreements that determine the rules of mutual cooperation between the former Soviet republics in the economic, social, defence and other areas, have been signed. 1995–1996 saw the formation of a Customs Union between Russia,

Belarus, Kazahkstan and Kirgizia. This has allowed a free movement of goods and capital within the common customs territory. In March 1996, the four governments signed an Agreement on accelerated integration in the economic and humanitarian areas. A joint organ of management of the integration of the four countries – Intergovernmental Council and Integration Committee (as an executive authority) – has also been created (ibid., p.20).

Of special significance is the agreement between the Russian Federation and Belarus on the creation of a Commonwealth of the two countries signed in April 1996. The Agreement envisages the establishment of a single economic space and a single market, the development of a unified transport, energy and information systems. It foresees the establishment of a minimum standard of social security, equal opportunity of education and access to the achievements of science and culture. The Russia–Belarus Agreement is an exception, since the other former Soviet republics do not appear to be following this example. Over the past five years there have been significant changes in the structure of the national economies of each CIS country. There has been a strong reorientation of the CIS countries toward closer links with the countries of the 'far-abroad' resulting in reduced interaction between Russia and the former republics.

A solution to these complex problems is seen in the creation of a common CIS market, but there are many obstacles on the way. A major impediment is the unequal level of economic development in CIS countries and the unequal distribution of fuel and raw material resources, which causes an imbalance in mutual trading relations. Another obstacle is the variation in the extent and direction of the economic reforms in these countries. Finally, according to Russian analysts, the policies of some Western countries are aimed at preventing full economic integration of the former Union republics. They point to the fact that the guaranteed credits that the international financial organisations and donor-countries of the 'far-abroad' have made available to former Soviet republics were more than twice as large as those granted to the Russian Federation.

Due to the above factors, Russia's position within the system of CIS partnership has changed significantly. During the period 1992–94, Russia's trade turnover with CIS countries had been falling steadily – it marked a sixfold decrease relative to 1991 – and the share of these countries in Russia's total trade turnover fell by 270 per cent. Russia's trade with the former republics has declined at the expense of their trade with foreign countries. During the first quarter of 1995, Russia's share in Turkmenistan's total foreign trade turnover was 9.1 per cent, while Turkmenistan's turnover with foreign countries was 77 per cent. Russia's share in Uzbekistan's foreign trade was 12.9 as compared to 72.5 per cent with foreign countries, with Georgia – 16.3 as compared to 66.9 per cent and with Azerbaidjan – 16.7 as compared to 67 per cent. Only with Kazahkstan did Russia retain her share of 53.6 per cent and with Belarus – 52.4 per cent. Trade with former Soviet republics is very important for Russia for it provides a market for Russian goods for which there are no outlets in the West. A document signed by President Yeltsin on 14 November 1996 places Russia's relations with the countries of the Commonwealth as a major priority (ibid., p. 25).

## AN ECONOMY IN TRANSITION

Six years after the beginning of economic reforms, a debate regarding the nature and direction of the Russian economy is taking place in Russia. The discussions turn mainly around the question whether Russia is heading toward a Western capitalist system or whether it is regressing toward the old system. Despite claims by many Western and Russian analysts, there is little evidence that Russia is reverting to the former centralised structure. All indications are that the type of economy that is emerging in Russia is neither centralised nor capitalist. It is an economy in transition, but a transition toward what? It will probably take many more years for a clear trend to emerge. In the meantime, there have been numerous attempts at defining the present Russian economic system, but the final outcome of the continuing process of transformation is hard to predict. In the West as well as in Russia there are some economists who are trying to develop a theory of transition from socialism into capitalism – so far, with little success. In the absence of a significant middle class and a class of capitalist-type entrepreneurs, it is difficult to define the Russian economic system or to make a prognosis as to its final form.

According to a majority of those who see Russia's future through dark glasses, Russia is developing a capitalism of a peculiar kind. It is neither European, North American, nor Latin American. Among those who are trying to classify the Russian economy is the Russian economist, Igor Gundarov. A feature of a capitalist system, says Gundarov (Gundarov, 1996), is the high rate of investment and growth of the economy. If one were to evaluate Russia's transition toward a market economy using the dynamics of investment and growth, then there is evidence that it is regressing rather than advancing toward capitalism. Evidence of such a regression can be found in statistics which indicate that in the 1970s, the economy of the former USSR performed better than the Russian economy today (ibid.). A possible conclusion one could draw, according to Gundarov, is that a market economy is less efficient than a 'socialist' one. The second conclusion would be that the reforms have not created a market economy but something quite different – one which he defines as being akin to a feudal system (ibid.).

The present Russian system contains features that cannot be found in any other industrially developed country. Russia is unique in the way it treats its reward for labour supplied – workers have to wait several months to be paid. Between 1992 and 1994, the amount of unpaid wages rose from 30 million dollars to 1 billion dollars, and in 1996 this amount reached 10 billion dollars, according to Aleksandr Livshits, Minister for the economy – a situation not found elsewhere (*Moskovskii komsomol*, 14 May 1996). The Russian economy is also characterised by a high degree of monopolisation. Two hundred Russian companies control about 60 per cent of total industrial production, which is an indication of the extent of monopoly in Russia unlike any industrialised country (*Ekspert*, 2 September 1996).

Despite the reforms, there is still a high degree of state intervention. The banking sector, for example, is still subject to non-market forces. The government has the power to close down any financial institution at any time. In 1996, the government revoked 38 banking licences (*Finansovye izvestia*, 5 November 1996), which could not be attributed to purely economic reasons. It is said that in order to protect its interests, the banking sector donated 5 billion dollars to the 1996 pre-election presidential campaign (*Nezavisimaya gazeta*, 22 November 1996).

A peculiar feature of the Russian economy is the volume of barter used in exchange of goods and services. Under the Soviet rule, barter deals were a common occurrence – particularly in agriculture where city dwellers would exchange consumer goods for agricultural products and enterprises would exchange goods and services for reciprocal favours. Barter became even more widespread in the post-Soviet area. Under Gorbachev, due to the high rate of inflation when farmers were reluctant to accept money, the government offered various incentives for selling agricultural products to the government in the form of industrial goods. Barter is used not only as a means of exchange of goods between individuals, but also among commercial and industrial enterprises. Almost one in three Russian enterprises is using barter operations to settle accounts with other firms (*Finansovye izvestia*, 9 July 1996). In the metal industry, for example, up to 80 per cent of supplies to the domestic market are channelled through barter in exchange for supplies of coal, electricity, and other materials. Barter is also being used in foreign trade. In September 1997, for example, Russia sealed a barter deal with Indonesia to swap Russian jet fighters and helicopters for Indonesian local products, including make-up and toys.

Another feature of the Russian economy and society is the decline in the number of people defined in the West as middle class, that is the group which contributes most to the advancement of an economy and whose standard of living is relatively higher than average. At the same time, the number of people in Russia living below the poverty line is increasing. In 1994–96 one family in four was considered poor because their per capita income was below the subsistence wage level. According to the latest estimate, over 42 per cent of the population is poor.

Despite Yeltsin's attempts to prove that things are getting better, there are many indications that the Russian economy is sliding toward a state of anarchy in which only criminal elements are the main beneficiaries of the reforms. A question asked by many Russians is 'how is it possible for individuals to accumulate within 1–2 years sufficient capital to buy out huge enterprises such as Uralmash, ZIL and even a sea-port?'. According to one opinion poll, the major contributing factor to the achievement of personal wealth in Russia is speculation, not honest labour (39 per cent of those polled), embezzlement of state property (34 per cent) and laundering of money (17 per cent) (Osipov, 1996).

The present situation in Russia appears paradoxical, according to Gundarov. Instead of a transition from socialism to capitalism, the Russian economy appears to be moving toward a feudal economic model. The regression seems to accelerate at a speed that would make it extremely difficult to stop. Those in favour of reforms and a market economy are more optimistic and are inclined to see an improvement in the quality of life. They use the abundance of goods in Moscow stores as an indicator of economic progress. According to President Yeltsin: 'today the shelves in shops are full of goods, while five years ago they were empty'. However such a criterion of quality of life is not seen as providing a complete picture of the economic situation in Russia.

First, the volume of supplies of goods in major cities is vastly superior to that of the periphery. Therefore, the surveys which were conducted mainly in large towns are not indicative of the real situation. There are still shortages of goods in some provincial towns. Second, according to Goskomstat and other selected surveys of households, the purchasing power of the average Russian has suffered a decline within the last five years. Over this period real disposable income has fallen sharply, with the exception of 1996 when the decline slowed down to one per cent (*Finansovye izvestia*, 10 October 1996). The abundance of goods would indicate a drop in demand due to falling earnings.

Some Russian economists see the solution of the present difficulties in a return to a system dominated by state intervention rather than attempting to imitate foreign economic models. A. Aksenov, former head of the Coordinating Working Group of the Russian Federal Government, advocates the adoption of a policy which would give the government stricter control over the activities of private business. He is strongly in favour of support for domestic producers. According to Aksenov, the present state of the Russian economy is due to experimentation which led to the '. . . complete destruction of the levers of governmental control over the economy' (Aksenov, 1993). In order to avoid a possible complete economic collapse, said Aksenov, it is essential to determine accurately Russia's national economic interests – something that ought to have been done in December 1991. 'The rejection of communist ideology does not signify a rejection of state interests, which due to objective economic reasons, may simply not coincide with the interests of the United States nor with the interests of West European countries.' Aksenov suggests the immediate denial of access to foreign advisers and consultants (who filled government corridors under Gaidar). It is necessary, Aksenov asserts, to look into the economic damage inflicted on Russia by foreign advisers who have access to much information, including planned sales of Russia's strategic resources. Russia, Aksenov maintains, should take into consideration the losses which arose as a result of sanctions against Iraq and the losses of markets for raw material and advanced technology (ibid.). It is obvious, Aksenov concludes, that strict government control over the distribution of resources cannot be avoided during the transitional period. 'Such measures cannot be considered anti-market since even traditional European economies are being regulated by similar methods. Practically all civilised countries have an effective system of government subsidies for the protection of low-profit enterprises in order to maintain their economic viability' (ibid.).

Russian economists see Russia's future industrial development as depending on the outcome of the battle between the supporters and opponents of a strong government, between those advocating state intervention and supporters of a free market economy (Narzikulov, 1996). Some economists see better prospects for the country in the fact that the government has begun to strengthen its presence in the economy. The main factor for this optimism was the admission by leading politicians of the disastrous consequences of the artificial limitations of the government's role in the economy. The revival of state intervention in the economy is said to be linked to the collapse of the belief in an automatic flow of foreign investments into Russia. The idea of strict government policy has been accepted by people who just a few years ago saw only negative sides in government intervention. Even men like Anatolii Chubais became apologists for the 'state of emergency' principle. The rise of the idea of state intervention has a material basis. Officially, the largest part of Russia's GDP is produced by private companies. However, it is the government that controls the financial resources of the country. By the end of 1996, for example, the share of the State Savings Bank in the total amount of deposits was 73 per cent, while all other 2000 commercial banks attracted only 27 per cent (at the beginning of 1996 the proportion was 65:35). Of great importance was the volume of short-term bonds issued by the Central Bank and Savings Bank. Their combined share in the total of government debts reached 80 per cent. The trend towards the monopolisation of financial resources is quite apparent.

Such views are becoming increasingly prevalent among Russian economists and political leaders. Some of the decrees issued by Yeltsin clearly indicate a return to state control rather than a move towards a free-market economy.

PRIVATISATION

A market economy implies in the first place freedom of business activities. This is proving extremely difficult in a country that for over seventy years was totally devoid of private initiative. A solution to this problem was seen in the privatisation of state-owned assets. Privatisation was considered as a means of improving the efficiency of production by introducing the profit motive. The subsidies provided by the government to state enterprises proved to be an economic burden resulting in a huge budget deficit. Privatisation was meant to be the solution to the financial problem as well as a step towards a free market through individual activity rather than a command system. In December 1991, the Russian government adopted a state programme of privatisation for 1992. The decision was prompted by the realisation that to liberalise prices without privatisation could further complicate the difficult economic situation (*Izvestia*, 27 December 1991). The privatisation programme included a provision which granted the workers collectives the right to receive up to 35 per cent of shares in privatised enterprises free of charge. The government also announced that it intended to issue to each citizen privatisation cheques which would give him/her the right to a share of unsold state property. The programme was formalised by decree in August 1992. Privatisation vouchers made their appearance on the Russian commodity exchange from the first day of their distribution. But most Russian citizens did not realise the value or even utility of the vouchers. Many Muscovites polled on that subject said they would sell the vouchers to the first buyer who offered 10 000 roubles (*Trud*, 6 October 1992).

Initially, most enterprises of the military-industrial complex were excluded, but since a large part of state productive assets were located in the military-industrial sector of the economy, it also became necessary to privatise part of that complex. The main reason for the conversion of the military-industrial complex was the excessive defence expenditure under decreasing militarisation and the changing role of military power in Russian politics. There was a decreasing emphasis on export of armaments as a political instrument. Russia ceased to offer weapons to its allies on political grounds but demanded payment in cash.

Armaments were considered the only competitive commodity which the former Soviet Union could export and one of the main sources of foreign exchange. At one stage, the USSR had been one of the leading exporters of armaments and military technology. At the end of the 1970s, Soviet exports of armament constituted about 50 per cent of the world total. According to American sources, the Soviets were exporting about 16 billion rubles' worth of armaments annually. Clearly, exports of armaments played a much greater role in Soviet foreign trade than they did in other countries. In the USSR they constituted over 15 per cent of its total exports, compared with 6 per cent in the USA and only 2 per cent in NATO countries. At the end of the 1980s, Soviet export of war matériel fell to about one-third of the world total. The cutback in the defence programme and the fall in exports of armaments had adversely affected enterprises included in the conversion programme. A number of enterprises ceased producing military equipment without replacing lost production capacities with civilian goods. Others continued to produce war matériel without government orders.

The defence complex has been affected by the difficult economic situation in Russia more than any other branch of the economy. Not only has the financial situation deteriorated, but the capability of the sector to secure the needs of the Russian army was also in jeopardy. According to official data, production of war matériel in 1995 fell by 20.5 per cent and in January 1996 it fell even further (*Nezavisimaya gazeta*, 14 March 1996).

Attempts of the defence complex to stabilise the situation by conversion and by increasing production of high-technology consumer goods proved unsuccessful because of the shortage of funds needed for the conversion. The situation within the complex has also been affected by the intensification of privatisation. The mass selling of shares of some defence enterprises resulted in a fall in the price of the shares to far below their nominal value. Over 80 per cent of the shares sold found their way into the hands of financial speculators who had no intention of investing in production but of controlling the operation of the privatised enterprises so as to derive maximum profit, or of reselling them at a price well below their asset value. Under political pressure by groups claiming that Russia was selling out its vital assets, Boris Yeltsin issued a decree 'On measures for securing the efficiency of state control over the privatisation of enterprises and organisations of the defence complex' (*Finansovye izvestia*, 16 April 1996). According to the decree, the government is to establish a list of enterprises of the defence complex in which privatisation will not be allowed, as well as a list of companies in which the state will retain a controlling interest. In December 1996, it was estimated that the military-industrial complex comprised over 1800 different enterprises employing over 3 million people. The state held 36 per cent of shares in the defence complex, while 34 per cent were owned jointly with private interests.

Privatisation of part of the complex faces an additional difficulty. Despite the steps undertaken by the Russian government toward restructuring the economy, a real market economy is still in the making. Market forces are not yet fully operational in Russia and former state monopolies are still operating – many at a loss. The government cannot afford to shut the gates of enterprises that are unprofitable or unable to produce goods that can be disposed of on the Russian or foreign markets. Letting such enterprises go under would throw out millions of workers and it would require huge funds to support the resultant army of unemployed. It could spell political disaster. Consequently, the government is forced to subsidise a large part of Russian industry.

Privatisation of agriculture presented difficulties and problems of a different kind. Simultaneously with the privatisation programme for industry and commerce, the Russian government also initiated a programme of agrarian reforms which included private farming. The main objective of the agrarian reform was the creation of a new type of agricultural enterprise – a private farm. It was expected that the small, owner-managed private farm would become a viable alternative to large-scale (collective) farming (*Finansovye izvestia*, 14–20 April 1994).

The law 'On private farming' introduced in 1991 was one of the first official acts of the agrarian reform. Three years after the adoption of the law, in early 1994, there were 270 000 private farms in Russia, but while 1992 saw a rapid growth in private farming, in 1993 the privatisation of farming slowed down significantly. In addition, a large number of private farms ceased to operate altogether. During the last quarter of 1993, the number of farms that ceased to operate was equal to the number of farms that closed down during the whole of 1992 (ibid.).

The main problem facing the private farming sector is access to finance and markets for agricultural produce. Previously, the farming sector relied exclusively on government support, but privatisation meant independence and reliance on individual resources. Another problem was the absence of infrastructure that would facilitate supplies of machinery and equipment as well as the distribution of produce to markets. Initially, there was also strong resistance from existing collective farms which made it extremely difficult for a farmer to leave the collective and to establish himself.

## FOREIGN INVESTMENT

In the early stages of privatisation, little was said regarding the role of foreign capital in the privatisation process because, as some Russians argued, national property was being sold at cheap prices. However, foreign investment in those branches of the economy in which the government has been reducing the level of subsidies, has become vital. Privatisation envisaged the possibility of attracting foreign investors – mainly in the unprofitable areas of the economy (*Finansovye izvestia*, 20–26 August 1993).

At the outset of the reforms, the Russian government has been trying to draw foreign investment capital. Foreign capital was thought to be necessary for the creation of new industries and foremost for the acquisition of Western know-how. In order to stimulate foreign investment in Russia, President Yeltsin issued a number of decrees in 1993 and 1994, which provided some taxation and customs concessions for foreign investors. The 'progressive' law on foreign investment adopted in 1991 was nullified by subsequent taxation legislation, which virtually abolished tax concessions granted earlier, and a law approved by the Duma abolished custom concessions as well. One Russian expert admitted that an analysis of all the factors that determine the risks involved in investing in Russia indicates that the investment climate in Russia is highly unfavourable.

The most widespread legal form of foreign investment in Russia is the joint enterprise. Official data indicate that at the end of 1993 there were 6500 joint enterprises operating in Russia. By mid-1994 the number of enterprises with foreign capital participation rose to over 14 000, but only half of them were actually engaged in productive activities (*Delovoi mir*, 13 May 1994). The bulk of foreign capital is invested in the sector that offers relatively high and safe returns – in oil and gas. Three joint projects – the oil and gas deposits in the Ob area in which the American firm Amoco participates, the Khayaginsk deposit with the participation of the French firm Total, and oil deposits on the island of Sakhalin exploited by the American Exxon Corporation – are some of the more important foreign capital ventures. The adoption of the law 'On agreements of production sharing of resources', offered the possibility of an early start on exploitation of oil-bearing areas located in the north of European Russia and on the Sakhalin shelf, but was rejected by the Duma.

Despite Russia's urgent needs for foreign capital and technology, the level of foreign investment in Russia remains low relative to the size of the Russian economy and in absolute terms. Total foreign investments in 1993 amounted to about 2.9 billion dollars. Overall, the share of foreign investment in the Russian economy is 2.7 per cent, which is insignificant when compared with that of other countries. One of the reasons for the reluctance of Western capital to invest in Russia is the absence of appropriate legislation that would guarantee the safety of investment. What also inhibits foreign investment is the poor business culture of Russian business partners.

The position of foreign investors in Russia is made complicated by the taxation regime. Foreign investors ceased to view Russia as a low tax country compared to the European levels of taxation. In reality, the tax burden in Russia is far higher because of a number of restrictions in the area of costs allowed as a tax deduction. According to the German company Siemens, Russian taxation rules do not allow a number of items to be considered as part of the costs of production. Depreciation of fixed assets, for example, does not make any allowance for inflation, with the result, that a foreign investor cannot accumulate funds for the replacement of old machinery and equipment. Interest paid for money borrowed to buy new equipment is not recognised as part of the cost of production. Expenditure on advertising, insurance and some other items, is also disallowed as a cost (*Nezavisimaya gazeta*, 19 November 1996).

The high level of taxation appears to be the result of the difficulties encountered by Russian authorities in collecting taxes; tax evasion and non-payment of taxes is a common occurrence. The Russian government is constantly busy revising the rules, but has so far not been successful in establishing a system of tax collection that would ensure a steady flow of funds into the state coffers. In response to the chronic underpayment of taxes and the subsequent refusal of the World Bank to transfer more of the earlier allocated funds to Russia, the taxation authorities decided to adopt strict measures for the collection of overdue taxes. The main victims of the measures were foreign firms who became subject to stricter government audit. As a result of these steps, a number of foreign accounts have been frozen. In some cases, significant funds have been automatically confiscated because of alleged irregularities in the payment of taxes (ibid.).


## FLIGHT OF CAPITAL

Another problem that has arisen as a result of reforms is the flight of capital from Russia. According to Russian officials, more than $US 1 billion is being spirited out of Russia every month, bleeding the nation of desperately needed investment funds. A senior official of the Russian Central Bank estimated that up to $US 15 billion a year was being sent abroad illegally. When the grey area of semi-legal capital export schemes is taken into account, it would be much higher. Some Russian economists estimate that since the beginning of the economic reforms in 1992, at least $US 60 billion has gone abroad either into foreign banks or into buying property in London, the south of France and other prime locations. A further vast sum – up to $US 40 billion – is thought to be kept in the form of cash dollars 'under the mattress' at home, as Russians do not trust the rouble and fear they will be hit by the taxman if they put their savings into Russian banks (*Daily Telegraph*, 24 June 1997). This is the so-called 'internal flight' or 'dollarisation' of the Russian economy. The dollarisation of the economy came as a result of the loss of confidence in the domestic currency. The rampant inflation that occurred soon after the introduction of reforms forced the Russian population to seek safer means of saving as the value of the rouble continued to plunge. The dollar soon became the dominant currency in Russia. According to the Russian Ministry of the Economy, during the three months April–June 1996, the Russians used 17.6 per cent of their gross income for the purchase of foreign currency (Interfax, 6 August 1996).

Until the first steps toward opening up the Russian economy were taken, the flight of capital was not an issue. Since the rouble was not convertible, the incentive and indeed the possibility of transferring funds abroad was practically non-existent, and the black market in foreign currency was an insignificant economic factor. It was only after the liberalisation of foreign trade and the privatisation within some branches of the economy, particularly banking, that the flight of capital from Russia became an important problem (Portanskii, 1997).

The main channel through which Russians manage to transfer currency abroad is foreign trade. The most widely used method of exporting capital from Russia is through transfer pricing. Often goods are exported from Russia at a low price and resold on the world market at a higher price, and a Russian exporter would receive the difference in prices either through a money transfer to his private account in a foreign bank or through a cash payment in Russia. Since new government regulations made it more difficult to apply these methods, the favoured option since 1993, is the so-called 'double invoicing'. A Russian exporting firm issues one invoice at a discount price and another containing the real agreed price. The difference is split between the Russian supplier and the foreign importer. This method is used for export as well as import. Another method is through the so-called fake credits when a Russian supplier either failed to receive payment for the goods supplied or to receive goods for money transferred abroad as payment for the goods. The money ends up in an account of a foreign bank. The accumulated funds in foreign banks are subsequently invested in foreign real estate or Western securities. Part of the capital leaving Russia is also linked to money-laundering operations organised by the Russian mafia. Because the illegal operations are serviced by Russian banks, many banks became associated with the illegal activities. Some of the measures to combat these activities introduced by the government have so far proved ineffective as the corruption has spread to the bureaucracy and the banking sector (Portanskii, 1997).

At one stage, the Russian government thought to rely on the financial reserves of the 'New Russians'; on their consent to repatriate some of the funds they invested in the West. However in the words of a Russian economist, 'even in the best of circumstances – internal stability and favourable political climate – the risk factor involved in investing in Russia is 3–4 times greater than in the West' (*Expert*, 1996, no. 33).

The question of flight of capital has been discussed in a paper presented at the Institute of Foreign Trade Research of the Russian Academy of Sciences in October 1996. Among several suggestions was the adoption of laws that would halt smuggling and would help to overcome the effects of crime in foreign trade operations. This latter problem would require stricter control over foreign trade operations as well as control over unofficial trade such as barter, trade in services and the transfer of funds as payments for imports (*Mezhdunarodnaya zhizn*, no. 10. 1996, p. 78).

## RUSSIAN OIL IN WORLD POLITICS

Oil has always played a major role in world politics because of its economic importance and the power it confers on those controlling its supply. On several occasions oil has been used as a means of exerting political and economic pressure on the industrialised West. Dependence on supplies of Arab oil has for a long time been of much concern to the industrialised world. After Iraq occupied Kuwait, an oil embargo was imposed on Iraqi and Kuwaiti oil, which led to a jump in the price of oil. Acting according to an earlier agreement, Saudi Arabia has increased its oil output and the price came down to its previous level. This broadly defined situation may soon change as a new player is about to enter the scene – the Russian Federation. This fact has not been widely publicised in the West, but has lately become a recurrent subject in the Russian press. Russian economists and political observers began to perceive Russia's endowment in oil reserves not only in terms of economic benefits, but as a significant factor of Russia's role in world politics. In contrast to the Middle East, Russia appears to the West as a potential supplier of oil and as a much more attractive alternative.

Figures speak for themselves. Proven reserves of oil on the territory of the former USSR are estimated at 8–12 per cent of world reserves (85 per cent of these are in the Russian Federation). Unproven reserves, according to Western experts, are of the order of 25 per cent, and according to the Russian company Hermes even higher – at 28–30 per cent of world reserves – which makes them nearly equal to those of Saudi Arabia (Neverov, 1992). However, due to the lack of financial and technical resources, Russia's output of oil has been steadily declining, and the political upheavals have severely affected the operations of the oil-producing sector of its economy.

Russia desperately needs foreign capital and know-how to increase production and to generate hard currency revenue which it requires to pay for essential imports. But in order to raise Russia's oil production to the appropriate level, billions of dollars must be spent – money which Russia does not have. Hence its interest in foreign investment. Western investment in the Russian oil industry is at the present time relatively low, but this is expected to change. A recent survey has shown that 67 per cent of Western entrepreneurs with links with the Russian market assign first priority to investment in Russian oil. The interest in Russian oil shown by Western investors is still to be translated into practical steps, but a battle for Russia's oil among the world's leading oil producers has already begun and some major Western oil companies have already concluded deals with the Russian government.

The French company, Total has been a buyer of Soviet oil for a number of years, but in the last few years it has concentrated on investment in oil exploration and production in Russia. One of the first joint ventures was the Romashkinsk oil deposit in Tatarstan. A joint enterprise – Total–Petro – in conjunction with the Russian Tatneft has been established for this purpose. Total intends to invest about 50 million dollars over the next few years. There are also other areas with good prospects, according to a spokesman for Total. Three oil-bearing deposits are located in the Republic of Koma in the Tomano-Pechorsk basin west of the Urals. Total has already signed a contract with the Russian company Ukhtaneftegazgeologiya for the exploration of the region estimated to contain reserves of 45 million tonnes of oil. Another project – the Kharyaginsk oil deposit located in the Nenetsk autonomous region – will also be jointly developed (*Trud*, 7 October 1992).

A contract for the exploration and extraction of oil in the Saratov and Volgograd regions was signed in Volgograd in April 1992 by the local authorities and the French company Elf. Elf intends to spend US $500 million on the first stage of the project. A consortium consisting of Mitsui, the Maraton Oil Company and Macdermott International, has signed an agreement with the Russian Government for an oil search on the Sakhalin continental shelf. Other Western companies have expressed interest in prospecting for oil in the Magadan region of Russia's Far East (*Rossiiskaya gazeta*, 18 April 1992).

It is not surprising that some of the world's oil giants such as British Petroleum, Chevron, Exxon, Amoco and many others are competing for the right of exploitation of the oil deposits. Mobil Corporation and Exxon Corporation have reached an agreement on joint oil exploration in Western Siberia. The exploration area extends over 86 million acres. The heads of the two corporations have offered Russia the latest technology, their experience in oil exploration and financial support for the project (*Rossiiskaya gazeta*, 8 August 1992).

An agreement on oil exploration was concluded in March 1996 between Royal Dutch Shell and the Russian company Evikon, and a joint company has been established for the exploration of oil fields in Western Siberia. A representative of the Dutch company said that the future of the joint enterprise depends on the adoption of the production-sharing law. The law was finally approved in December 1994 (*Finansovye izvestia*, 2 April 1996).

American oil companies are not far behind. Polyarnoe siyanie, a joint enterprise whose founders are the American company Conoco and the Russian Arkhangelskgeologiya, has announced the imminent start of joint exploitation of oil deposits in Russia. Conoco is part of the giant Du Pont Corporation. Conoco together with its Russian partners has also begun exploring oil deposits in the Arkhangelsk province. An agreement to this effect has been concluded between the American company and the Russian government. According to Konstantin Nikandros, a spokesman for Conoco, capital investment of the company and its Russian partner Arkhangelskekologia could reach 3 billion dollars.

The question of America's interest in Russian oil has been raised by an American senior policy analyst at the Heritage Foundation (Cohen, 1997). He suggested initiating a hearing in the Senate on US access to oil and gas resources in the Caspian Sea basin and Central Asia. The increasing instability of the Middle East makes the tremendous energy reserves in Central Asia more important for US and Western economic development. Russian energy companies such as Lukoil and Gazprom play an important role in the race to control the production and transportation of oil and gas from the Caspian Sea region and Central Asia. Turbulence in the Middle East may make these resources more important to the economic stability of the West.

With the war in Chechnya settled, Russia renewed its demands that the flow of oil from the Caspian Sea be directed to its own Black Sea ports rather than routed through Georgia and Turkey, while the United States has been seeking to limit Russia's control over future oil exports by encouraging multiple pipeline routes that would bypass Russia. Russia's request was successful, and in October 1997, oil began flowing out of the Caspian Sea region through Russia for export to the West. The pipeline stretches hundreds of kilometres north-west from Baku on the Caspian Sea to the Russian port of Novorossiisk. The route runs also through Chechnya. The initial flow of oil is just the beginning of what may become a torrent, rivalling the Middle East as a source of energy for the world (*Washington Post*, 30 October 1997). Barring political upheavals, it seems certain that in the long run Russia will become a major world supplier of oil. When this happens it may determine not only Russia's future, but that of the world economy and world politics.

## THE RUSSIAN ECONOMY IN 1997

Most Russian economic analysts agree that the economic reforms have failed so far and suggest various solutions to the present difficulties. The failure of economic reforms can be seen in the fall of the volume of investment. By the end of 1995 it has been estimated that the volume of capital investment was only 29 per cent relative to 1990. In 1996 the fall in investment accelerated and fell by a further 15 per cent relative to the corresponding period of the previous year. Some Russian economic analysts suggest that the fall in investment was due to the flight of capital from Russia. Others argue that the flight of capital was balanced by the inflow of capital in the form of foreign aid. Between 1991–96, Russia received 79.2 billion dollars from international aid, technical cooperation, export credits, budget support and investments (*Finansovye izvestia*, 5 November 1996).

Another indication of the economic crisis is the dramatic collapse of industrial production. The total volume of production in 1995 was 50 per cent of the 1990 level. That means that the fall has affected all branches of the economy including those that are usually the sources of foreign exchange. In 1995, the level of production of goods in which Russia was still competitive – the metallurgy and machine-building industries for example – was only 71 per cent of the 1990 level. There was also a significant fall in output of resources which were traditionally a source of considerable inflow of funds for the government such as gold and diamonds. Investments in the exploration of diamonds fell by almost 90 per cent. Even the extraction of gold became unprofitable. Gold output in 1996 declined by 14 per cent. The main cause for the decline in the production of gold is attributed to the inability of the government to meet its financial obligations to gold producers (*Nezavisimaya gazeta*, 19 September 1996).

1997 does not augur well for the Russian economy, according to the well-known Russian economist Leonid Abalkin. Further falls in industrial production are expected. At the beginning of 1997

*Table* 6.1    Main macroeconomic indices for Russia in 1996 (percentage changes)

|  | 1996 Nov. | Dec. | 1997 Jan. | Feb. | 1996 |
|---|---|---|---|---|---|
| GDP | −0.4 | 1.0 | −17.0 | −5.0 | −7.0 |
| Real per capita income | −0.9 | 5.0 | −10.0 | −0.3 | −1.5 |
| Real wages | −0.9 | 8.0 | −4.0 | −1.0 | 13.0 |
| Consumer goods prices | 1.9 | 1.4 | 2.0 | 1.3 | 22.0 |
| Wholesale prices | 0.9 | 0.7 | 1.3 | 1.0 | 26.0 |
| Retail trade turnover | 0.0 | 7.0 | −15.0 | −8.0 | −4.0 |
| Export to far-abroad | −7.0 | 10.0 | 19.0 | 7.0 | 7.0 |
| Imports from far-abroad | 14.0 | 12.0 | −31.0 | 19.0 | 9.4 |
| Registered unemployment | 2.0 | 2.0 | 1.8 | 4.8 | 9.6 |
| Industrial production | −6.0 | 2.0 | −8.0 | 4.0 | −8.0 |
| Housing construction | 30.0 | − | −98.0 | 22.0 | −8.0 |

*Notes*: November – actual; December–February – estimates; 1996 – estimates

*Source*: *Finansovye izvestia*, 23 January 1997.

the number of unemployed in Russia was estimated at seven million according to official figures, but some unofficial sources put the figure at ten million, not including hidden unemployment (*Finansovye izvestia*, 18 February 1997). Russia ranks last on the list of 49 countries producing 94 per cent of the world GDP. Even among the CIS countries Russia ranks as one of the last in economic efficiency. The level of industrial production in Russia in 1996 was 47 per cent relative to 1990, compared with Uzbekistan at 106 per cent, Turkmenistan – 81 per cent, Belarus – 63 per cent, and Ukraine – 55 per cent (*Nezavisimaya gazeta*, 22 November 1996).

The only discernible economic success was a significant reduction in the annual rate of inflation to between 22 and 24 per cent. However, the volume of government internal debt (mainly government short-term bonds) reached almost 250 trillion roubles (about 50 billion dollars) (Narzikulov, 1996). The fall in the rate of inflation has been accompanied by a rise in defaults in payments. At the beginning of October 1996, the shortfall in budget revenue exceeded 100 trillion roubles, while the total indebtedness of enterprises and other institutions reached almost 500 trillion roubles. The level of investment in the real sector of the economy was also extremely low.

Table 6.2   Major macroeconomic indices for the period 1996–2000

|  | 1996 | estimate 1997 | 1998 | 1999 | prognosis 2000 | 2000 as % 1996 |
|---|---|---|---|---|---|---|
| GDP as % of previous year | 94 | 100–102 | 103.0 | 104.5 | 105.0 | 114.0 |
| Inflation: average per annum | 147.7 | 115.0 | 109.1 | 107.2 | 106.6 | 143.0 |
| Industrial production % of previous year | 95.0 | 100–102 | 104.0 | 106.0 | 108.0 | 120.2 |
| Gross agricultural production % of previous year | 93.0 | 98.0 | 103.0 | 104.0 | 104.0 | 109.0 |
| Capital investment trillion roubles | 350 | 425 | 510 | 612 | 740 | |
| as % of previous year | 80–82 | 100–101 | 107.0 | 110.0 | 112.0 | 132.0 |
| Foreign investment billion dollars | 6 | 9 | 10 | 11 | 12 | |
| Retail trade turnover as % of previous year | 96.0 | 101.0 | 102.0 | 103.0 | 104.0 | 111.0 |
| Unemployment: million | 2.6 | 3.6 | 4.2 | 4.4 | 4.6 | |
| Rate of unemployment % | 3.6 | 5.1 | 5.8 | 6.1 | 6.4 | |
| Export to far-abroad billion dollars | 69.5 | 73.0 | 76.0 | 82.0 | 89.0 | 128.0 |
| Import from far-abroad billion dollars | 46.3 | 50.0 | 59.0 | 69.0 | 78.5 | 169.5 |

Source: *Finansovye izvestia*, 23 January 1997.

According to one Russian economist, 'the luxury of the bank's offices cannot hide the industrial crisis because the redistribution of capital from the basic branches of the economy to the financial sector have usually a tendency to come to a halt'. This has already occurred in 1996 during the crisis of the banking system. The total of gross balances of banks declined by almost half (even when allowing for inflation). There was practically no growth in the amount of funds of enterprises held on their current bank accounts. The volume of long-term loans by the banks fell by 25 per cent over the year (ibid.).

## THE RUSSIAN ECONOMY TOWARD THE YEAR 2000

Early in 1997, the Russian government submitted to the Duma its 'Basic directives for a medium term programme for 1997–2000 – structural transformation and economic growth'. The main objective of the programme – stable economic growth of not less than five per cent per annum and the creation of conditions for an increase in investment – is to be achieved by the end of the century.

The government plans to establish macroeconomic conditions for a further structural transformation of the economy – a rate of inflation of no more than 6–8 per cent per annum, and a budget deficit of no more than 1.5 per cent of GDP by the end of the period. Government borrowings will be cut down and returns on government bonds will be kept at 2–3 per cent above the rate of inflation. At the end of the period, the inflow of foreign investments is expected to amount to about 12 billion dollars (Pismennaya, 1997). 1997 is to be the beginning of the restructuring of some problem enterprises with the government's participation, as well as structural transformation of the branches of natural monopolies (introduction of a new system of price formation, and a reduction in cross subsidies). There will also be a restructuring of budgetary expenses – particularly military expenditure. In order to encourage savings, the government intends to introduce a system of insurance of bank deposits in 1998.

The government programme was met by much scepticism in the parliament. Most participants in the parliamentary debate criticised it – they simply did not believe in its feasibility. It was also criticised by economists of the Institute for Economics of the Russian Academy of Sciences who noted that the programme does not take into account the steadily increasing corruption in the economy. According to some expert estimates, two-thirds of the market is controlled by criminal elements. It was also pointed out that the previous medium-term programme adopted by the government in 1995 – 'Reforms and development of the Russian economy' – which was to be completed within three years, is still in the course of being realised (ibid.).

FOREIGN TRADE

One of the bright spots in Russia's economy is the foreign trade sector. For a number of years, Russia had a positive balance of trade, which contributed to the financing of vital imports. Foreign trade reforms were mainly aimed at liberalisation of international trade by opening the Russian market to foreign competition. According to preliminary data, the official foreign trade turnover in 1996 with countries of the near- and far-abroad was 5.2 per cent higher than in 1995 and amounted to about 133 billion dollars. Russia's positive balance of trade rose by over 6 billion dollars, and by the end of the year amounted to almost 40 billion dollars. This came as a result of maintaining a constant level of imports and a significant increase in exports (Kuzmichev, 1997). A less positive factor is the large share of fuel and energy resources within the total volume of exports (45 per cent). In 1996 Russia exported 127 million tonnes of oil and 200 billion cubic metres of natural gas. At the same time, the value of total exports of machinery rose by 10 per cent and to countries of the far-abroad – by 15 per cent (ibid.). The volume of imports in 1996 did not exceed the level of 1995 and amounted to about 46.6 billion dollars. Machinery and equipment constituted about one-third of Russia's total imports. In 1996 there was a geographical shift in the sources of imports. Imports from far-abroad countries fell by 4.6 per cent while those from CIS countries rose by 8.3 per cent, but 70 per cent of total imports in 1996 came from far-abroad countries. Among Russia's leading trading partners in Western Europe are Germany, Italy and Holland. Among the countries of Central and Eastern Europe, Poland has become Russia's major partner in this region with a total of 4.2–4.5 dollars in 1996 (ibid.).

There are two important indicators of Russia's foreign trade activities in 1996 which show a clearly discernible trend. The first is a 10 per cent increase in trade with the CIS countries, the second, the most dynamic change in Russia's foreign trade, is the rise in trade between Russia and the United States. According to preliminary estimates, Russia's trade with the US in 1996 rose by 5–7 per cent.

While Russia can boast some successes in foreign trade – a significant increase in turnover and a positive balance of trade – many Russian economists claim that foreign trade successes are at the expense of domestic producers and affect all sectors of the domestic economy. An argument put forward is that by opening the Russian

*Table* 6.3   Preliminary results of Russia's foreign trade in 1996 (billion dollars)

| Region | turnover | export | import | balance 1996 | 1995 |
|---|---|---|---|---|---|
| Far-abroad | 102.4 | 70.5 | 31.9 | 33.6 | 32.5 |
| change (%) | +3.7 | +7.4 | +4.6 | | |
| CIS countries | 30.7 | 16.0 | 14.7 | 1.3 | 0.7 |
| change (%) | +10.4 | +12.4 | +8.3 | | |
| Total | 133.1 | 86.5 | 46.6 | 39.9 | 33.2 |
| change (%) | +5.2 | +8.3 | −0.1 | − | − |

*Source*: *Nezavisimaya gazeta*, 14 January 1997.

market to foreign competition, the Russian government is destroying the domestic industrial potential (Blinov, 1996). They see much merit in the former command system because it controlled the volume and selection of imported goods. They also see an advantage in the old system of price formation, which aimed at satisfying domestic consumer demand rather then profitability. Exports on the other hand had been controlled in such a way as not to deprive the country of resources in short supply. Generally, the benefit of the old system is seen in the 'primacy of the public interest and in the securing of Russia's economic independence' (ibid., p. 48).

There is also much criticism of the present Russian government regarding its response to action by foreign countries which harm the Russian economy. It is suggested that Russia act independently rather than submit to the dictates of international agencies such as the IMF, the World Bank and Russia's other Western partners. The argument is that in many countries, including highly developed ones, there are sections of the economy which cannot compete on the world market but are capable of becoming competitive under an appropriate protectionist policy and government assistance. To protect the interests of its producers, it is pointed out, the European Union introduced quotas on exports from Russia of some items of light industry and non-ferrous metals, that is products whose export may affect Western domestic producers. One of the problems Russia must overcome is the anti-dumping measures and prohibitive tariffs applicable to certain Russian goods. If necessary, Russia should take coutermeasures for the protection of her economic interests (*Mezhdunarodnaya zhizn*, no. 10, 1996). A complex problem in this respect will arise with Russia's intention to join the GATT and World Trade Organisation. Russia's participation in world trade is very important for her economic progress, but it may have negative consequences given the unpreparedness of Russia's industrial base and its financial system to meet the strict requirements of these organisations.

The 1996 legislative programme of the Russian Federal Duma included action of practical importance aimed at providing protection for Russian producers. Among the proposed laws were the laws 'On protection of Russia's economic interests in foreign trade', 'On agreements on concessions', and 'On currency and export control'. There were also proposals for the introduction of changes and additional laws 'On state regulation of foreign trade activities', 'On customs tariffs', 'On currency regulations and currency control', 'On agreement on production-sharing', and 'On foreign investment in Russia'.

A middle ground is taken by many Russian economists who believe that the Russian economy should be open to international competition, but its openness should be determined by the degree of preparedness of basic sectors of the economy, their production potentials and competitiveness on the domestic and world markets. This assumes a carefully thought-out combination of liberalisation of foreign trade activities and selected protectionist measures. The subjects of protection should be, in the first place, the branches and types of production which, when supported by the government, could in the short and medium-term become competitive and could replace imported goods on the domestic market. In order to achieve the above objective it would be necessary to clearly determine differentiated customs tariffs. An effective means of protectionist policy would also be some non-tariff instruments such as import and export restrictions, licensing, stricter application of technological standards, health, veterinary and ecological control, anti-dumping and compensation duties etc. At the same time, Russian economists recognise that protective duties and the introduction of import quotas are not always a stimulus for improvement in the competitiveness of domestic production. Nonetheless, the realisation of such a foreign trade strategy, particularly during the present period of economic crisis, is impossible without a significant increase in the role of the government (ibid., p. 72).

The conclusion reached by some Russian economists is that the development of Russia's foreign trade relations must be orientated toward the principle of diversification of export and import markets in order not to become economically dependent on individual countries or regions. This is particularly relevant to trading and economic relations with the CIS countries. A strategic course for the gradual creation of an integrated Commonwealth, above all a customs and monetary union, requires the strengthening of Russia's economic position *vis-à-vis* these countries.

## FOREIGN TRADE AND INTEGRATION INTO THE WORLD ECONOMY

Despite Russia's apparent successes in foreign trade, the situation of Russia's foreign currency reserves is deteriorating. Russia's gold reserves inherited from the former USSR, which were originally estimated at 2500 tonnes, fell to 115 tonnes at the beginning of 1996 (*Nezavisimaya gazeta*, 23 November 1996). In October 1996, the Russian Prime Minister announced the government's intention of selling the rest of the gold reserves (*Nezavisimaya gazeta*, 29 October 1996). In April–May 1996, Russia's foreign currency reserves fell from 8.7 billion dollars to 4.3 billion dollars. At the same time, Russia's external debt doubled to more than 120 billion dollars.

The Russian government placed much hope on Western financial aid, but this proved disappointing. The fact is that Russia requires hundreds of billions of dollars to be able to restructure its economy – an amount that Western banks do not have readily available or are unwilling to provide (*Moskovskii komsomol*, 11 March 1995). Some Russian analysts see the Western banks' interest in maintaining this situation as a means of exercising control over the Russian economy. Nevertheless, since 1991, the international community appears to be cooperating with the Russian Federation in its transition to a market economy, as well as assisting Russia in becoming a member of international financial institutions. The aid allocated to Russia so far amounts to about 79.2 billion dollars. 47.3 billion dollars, or 60 per cent of the total aid, came from the G-7 group and the European Commission – Denmark, Finland, Holland, Norway, Sweden and Switzerland, while 29.7 billon dollars, or 37 per cent, came from international financial institutions. The remaining 22.2 billion dollars, or 3 per cent, are from other sources (*Finansovye izvestia*, 5 November 1996). These figures do not include the extension of Russia's debt repayments. Although it is difficult to determine the exact amounts already paid out, according to some estimates, out of the allocated total amount of 79.2 billion dollars, 52 per cent has already been transferred (ibid.).

A conference that took place in Washington on 24–26 April 1996 as part of the half-yearly session of the World Bank and IMF, debated, among other items on the agenda, the question of financial aid to Russia. It proved disappointing from the Russian point of view (Vasilchuk, 1996). The treatment Russia received at the conference is a harbinger of a 'cold peace', according to an article published in the respected *Finansovye izvestia*. In 1995, the Russian government and the Bank of Russia did everything that was possible to conform to the recommendations by the IMF regarding strict monetary policy. The Russian budget deficit did not exceed 3–4 per cent of GDP (compared with 6 per cent in France, 7 per cent in Britain and 10 per cent in Italy). The domestic market of government securities has been growing, which allowed the financing of over one-third of the deficit. In 1995, the Bank of Russia succeeded in reducing the rate of increase of money supply to 1–2 per cent per month compared with 9 per cent in 1994, and April 1995 was the third month in a row showing a slow-down in the rate of price increases (ibid.).

Another problem Russia faces is foreign debt. According to data supplied by the Russian Ministry for Finance, at the beginning of 1996 Russia's foreign debt amounted to 120.4 billion dollars of which 103 billion was owed by the former USSR. Russia's debt of 17.4 billion dollars was accumulated after 1 January 1992 (*Finansovye izvestia*, 6 February 1997). At the same time, Russia has a significant amount of accumulated debts owed to the former Soviet Union by its former allies. At the beginning of 1997 they amounted to 150 billion dollars – debts which Moscow considers almost irrecoverable. Russian officials hope to recover part of the debt – about 50 billion dollars – once Russia becomes a member of the Paris Club of creditor countries. It hopes to be able to sell those debts on the secondary market to banks and other financial institutions (*Mezhdunarodnaya zhizn*, no. 10, October 1996, p. 77). Russia agreed to take over the responsibility for the debts of the former USSR and in return expected mutual recognition of her right to all foreign assets of the Union. Russia was granted the rights to foreign real estate, but regarding the rights to the debts owed to the former Soviet Union by third countries, the situation remains complex. It is not only a question of immediate settlement of this amount, but primarily of the acknowledgment of the debts by the debtors (Shokhin, 1996).

The Russian delegation to the April 1996 World Bank and IMF conference in Washington hoped that its proposal for a new initiative on a long-term restructuring of Russia's foreign debts and on granting in 1996–97 an additional loan of nine billion dollars would be approved by the IMF. However, Russia's proposals have not been accepted. According to one opinion, the change in the IMF and the 'Big Seven' position, was caused by Russia's claims to the right of conducting its foreign and domestic policies according to its own national interests without outside interference (Vasilchuk, 1996). According to this view, the more steps Russia undertakes toward economic reconstruction the more she is seen by the developed countries as a potential competitor. Accordingly, the interests of the international financial bureaucracy run counter to Russia's national interests (ibid.). Simultaneously with the requests for financial aid, Russia undertook diplomatic steps to join the World Trading Organisation. This action conforms with Russia's foreign policy aimed at securing her a place within the world community of nations. Russia submitted its application to join WTO in 1994. During 1994–96, in the course of a number of meetings of the so-called working group on Russia's participation in the WTO, the Russian side presented a memorandum on Russia's trade policies and generally additional information on Russia's foreign trade activities. In February 1997, the head of the permanent delegation to the European Commission in Moscow stated that Russia will become a member of the WTO within 18 months.

The main obstacle to overcome before Russia joins the WTO is the fact that Russia has so far not been recognised as a country with a market economy, according to the head of the directorate of the European Commission. There are also other obstacles. A year earlier, in 1996, Russia was required to lower the average import tariffs to the level of the WTO's 10 per cent. This, the Russian side claimed, was impossible for a country with an economy in transition. The level of Russia's average import tariffs at the beginning of 1997 was 15 per cent.

An additional condition for Russia's membership of WTO was that Russia accept a number of international agreements, especially regarding state purchases and trade in aviation technology in which Russia has a great deal of expertise. This means that Russia must offer tenders for amounts exceeding 300 000 dollars that are open to companies of member states. The Russians thought such a condition unrealistic and unacceptable because it would mean the abolition of subsidies to the Russian aviation industry and lowering of tariffs to zero. The Russian market is still far from being able to meet such requirements.

Russia's membership of WTO is also dependent on significant changes in the current legislation, which must conform to WTO standards and other international agreements. The problem for Russia is that given the present membership of over 120 countries, she must conclude separate agreements with each of these countries whose interests very often clash with Russia's interests. There are also difficulties with regard to US–Russia economic relations. Russian sources point to the Jackson–Vanik amendment which was still in force at the beginning of 1997.

In the meantime, the World Bank is preparing a two-year, $US 6 billion loan to help the Russian government pay off huge arrears in wages and pensions. The Bank's president, James Wolfensohn, said that the World Bank considered the loan necessary to ensure social stability within Russia, where millions of workers are going without pay (*The Age*, 16 April 1997).

Two more meetings of the working group are scheduled for 1997, during which the final decision will be taken regarding Russia's membership in 1998. At the last meeting in Geneva some members of the WTO insisted that Russia accept the principle of the so-called 'standstill' – a voluntary commitment not to introduce any negative changes into its trading legislation (raising tariffs or other trading restrictions) over the period of negotiations. Russia objected to this condition.

Russia's present financial situation does not show any signs of improvement – its foreign debt continues to grow, for which there are two reasons. First, since Russia took over the indebtedness of the USSR, she was unable to pay even the interest. As a result, the debt of the former USSR increased from 97 to 103 billion dollars. Second, Russia's current indebtedness continues to grow on account of new loans. For the time being, Russia fulfils her obligations regarding her own debts, and since 1992, Russia began to be more selective in its borrowings. The government no longer finances the purchases of grain and other goods. Loans are being primarily used for the acquisition of equipment and the restructuring of industry. The Russian parliament has limited the volume of borrowings for 1996/97 to 9.2 billion dollars.

THE ECONOMY AND FOREIGN POLICY

The deterioration in the Russian economy and the decline of Russia's economic and industrial potential generally, has become, for the first time since the introduction of reforms, a real threat to the stability of the government and public institutions, according to a report by the Russian Institute of Economic Forecast (Vasilchuk, 1997). The report singles out six basic problems of the Russian economy in 1996–97.

(i) The low level of tax collections, which does not cover the necessary minimum of government expenditure.
(ii) Deterioration in the export sector. Export revenue is not sufficient to cover the cost of imports and the servicing of foreign debts. The foreign trade surplus of 20 billion dollars in 1996, is in fact a transfer of Russian resources abroad.
(iii) Insufficient flow of finance for capital investment needs.
(iv) Uncontrolled curtailment of the agricultural sector.
(v) Critical decline in consumption due to high prices and low disposable incomes.

The report does not offer any solution to these problems, but notes that over the period of reforms, the government has not been able to adopt a policy that would be clear and accessible to all – a basic requirement of any socio-economic system. Meanwhile, in May 1997, the Russian leaders declared an end to the post-communist era of economic depression with news of the first growth in quarterly economic indicators since capitalism dawned in Russia. The statement was based on figures that included a 0.2 per cent rise in gross domestic product. Coming after at least six years of steady and severe decline, and coinciding with other signs of improving economic health, the slight January–March 1997 expansion was greeted in Moscow as the start of a long-awaited turnaround.

The situation in the Russian economy appears to be the reason why the Russian government is devoting most of its attention to domestic problems rather than to foreign policy. This would explain the acceptance by Russia of most of the American initiatives related to the expansion of NATO in Europe. Moscow's apparent concession to the enlargement of NATO, has been prompted by the early acceptance of Russia becoming an equal member of the G-7. A Russian economic commentator, Aleksei Portanskii, expressed his doubts about the enlargement of the G-7 being transformed into G-8 if Russia is accepted. He underlines the fact that the 'Seven' is a club of the richest, most industrially developed and democratic countries whose influence over the world economy and finances is decisive. It was precisely on account of its economic power that the club had been created. The endorsement of a new member whose economy is inferior to that of the other members, would make the functioning of this body ineffective. The acceptance of Russia into the club would be a political gesture rather than a practical step, according to Portanskii (Portanskii, 1997).

Russia's membership of the WTO is a priority objective of Russia's foreign economic relations and foreign policy. Joining WTO would signify the removal of discriminatory barriers for Russian exports and access to world markets. There is strong opposition in Russia against what it sees as economic discrimination in the form of restricted access to world markets and the imposition of measures aimed at curbing this access. The Russian government is also critical of the slow progress in providing Russia with financial aid.

Seen from a Western perspective, the reluctance by Western financial institutions to transfer the promised financial aid to Russia is justified by the state of the Russian economy and the way it is regulated by the government, according to a Russian analyst. The West demands a speeding up of reforms so as to bring the Russian economic system closer to a Western model. This may be a rational expectation, but in reality the Russian government has only limited possibilities to accelerate the rate of reforms, let alone to put them into practice. The resistance against reforms is still very strong. Another reason for Western caution in providing aid is a perception that once the Russian economy recovers from the present crisis, the Russian government will begin to conduct a more active and perhaps aggressive foreign policy – there are many voices in Russia who demand that Russia have a more assertive position in international affairs.

# 7 Russia and the World

Prior to the dissolution of the Soviet Union, the foreign policy of the former USSR had always been reasonably well defined. During the Cold War it was thought to be determined by the ideological conflict with the United States, and Soviet relations with a foreign country were conditioned by the degree of the latter's opposition to the policy of the United States. The USSR could usually rely on the support of the 'progressive forces' in the United Nations, and Soviet influence on world affairs was also determined by its power of veto in the Security Council. Soviet foreign policy was then operating within a bipolar world system in which the United States and the Soviet Union were the dominating powers. From the Soviet point of view it was a satisfactory state of affairs because it placed the USSR on the world stage as an equal major player.

The bipolar world system signified a political division of the world into countries considered as belonging to the Western free democratic world and those that supported communism under the guidance of the Soviet Union. The division into the two camps did not make a clear distinction between countries according to the regime under which they operated. The Western camp contained many countries with an undemocratic, often dictatorial government, but as long as it showed its opposition to communism, it gained the support of the United States. Similarly, within the socialist camp were regimes that could hardly be defined as communist, but as long as they opposed imperialism, they were considered by the Soviets as fraternal states and received material support, mainly in the form of supply of weapons either on credit or simply free of charge.

The change in the Kremlin leadership in 1985, signalled a change in the direction of Soviet foreign policy. While Gorbachev declared his willingness to compromise on many issues of international politics, he continued to assert the existence of the two political systems, but attempted to show that peaceful coexistence is possible and indeed desirable. This was considered at the time as the end of the Cold War.

There was a great deal of confusion regarding the role of the USSR in the world. For the Soviet Union it was a question of determination of its position – real or desired – within the world's economy and politics (*Kommunist*, no. 12, 1990). A major problem facing the USSR at the time was the internal economic situation and the lack of adequate resources for asserting its role on the international arena. Its strategic and political international position has been steadily deteriorating. Its standing was for a long time determined by the parity of missiles, but with the rising internal chaos, the intellectual 'superpower' concept was being eroded. In the words of a Russian analyst, 'one cannot get very far with missiles alone' (Bovin, 1991). In the area of military power, however, the USSR acquired strategic parity with the US and preserved it despite the apparent effort by the American military to achieve superiority.

Until the advent of *perestroika* Soviet foreign policy was based on the outside threat factor. It dated from the time of the Revolution and even during the post-war years it was used to rally general support. Some post-Soviet political analysts, describe this period of threat of a global conflict and of the use of nuclear weapons as having had a deforming influence upon the Soviet Union's role on the world arena (*Kommunist*, no. 12, 1990, p. 115).

With the rise of Mikhail Gorbachev, the most important task of Soviet foreign policy was the destruction of the old mechanism of confrontation and the removal of the ideological myth. It proved to be a very slow process compared with what took place in former Soviet satellites. Ideological dogma and other Stalinist attributes had much deeper roots in the USSR than in its Western neighbours. For the Soviet Union, 'Stalinism was an indigenous creation, a monster raised on the national soil, while in Eastern Europe it was imported by force' (Kortunov, 1990, p. 117). Under Gorbachev, the process of democratisation and formation of foreign policy was still in its initial stage. Despite the economic and political failures on the domestic front, the New Thinking had moved Soviet foreign policy to the forefront of international politics. Gorbachev became fashionable in the West as the man 'with whom one could do business'. He created much interest and his speeches were being listened to with great attention.

Between 1985 and 1991 the Soviet government was in full control over its foreign policy. However, events within the USSR and in Eastern Europe, took away from the Soviet government the ability to formulate an independent foreign policy. Following the coup of August 1991, when all former republics declared their independence, Soviet foreign policy entered a period of transition during which it had to define its place not only in relation to the outside world, but within a fragmented group of independent states. Earlier, in June 1990, Russia had declared its sovereignty and entered international politics by establishing a Ministry of Foreign Affairs with Kozyrev as the Minister (Bovin, 1991). While one could still speak of Soviet foreign policy, its direction became increasingly dependent on the position of the largest republic – Russia. There was a discernible trend to identify the former Soviet Union with the Russian republic, and the creation of a separate Russian Ministry of Foreign Affairs was evidence of that trend. Russian political analysts saw future foreign relations determined by Russia rather than by the Union (ibid.).

After the final act of disintegration of the Union into a number of independent states and the collapse of the Warsaw Pact Organisation, one could no longer speak of Soviet foreign policy. The USSR's place on the international stage had been taken over by the Russian Federation, and since the end of 1991 Russia has been attempting to find its proper place on the world stage.


## TOWARDS A MULTIPOLAR WORLD – A RUSSIAN VIEW

With the collapse of the socialist camp, the period of the bipolar world system came to an end. In his extended review of new Soviet policies, Gorbachev clearly indicated that with the approaching end of the bipolar world system, the USSR placed increasing emphasis on the role of the United Nations in resolving conflicts. It was an attempt to prevent the US from dictating its rules to the world by bypassing the United Nations, where, Gorbachev hoped, the Soviet Union would still maintain its authority (Gorbachev, 1988, p. 142). This approach to international politics prevails today and is reinforced by the perceived attempts of the US to dictate its rules in Europe through NATO. After the dissolution of the Soviet Union, the NATO block basing itself on the principle of 'political realism', began actively to fill the emerging geopolitical vacuum, according to Arkadii Vartanyan, a Russian commentator. 'The new direction is leading toward a definite objective – absolute domination and the creation of a renewed world order which conforms with NATO's social, economic and political interests' (Vartanyan, 1996).

For Russia it implied the necessity for a speedy resolution of a vital question: should, and is Russia capable of occupying her proper place on the world political map and if so what are the possibilities? It is not a simple question to answer – the situation in Russia is unclear and complicated. With the collapse of the Soviet Union and the emergence of Yeltsin as President of Russia, it seemed as if Russia's path led to the West. Russia's foreign policy under Yeltsin clearly indicated a trend toward joining the industrially developed countries, toward a system of liberal governments, and a definite break with the messianic ideas of the former Soviet Union (Timmerman, 1994). This signalled to the West that, in contrast to the former Soviet Union, Russia considers Western countries as basically non-hostile, but as partners and possible allies. The Yeltsin leadership took as its point of departure the notion that Western attitudes toward Russia would be favourable on account of the radical domestic reforms, which would create a basis for common values and eradicate the ideological conflicts of the past. It was thought that the West would accept Russia as a great power, as a full partner in the international community, and respect its interests.

It looked as if Russia had found its basic direction. But the Russian government was subjected to pressure from various political forces, which often express extreme and conflicting ideas on political matters and on the question of Russia's future role within the system of international relations. This question remains the subject of heated disputes and is increasingly being transformed into an instrument of internal political struggle for power and for an alternative direction.

A major problem in analysing Russia's foreign relations is the fact that at present Russia does not seem to have a well-defined foreign policy. Its foreign policy must be looked upon as an amalgam of relations with a number of separate entities, such as the European Union, the United States, former East European satellites, former Soviet republics, and other countries of no less importance such as China and Japan. Russia's foreign policy is not a single all-embracing policy but several policies that determine not only the relationship between Russia and the United States in general, but also relations between Russia and many world regions and states. The reason for the apparent fragmentation of Russia's foreign policy is that Russia is still in the process of determining its national interests and its proper role in world affairs. However, the real causes of the increasingly acute conflict lie much deeper; they lie within the disagreements over the question of Russia's future identity, and in this context its relationship with the rest of the world (ibid., p. 17). In this respect Russia's relations with the

United States are still of prime importance. They are conditioned by a kind of rivalry between the two world powers – a rivalry, which on the surface has no competitive military or strategic connotations, but which expresses Russia's aspiration to retain its major role on the world stage.

The end of the period of confrontation between the former USSR and the United States is generally seen as the end of a bipolar world and as a gradual emergence of a multipolar world order, of which Russia appears to be the main champion. The advancement of the idea that world politics should no longer be determined by the most powerful state, the United States, was at the same time an admission that Russia had lost her place as a superpower on the world arena. While Russia may still be considered as a superpower in a military-strategic sense in that it maintains its nuclear potential, its role in international politics has been downgraded to a secondary position. The attempt by the United States to offer Russia what seemed to be an equal voice in decisions affecting international conflicts, such us Bosnia Herzegovina, the Gulf War and in the Middle East, could not hide the fact that Russia is no longer an equal partner. Russia's position became weak not only in the West, but in the Balkans, in the Middle East and in the Asian-Pacific region as well. The Serbs, Muslims and Croats were pacified by American diplomats, the Bosnian peace agreement was signed in Dayton and Paris, and the Palestinian–Israeli peace declaration in Washington (Gornostaev, 1997).

The realisation of this fact, forced Russia to assert its place by strongly supporting the role of the United Nations, where Russia's seat at the Security Council gives her the right of veto of any UN resolution sponsored by the United States. This became evident when the question of European security surfaced in connection with the plans for extending NATO. According to the Russian official stance, 'a model of European security should be based on all international organisations such as the UN, OSCE (Organisation of Security and Cooperation in Europe), Council of Europe and the European Union. NATO should function only in conjunction with 'Partnership for Peace'. According to the Russian view, the central function of the new model of European security should be taken over by OSCE – an organisation created on the principle of consensus which guarantees the rights of all participating countries whether large or small. Consequently, Russia sees the necessity of avoiding the inclusion into the new system of those elements that would assure the security of some participants at the expense of others (meaning Russia). Such a model should envisage the application of measures aimed at the resolution of conflicts beginning with preventive diplomacy and finishing with 'enforcement of peace'. However, such a model of European security should not take on the functions of the United Nations (Primakov, 1996, p. 10).

According to one Russian analyst, the collapse of the bipolar world, does not take place in a symmetrical fashion; the position of the East has weakened while the West has retained its position (Bovin, 1991). The perception of the US striving to establish a new world order in which Russia would participate as a minor partner, was reinforced by America's victory in the Gulf War. Although formally the Soviet Union supported the American military effort, in reality it saw the operation 'Desert Storm' as a purely American initiative undertaken for its own national interests. President Bush's talk of a new world order acquired a different connotation from the Soviet and later Russian point of view.

A critical analysis of the 'new world order' was presented by the then Deputy Minister of Foreign Affairs of the USSR, V. Petrovskii in August 1991. His analysis is still relevant today and was later confirmed by Yevgenii Primakov. The term new world order is not really new, said Petrovskii. It appeared every time that the system of international relations was undergoing a drastic change – for example, when the old Versailles system was replaced by the Yalta–Potsdam system. This in turn was replaced by the Cold War which established a new, although far from ideal, world system. It was only when the 'New Political Thinking' became transformed into a real factor in international relations, that the need arose to re-think the structure of world society (*Izvestia*, 13 August 1991). To the question of whether the Soviet Union, despite its internal difficulties, would be able to integrate into the new world order, and whether as a result it would lose its superpower status, Petrovskii answered in the affirmative to the first part. As to the second part, he categorically disagreed with an American political scientist who in a recently published article in *Izvestia* said that the 'new world order' is the old order minus the USSR, plus Germany and Japan (ibid.).

It was the latter point – the complete denigration of Russia's importance in world affairs – that provoked a reaction from those in Russia who saw the slow erosion of Russia's importance as being a result of American domination. One of the critics is the new

Russian Foreign Minister, Yevgenii Primakov. According to Primakov, after the end of the Cold War there emerged a trend toward a transition from a bipolar to a multipolar world order. Western European countries began to assert their independence from the American nuclear umbrella. Japan also began asserting its political and military independence from the US. However, Primakov stated, it is still too early to speak of a multipolar world order. The inertia of former political thinking is still in evidence, and the stereotypes that became entrenched during the forty years of the Cold War in the minds of political leaders have not yet disappeared despite the dismantling of strategic missiles and the destruction of thousands of tanks (Primakov, 1996, p. 3).

Primakov saw the new world order as being composed of 'leaders' and those that are 'led'. This mentality, he said, is being fed by the illusion that in the Cold War some countries have been victorious while others were defeated. Such mentality indirectly encourages a tendency to create a unipolar world. Primakov accused the United States of adopting the role of policeman of the world and exploiting its economic and military power to attain its political objectives. As an example he quoted the Helms–Berton law which punishes those who economically cooperate with Cuba. Similar pressure against Iran's and Libya's trading partners resulted in attempts aimed at continuous intensification of the economic blockade. Resolution 986 of the Security Council of the UN 'oil in exchange for humanitarian aid to Iraq' is being artificially withheld. Since the end of the Cold War, some of the discriminatory trade restrictions are still in force and Russia is still included among the developing countries. Under the pretext of 'non-market status' of the Russian economy, the West is applying anti-dumping measures to Russian exports (ibid., p. 5).

By the end of 1996, Primakov clarified the principles guiding Russia's foreign policy. In an interview with ITAR-TASS, Primakov stated that the major objective of Russia's foreign policy remained unchanged – the creation of favourable conditions for the democratisation and economic transformation of the country. During the past few years Russia has striven to adopt a formula that would meet its aspirations as a world power – equal partnership. On the global scale it was achieved through the strengthening of Russia's position within the 'Big Eight'. It was part of Russia's policy aimed at the creation of a multipolar world order (ITAR-TASS, 1997). As a second objective Primakov saw the diversification of Russia's international links. Russia, Primakov said, is attempting to correct its former excessive leaning toward the West. As a great power, 'with significant interests in Asia and the Middle-East, Russia cannot march forward with one foot in the West', Primakov concluded (ibid.).

## RUSSIA AND THE CIS

It is generally recognised in Russia that Russia's national interests and its security are dependent to a great extent on its relationship with the former Soviet republics turned new independent states. A major principle of Russia's foreign policy, approved by the Federal Security Council in April 1993, has been defined as the 'need to secure stable mutual relations with the countries of the near abroad'. It has also been defined as a prime condition of Russia retaining its status as a great world power. Activities aimed at undermining the integration process of the CIS, are considered in Russia as a major threat and a challenge to its national security. Recognition of the rights and interests of national minorities – members of the peoples of the Russian Federation residing in the countries of the former Soviet Union – is also considered as part of Russia's vital interests. But, according to most Russian commentators, Russia's attempts at securing her legitimate interests in this area have been met by disapproval from the West (Kolchin, 1995).

Russian observers generally consider Western assessment of the post-Soviet space as negative. This, they say, was explicitly stated in an article by Z. Brzezinski published in a Russian newspaper (*Nezavisimaya gazeta*, 20 May 1994). Brzezinski quoted the then French foreign minister, A. Juppé, as saying that 'the Russians are slowly beginning to take control of the entire territory of the former USSR into their hands'. Although it is understandable, Brzezinski said, that Russia wishes to play an important role in what is known as the CIS, it does not follow that 'Russia could do whatever she likes – she cannot play the role of a gendarme'. Russia's diplomatic activities aimed at regaining influence in all parts of the world and in particular its efforts toward the integration of the CIS, are seen by some American observers as an attempt to establish a block of countries to counterbalance NATO's strategic and political position in Europe. According to another Russian newspaper (*Segodnya*, 24 June 1994), Russia's policy towards the near-abroad has disturbed the West. Although the West accepts Russia's interests in the CIS, it nevertheless strives to prevent the 'imperialisation' of Moscow's foreign policy. President Clinton has declared that the US does not object to the unification of the former Soviet republics provided it is done on a voluntary basis and according to their free will.

Russian commentators, generally, see the reintegration of the former Soviet republics as being in the interest not only of Russia but of her former partners as well. One Russian analysts draws attention to the fact that the Russian periphery has benefited more than did Russia from the exploitation of Russia's resources – an argument put forward by many Russian analysts (Kolchin, 1995).

The CIS and the Baltic states first appeared as a subject of Russia's foreign policy on 10 December 1991 – that is just before the endorsement by the Supreme Soviet of the Russian Federation of the Belovezh Treaty, which created the CIS. The emergence of independent states on the territory of the former USSR not only led to a cardinal change in the political map of the Euro-Asian continent, but also created an entirely new system of international relations, according to a Russian observer (Pechenev, 1996). Since the autumn of 1994, integration processes in the military area began to acquire a practical form. On 21 October 1994, the heads of the governments of the CIS signed a Memorandum of the Council of Heads of Governments of the Commonwealth entitled 'Basic directions of the integration developments of the CIS'. The process of integration entered an active phase in 1995. On 10 February 1995, all CIS governments (with the exception of Azerbaidjan) signed 'The Concept of collective security of countries – participants in the Treaty on collective security.' A united system of air defence was created in 1995, and negotiations are also taking place regarding military and technological cooperation and a programme of production and maintenance of armament (Korotchenko, 1996). The signing of the Treaty on the creation of a Russia–Belarus Commonwealth and the 'Treaty of Four' on closer economic and cultural cooperation between Russia, Belarus, Kazahkstan and Kirgizia were two important steps towards the integration of the CIS. Russia also concluded an agreement on confidence building measures with the participation of Kazahkstan, Kirgizia and Tadjikistan.

A serious problem is Russia's relations with Ukraine, particularly the disagreement regarding the location of the Russian Black-Sea navy in Sevastopol. The recent agreement between Russia and Ukraine seems to have defused the situation. However, the declared warming up of Russia–Ukraine relations after the visit by

Leonid Kuchma in Moscow, has rapidly changed; Ukraine does not foresee the possibility of joining the Customs Union while considering the probability of special relations with NATO (Kasaev, 1996).

The visits by Primakov and the then Russian Minister for Defence Grachev to Central Asia in January 1996, clearly indicated Moscow's priorities – the countries of this region are now being viewed as potentially its closest allies. Russia's attempts at renewing relations with former Asian republics are considered successful. The transfer to Russian control of a number of large enterprises and military plants of the former USSR in Kirgizia, indicates that Russia–Kirgiz links are developing in a favourable manner (ibid.). The warm welcome of the Russian military delegation in Alma-Ata and the concluded agreement on Russian aid for the creation of a Kazakh war navy, coincided with the 'pardon' bestowed upon the ataman Nikolai Gunkin, a staunch supporter of a union between Kazakhstan and Russia.

Even the Central Asian politician Islam Karimov of Uzbekistan, who was no friend of the Kremlin's appears to agree to the establishment of closer ties with Russia. This step, according to a Russian observer, is forced upon him by the deteriorating economic situation in Uzbekistan and problems in neighbouring Tadjikistan.

It would appear as if the CIS is again undergoing another stage in the slow process of establishing a Commonwealth, which may lead to the creation of a new grouping of states. The decision taken by the Russian government in autumn 1996 to render increased technological assistance and credits to the countries of the near-abroad, are another indication of the reorientation of Russia's foreign policy from the Western direction toward the East (ibid.).

According to one Russian analyst, 'in today's multipolar world Russia requires strong and reliable partners and allies (Rogov, 1995, p. 11). What Russia needs 'is to be surrounded with friendly neighbours', and it must, therefore, devote its attention to the strengthening of its new borders. 'The latter has become more important on account of the expansion of NATO to the East' (Pechenev, 1996).

The signing of an agreement with Belarus and the union of four – Russia, Belarus, Kazakhstan and Kirgizia – is still at an early stage and cannot be considered as a complete success for Russian diplomacy. The formation of a well-defined policy toward former Soviet republics that will meet Russia's long-term interests, is thought to be a problem which must be solved if Russia is to retain its status as a great power. For the foreseeable future, the relations with these republics will remain a priority in Russian foreign policy (ibid.).

General Igor Rodionov, Russia's former Minister of Defence and Chairman of the Council for Defence of the CIS, presented his views on Russia's national security at a conference devoted to the question of military and political integration of the CIS countries in December 1996. His speech was reported as being held in a confrontational spirit, which reflected the point of view among the Russian military leadership concerning Russian national security (Korotchenko, 1996). Rodionov noted that practically all actions of the West are aimed at disturbing the unity of the CIS and at reinforcing existing frictions within the CIS. The West, he said, exploits the existing inter-ethnic, inter-religious, territorial and other problems that have arisen in the post-Soviet space. It is attempting to directly destabilise the political situation within individual CIS countries and to curb integrational processes (ibid.). Speaking of the sources of military dangers for the CIS countries, Rodionov included territorial claims by a number of foreign countries. Among such claims are the Kuril Islands, Sakhalin and Kaliningrad. Kaliningrad has been the subject of Lithuanian demand for immediate withdrawal of Russian troops, and some Russian observers have expressed fears about a possible German claim of lost territory in what was formerly East Prussia annexed by the USSR in 1945.

Among other military dangers he sees local wars and conflicts in the close proximity of the borders of the CIS, the proliferation of nuclear armaments and other means of mass destruction and the means of their delivery. Especially dangerous, according to Rodionov, are attempts by the US aimed at the retention of its unchallenged world leadership based on the NATO bloc, including its decision to expand to the East. Rodionov also underlined the dangers inherent in the proliferation of religious extremism and of its attempts aimed at the destabilisation of the situation within the CIS. Under these circumstances, according to Rodionov, the cooperation in the area of military security between the CIS countries acquires major importance. The strategic factor which could provide such security would be the creation of a system of collective security. Based on mutual interests and on military and political objectives, it is possible to create a defence alliance between a number of CIS countries with a view to creating a unified military force (ibid.).

## THE EASTERN SECTOR

The Eastern border area is also receiving significant attention in Russian foreign policy. Indicative of its importance was the meeting of the Russian Foreign Ministry's Foreign Policy Council in November 1994 devoted to 'problems of security, stability and integration into the Asia-Pacific Region and Russia's interests'.

The process of replacing an essentially bipolar, military and ideological model of confrontation, typical of the greater part of the twentieth century, by a system of major, mostly economic regional entities, is seen by the Russians as taking place in all parts of the world. 'From this point of view the APR [Asia-Pacific Region] may be seen as a laboratory of new regionalism' (Kulagin, 1996, p. 35). The disintegration of the Soviet Union and the loss of mineral deposits outside the Russian republic (in Ukraine, Kazakhstan, Kirgizia and the Transcaucasian republics) set the strategic task of developing in Siberia and the Russian Far East large deposits of iron ore, copper and other non-ferrous metals such as gold, aluminium and so on that have not been adequately exploited. This in turn demands building a new transportation and communication infrastructure in the region. In addition, Russia's loss of many Baltic and Black Sea ports has increased the importance to it of the Far Eastern ports. Serious difficulties in economic cooperation with the European part of Russia, has caused Russia's eastern region to gravitate naturally toward the dynamic economy of the ARP, the foreign region closest to the Russian Far East. It is also in this region that Russia shares borders directly with three major military powers – the US, Japan and China.

There are however serious obstacles to large-scale Russian participation in the processes going on in the ARP. Russia's territories directly adjoining the ARP (the Maritime and Khabarovsk territories, the Republic of Sakha-Yakutia, the Magadan, Kamchatka, Sakhalin and Amur regions, the Jewish Autonomous Region) account for roughly 5 per cent of the Russian GDP and about as much of its population. The barriers that separate the Russian Far East from the economy of the European part of Russia and the Urals make it difficult to market in the ARP products of the western part of Russia. Today the Trans-Siberian railroad does not unite Russia in this respect but cuts it in two due to high transit charges and because its carrying capacity is limited. Another bottleneck in large-scale Russian exports is the limited handling capacity of Far Eastern ports (ibid., p. 37).

A serious barrier to wide-ranging business cooperation between Russia and the ARP economic complex is the position adopted by Japan, which still refrains, primarily for political reasons, from giving its leading companies and banks the green light for extensive business with Russia. As is well known, the Japanese have been demanding for decades the return of the islands which they lost following the end of the Second World War. There are circles in Japan who demand the transfer of South Sakhalin to Japan (Lazarev, 1991). The dispute between the USSR and Japan mainly concerns territories, which the Soviet Union has denied to Japan for many years. There were several opportunities for solving the problem. The last one was in 1956, when the USSR agreed to return two islands – Khabomai and Shikotan – conditional upon the signature of a peace treaty. Many Soviet political scientists consider that a return to the 1956 agreement could result in the desired relaxation of mutual relations (ibid.). But due to Soviet procrastination, and the signing of the Japanese–American Treaty of 1960 which provided the US with the right to establish military bases in Japan, the USSR refused to adhere to the previous agreement and declared the dispute definitely resolved. Subsequently, Japanese diplomacy has brought up the territorial question – it now speaks of the return of all four islands, the so-called Northern Territories (Vorobev, 1991).

For some time, Moscow tried to ignore the Japanese claims. But soon Japan found the lever with which they thought they could solve the question; growing economic difficulties within the Soviet Union would force Moscow to compromise in exchange for credits and technical cooperation. Indeed, according to some Russian commentators, the internal situation in Russia has brought about the talk of a possible 'sale' of the islands to Japan (ibid.). Nevertheless, Russia–Japan relations remain a serious problem.

In December 1996, Primakov went to Beijing, while China's Prime Minister Li Peng visited Moscow and was received by Yeltsin. Despite the progress in Russia's relations with China, it was not a restoration of the ideological alliance of the 1950s. Russia managed to solve the question of its common borders with China the demarcation of which is to be completed in 1997. Russia sees its rapprochement with Beijing as a response to the expansion of NATO.

The Russian foreign minister, Yevgenii Primakov, after his visits to several countries could boast of one success – the statement by the Chinese Minister for Foreign Affairs, Tsian Tsichen, in which he said that during the forthcoming Chinese–Russian summit in

Moscow in spring of 1997, both countries are to sign the long-awaited agreement of border troop reduction (Kondrashev, 1996). Primakov's medium-term prognosis is that Russia does not envisage any problems between the two countries in the next ten to fifteen years (ibid.).

## RUSSIA AND THE MIDDLE EAST

The news of Iraq's invasion of Kuwait came on 2 August 1990 during a meeting between Shevardnadze and James Baker in Irkutsk. At first the news was met by both the Russians and Americans with a certain degree of indifference – it was thought to be one of the many border crossings by Iraq. The Soviet–American meeting concluded the same day and Baker continued his journey to Mongolia while Shevardnadze went back to Moscow. The next day, 3 August, a mini conference took place in the Kremlin during which the position of the USSR in the conflict was discussed. It was decided to join the United States in condemning Iraq's aggression. But the position of the Soviet Union was rather ambiguous. Shevardnadze in his speech at the United Nations supported the resolution calling for appropriate measures against Iraq and he also suggested that the Security Council should initiate steps to activate the work of the military committee on the allocation of national contingents. 'It is possible', said Shevardnadze, 'that the Security Council on the recommendation of the military committee, will consider it necessary to create units of "speedy reaction" in which troops of the five permanent members would participate.' At the same time, Shevardnadze issued an assurance that the Soviet Union would not send any military personnel to the Persian Gulf (Vasiliev, 1991).

Despite the apparent contradiction, Shevardnadze's speech, according to one Russian commentator, should have been seen in the context of the 'New Thinking'. It was a continuation of Soviet foreign policy of the last five years – a policy of accommodation with the West (ibid.). But intervention was far from the Soviet mind. The Soviet Union tried for a peaceful solution by sending Primakov to Iraq. His position was also not well defined. When questioned, he said that he was against a resolution calling for military sanctions, but at the same time expressed an opinion that if a resolution was not to be followed by concrete action, it would reinforce Iraq's position. According to one Russian analyst 'it was not an automatic approval of any actions by the United States, but a practical application in international relations by the Soviet Union of the principles of its new political thinking' (Pogorelyi, 1991). This was despite the fact that according to Article 10 of the Iraq–USSR 1972 Treaty: 'each side declares that it will not enter into an alliance or participate in any group of states or any arrangements directed against the other side' (Korolev, 1991).

The war in the Persian Gulf erupted at a time when East–West relations were undergoing radical changes. It again stirred up the question of Soviet national security. The war in the Persian Gulf presented the USSR with one basic question: was there a change in the nature of Western government policies? The answer, according to one Soviet commentator, was negative. The West was still pre- pared to apply any means, including military force, for the attain- ment and security of their own interests. The economic interests of the United States and Western Europe were the main catalysts of the Gulf War. 'It was clear from the outset that the objective of the US was not only the liberation of Kuwait, but the elimination of Iraq from the military-economic map of the region and the taking over control of the oil wealth' (Gudkov, 1991).

Russia's position in another Middle East conflict was determined by American insistence that the Soviet Union co-chair the Israel– Palestinian peace conference. The reason for America's attitude in this respect can be explained by the fact that the United States, despite its victory in the war against Iraq, could not solve the problems of the Middle East without Soviet participation. The Soviet Union despite its internal difficulties was still seen by the Arabs as a counter- balancing factor to the US–Israel alliance. However, after the dis- solution of the Soviet Union and its replacement by Russia on the international stage, Russia's participation in the peace process had become only a formality.

Renewing diplomatic relations with Israel and the mass migra- tion of Jews to Israel had introduced a new element in Russia's relations with that country. The presence of over 700 000 former Soviet citizens in Israel provided favourable conditions for mutual trade and served as a bridge between the two countries. It led to closer economic links thanks to the large number of Russian-speaking Jews who still retain their connections with Russian authorities and are instrumental in establishing joint ventures. On the international arena, however, Russia appears to be adopting an even-handed position not much different from the US and the European Union.

The Russian press, by contrast, is much more favourably inclined toward Israel.

Russia has a vital interest in that region for economic rather than political reasons. The loss of influence in the Middle East has affected Russia's trade in armaments – an important source of Russia's foreign currency reserves. Previously, export of armaments by the former Soviet Union was determined by political considerations as a countervailing factor against American interests. In the post-Soviet era it was the volume of dollars received from the sale of weapons that became the decisive factor. The decline in Russia's supply of armaments to this part of the world, is seen by the Russians as a result of America's aggressive trade policy.

The latest trend in Russia's foreign policy in this region is an attempt at regaining the role of a superpower on the world stage and in the Middle East in particular. According to Aleksei Chistyakov, Deputy Director of the department of the Middle East and North Africa of the Russian Foreign Ministry, the end of the US–Soviet confrontation placed the Middle East among Moscow's top priorities because of the downgrading of economic relations between Russia and the countries of the region (Chistyakov, 1994). There was a particularly visible reduction in Russian arms sales. In 1988, the Soviet Union supplied to the Middle East arms worth over 14.5 billion dollars. In 1992 it fell to slightly over 2 billion dollars. Thus, said Chistyakov, Russia's interests in the Middle East are purely economic. In respect to its former clients such as Iraq, Libya and Syria, it is their indebtedness to the former USSR that makes the lifting of restrictions a Russian objective. In this way Russia hopes to recover some if not all of the debts incurred by these countries for arms supplied by the former USSR. The current period, said Chistyakov, also offers opportunities for cooperation with other countries with which Russia either kept limited relations or had no relations at all [Israel] (ibid.).

Furthermore, according to Chistyakov, Russia is a country where Muslims number about 20 million. This makes the Islamic factor an internal political reality. It has a strong impact on relations between Russia and the Middle East and should be seen as a national security factor. 'The understandable lack of tolerance towards a number of Muslim extremist groups and movements should not become an established trend which places almost the entire Muslim world into the camp of opponents of modern civilisation' (Primakov, 1996, p. 4). Russia also has interests in other countries in which the Muslim factor is predominant. In the eyes of millions of Muslims, the victor in Chechnya was Islam. The situation in all these countries, strange as it may seem, suits Russia to the ground. The victories of the Taliban in Afghanistan, have again forced some of the Central Asian republics to seek Russia's protection. The excessive attention devoted to Chechnya by Muslim politicians, forced the West to close its eyes to Russia's violations in the area of human rights and to help Russia as 'bastion of Christian civilisation', as a 'cordon sanitaire on the path of the Islamic Revolution'. Russia attempts to become a 'shield' for Europe. It is attempting to do in the East (in the south-east to be more precise) what NATO is doing in the West – expand its influence over neutral countries under the pretext of protecting them against foreign threat. However, the role of the 'threat of world revolution' is played not by communism but by the Muslim radical movement.

Prior to the December 1995 elections to the Duma, several leaders of Russia's major political parties stated their foreign policy platform. They referred to Russia's role on the international stage and in the Middle East. According to Sergei Belyaev, First Deputy Chairman of Our Home Russia movement council, 'Russia must expand its traditional links with leading countries of the Islamic world and raise her role in the Middle East peace settlement.' Similar views were expressed by Alexander Shabanov, Deputy Chairman of the Russian Communist Party Central Commitee. In reference to the Middle East, Shabanov was for the restoration of 'traditional links with those allies who continue to have a stake in cooperation with Russia' (*International Affairs*, Moscow, nos. 11–12, 1995). Vladimir Lukin, Vice-President of Yabloko and Chairman of the Committee for International Affairs of the State Duma, shared similar views. Exaggerated warming up to the West by Russian leaders has done little good for Russia, according to Lukin. Russia is the biggest Eurasian state with centuries of relations with the Muslim and East Asian civilisations. 'Russia must vigorously resist Islamic fundamentalism, but should not be drawn into a confrontation with the largest Islamic countries (including Iran). It should seek avenues of agreement and develop mutually beneficial relations' (Chistyakov, 1994).

AN AMERICAN VIEW

An American view on the post-Cold War US–Russia relations, was presented by Ariel Cohen, a senior policy analyst, in March 1997. Although his views may not represent the opinion of the majority of American political analysts, they may be taken as evidence of an emerging trend in US policy toward Russia. Cohen's conclusion is rather similar to the Russian interpretation of the American position; it suggests that the American Administration develop a new paradigm to govern its relations with Russia – a policy that he calls 'proceed with caution' (Cohen, 1997).

According to Cohen, during the Clinton Administration's first term, foreign policy principles such as protecting democracy and safeguarding American strategic security interests were forfeited in favour of the Administration's belief that it could gain from its uncritical embrace of Boris Yeltsin. By overemphasising its support for Yeltsin, the Administration promoted other democratically oriented Russian leaders, but at the same time, generated anti-American sentiments among important segments of the Russian elite. Moreover, despite the multi-billion dollar economic support from the US, the IMF and the World bank, the Kremlin has not yet efficiently implemented the much-needed economic reform package. The slow implementation of the reforms in Russia is seen by the analysts as a deliberate policy aimed at retaining the old system. This is why some people in the Administration demand a nexus between reforms in Russia and Western economic support. Further multilateral support should be focused more on structural reforms such as breaking up monopolies, agricultural reform, legal reform and the promotion of rule of law, and military reform that would include a cutback in the armed forces.

This is in fact part of the Russian government programme, but its implementation is very difficult given the complex problems Russia is facing. American analysts of Russia's policy do not take into account the fundamental differences between the type of society in Russia and that of the West, and the kind of system that Russia inherited from the former Soviet Union. Nothing is said about the problems that Russia is facing in its attempts to transform a centrally planned system into a free market. It is an approach which is also adopted by the international financial institutions such as the IMF and the World Bank. Both apply Western criteria to Russia without taking into account the specificity of that country.

The Soviet Union has never had the economic might to match its military muscle, but Russia today lacks even the latter. The Russian government has lost the ability – at least for the present – to project conventional power effectively outside its borders. Since the end of the Cold war, Russia is seen in the US as a weak regional power in need of Western assistance. At the same time, Russia makes unfair security demands on its neighbours by trying to block Poland, the Czech Republic, and other countries from joining NATO. 'It is reminiscent of efforts by the Soviet Union and the Romanov Empire to carve out spheres of influence and assure that Soviet or imperial Russian security interests prevailed over those of neighbouring countries' (Cohen, 1997).

An extreme policy agenda is suggested: the US should refrain from making too many concessions to gain Russian acceptance of NATO enlargement. It should step up pressure on Russian nuclear proliferation activities. Russia is selling the 'crown jewels' of its military-industrial complex, such as guided missiles cruisers, modern aircraft, and nuclear weapons technology to China. It has signed agreements to transfer to China its advanced gas centrifuge technology, used in uranium enrichment, and nuclear missile technology to build multiple independently targeted reentry vehicles (MIRV). Russia has also signed an agreement to sell two nuclear power stations to Iran.

The threat of a new Russian Empire seems to be pervading some American political observers. They accuse the Clinton Administration of a lack of willingness to halt Russian imperialism, which they say, may come back to haunt the US in the near future. The possible emergence of an anti-Western, nationalist Russia with a considerable nuclear arsenal cannot be ruled out. Preventing the emergence of a new Russian empire in the lands of the former Soviet Union should be a priority for the US and its allies.

> While the majority of those in power in Russia regard themselves as culturally European and Westernised, some politicians from the communist era, like Foreign Minister Evgenii Primakov, Nuclear Industry Minister Victor Mikhailov and CIS integration minister Aman Tuleev, remain proponents of the old Soviet-style outlook (ibid.).

An example of the 'old guard' in action is Kremlin's moves to consolidate its influence in the CIS, which Primakov clearly perceives as a top priority for his ministry. Under Primakov, Moscow is creating strategic alliances with Beijing and Teheran, and forming a sphere of influence in the former Soviet area known as its 'near-abroad'. The union between Russia and Belarus is seen as bringing Russia's borders back to Poland, and as greatly expanding Russia's frontier with Latvia and Lithuania. It would also lengthen the Russian–Ukrainian border by hundreds of kilometres.

This mirrors Russia's accusation of NATO's expansion as aiming to push back Russia's frontiers further east. NATO's expansion to the East, looms as a significant, if not the most significant, factor in US–Russian relations. What began as an attempt at transforming NATO into a non-military institution in response to the dismantling of the Warsaw Treaty Bloc, has become a stumbling block towards creating normal relations between Russia and the West.

# 8 Russia and NATO

## THE COLLAPSE OF THE WARSAW TREATY ORGANISATION

The revolution in Eastern Europe had raised some fundamental questions about existing European security affiliations and institutions. In 1990, the Warsaw Pact appeared to be disintegrating, and there were indications that the Soviet Union wished to transform the Warsaw Pact alliance from a military into a political institution. Gorbachev spoke of the Warsaw Pact as having a future as a political consultative organisation, but in the West, there was much scepticism whether there was enough common ground to hold the organisation together (Sloan, 1990, p. 6).

The then Soviet Marshal V. G. Kulikov while analysing the stages of development of the Warsaw Pact Treaty organisation came to the conclusion that the responses of the Warsaw Bloc to the military challenges by the West were not always adequate (Kulikov, 1990). Kulikov saw a new stage in the development of the Warsaw Treaty Organisation as beginning in 1985 when a transition to the new thinking in international affairs had been taking place. The international climate was much improved thanks to the steps taken by the Warsaw Treaty Organisation such as the adoption in 1989 of a new military doctrine based on defence and the unilateral reduction of armed forces. 'It cannot be denied', said Kulikov, 'that the lowering of the level of tension has been a result of both the East and the West. But the trend toward disarmament and the exclusion of force in solving international problems has yet to become irreversible' (ibid.). At the same time he also foresaw the distinct possibility of dissolving both blocs. It was the first Soviet objective analysis of the international situation which placed equal responsibility on both sides of the Cold War. An additional reason for the dissolution of the Warsaw Treaty Organisation was seen in the economic burden that the maintenance of the organisation imposed upon the Soviet Union. The withdrawal of Soviet troops from Eastern Europe was seen not only as a political and military gain but an economic one as well.

The impending dissolution of the Warsaw Pact presented a number of problems for the USSR. Foremost was the question of national security when the responsibility for it would lie exclusively on the shoulders of the Soviet army. After all, NATO remained a military bloc in which the forces calling for restoration of Cold War structures were still active. US Secretary of Defence William Perry warned: 'NATO is not a social club. It is not a fraternity. It is a military alliance' (Zheglov, 1991). On the question whether the dissolution of the Warsaw Bloc would result in an imbalance of forces in Europe to the detriment of the Soviet Union, some Russian analysts thought that since the main military force of the Warsaw Bloc was in the hands of the USSR, including nuclear weapons, the dissolution would not affect the security of the Soviet Union (*Trud*, 19 March 1991). Some analysts suggested transforming NATO and the Warsaw Bloc into one common European organisation which would function under the direction of European institutions and the United Nations. It was thought that 'European security was also the security of the USSR' (Zheglov, 1991)). Eventually, the Soviet Union put forward a proposal to dissolve both military-political blocs, to gradually create a new system of European security without blocs but based on the Helsinki process of which the first step was the signing of the Paris Charter (Zagorodnikov, 1996).

But as subsequent events have demonstrated, the process of the 'deblocking' of Europe has acquired an unexpected shift. Instead of a gradual and parallel scenario for the two blocs, for which Moscow had a distinct preference, strong centrifugal tendencies have appeared within the Warsaw Treaty Organisation, while the position of NATO has remained more or less static. These centrifugal trends became more powerful after the peaceful revolutions leading to a change in the systems of Hungary, Poland and Bulgaria and the reunification of Germany which meant the loss of the GDR – a member of the Warsaw Pact. On 27 October 1989, the Warsaw Pact nations issued a statement endorsing the right of each member country to seek its own political doctrine. The following day, Yevgenii Primakov, declared that member states were free to leave the alliance. Finally, during the extraordinary meeting of the Political Consultative Committee of the Warsaw Pact in Budapest on 25 February 1991, it was decided to dissolve the military organisation of the alliance.

There were several reasons that brought about the decision to disband the Warsaw Pact, according to one Soviet analyst of the time (*Trud*, 19 March 1991). These were the end of the Cold War

and the end of the policy of military confrontation based on ideological principles, but a major cause lay in the countries of Eastern
Europe – in Hungary, in Czechoslovakia and, to a lesser extent, in
Poland – political forces which had previously opposed the military structure of the Warsaw Pact, came to power. Their past experiences could not strengthen the bonds of friendship between
the Warsaw Pact countries and the USSR, neither did they make
them feel more secure (ibid.). Consequently, in the absence of
voluntary support for the alliance, it became futile to maintain it.
The subsequent unification of Germany and the disappearance of
the GDR – a mighty link in the alliance – only intensified the centrifugal trends within the Warsaw Pact. In addition, some of the
initiators of the dissolution of the Warsaw Pact, began to declare
their intentions of becoming integrated into the Western security
structure including NATO.

Russian commentators began to draw attention to those voices
in the West who suggested that NATO should be preserved as a
stabilising factor within the European collective security system.
The Russians thought that to base collective security on NATO
would be a grave mistake and a manifestation of old Cold War
thinking. Other Russian observers did not believe in the likelihood
of NATO expanding to the East. After all, the Warsaw Pact had
just been dissolved and with it the danger from the East had receded. Doubt was also expressed whether NATO would be willing
to widen its sphere of influence by accepting former members of
the Warsaw Pact into its ranks and whether NATO would allocate
enormous funds for the re-equipment of the armed forces of Eastern Europe. A question was also asked whether NATO would be
prepared to accept countries which were known for their instability?

## A VIEW FROM WASHINGTON

The dissolution of the Warsaw Pact Treaty Organisation has raised
serious questions about NATO's future. US Secretary of State, James
Baker, and other Western politicians adopted a stance similar to
that of the Soviet Union, and proposed that NATO become a political alliance in the future. Some observers, however, doubted
whether NATO could continue as an effective organisation without a Warsaw Pact threat as its *raison d'être*. Even those who agreed
that NATO could be maintained as a Western political identity,

did not agree as to the main objective for its existence. The Bush Administration said that it supported free Europe with a continued role for NATO and the United States. At this stage, the Administration did not clearly define its position regarding European security arrangements. The main argument for American involvement in European affairs, which until recently was based on the Soviet threat, was no longer valid.

Some political analysts thought that Mikhail Gorbachev had decided that the Soviet Union was either no longer needed or could not afford such a costly security blanket [the Warsaw Pact] on its Western borders. The fact on the ground, however, was that the Soviet Union despite its political and military retreat from Central Europe remained a superpower with sufficient military forces to play a major role in European affairs.

The changes in Eastern Europe and in the Soviet Union itself, sharpened the debate over the role of the US in Eastern Europe. Some American experts urged the Administration to become more involved in the affairs of these countries. They argued that close links with Eastern Europe would strengthen American's long-term position in Europe. This was important for the US, according to some observers, because of the prevailing view at the time that NATO might also recede as a military factor in Europe due to the changed attitudes of the Soviet Union (Miko, 1990, p 4) There were already voices advocating the integration of Eastern Europe into the Western system of nations. Although NATO, at the time, had not been considered as a unifying organisation, it was thought that a new structure should be created in order to avoid fragmentation and instability in the East. The future role of the United States and the Soviet Union were not positively defined, except by those who were sceptical about the new Soviet policy and maintained that the US should continue to exert pressure on the USSR. Of crucial importance was the attitude of those in the US who advocated NATO's expansion and who spoke of the necessity of consolidating the results of 'western victory in the Cold War'. Others expressed concern about the destabilising effects of the moves in the region, especially after some of the initiators of the dissolution of the Warsaw Pact unambiguously declared their intentions to integrate into the Western structures of security.

The state of uncertainty about the future role and objectives of NATO did not entirely disappear with the declaration of political sovereignty by the Russian Federation in June 1990 and the dissolution of the Soviet Union in December 1991. Since Russia, as the largest republic in the Union became the successor to the USSR, the United States began to revise its position regarding NATO's role in Europe. Initially, there was an apparent attempt by the West to discourage East European countries from undertaking a step which could lead to serious complications in relations with Russia. It suggested neutrality instead on the Austrian or Finnish models. As one American official stated: 'One must admit that Russia has valid security interests and it is doubtful whether it would accept the establishment on its Western borders of a kind of "sanitary cordon" which existed in the 20s. As a strict minimum, Russia would probably accept, as would the West, a buffer zone of neutral countries' (Zagorodnikov, 1996). Some analysts thought that the expansion of the alliance without considering Russia's interests, would undermine the existing European system recognised by Russia. 'Russia as a great nuclear power will unavoidably seek other alternatives' (Pushkov, 1997). At the same time, voices in the West asserted the necessity of maintaining NATO in its present form. The General Secretary of NATO, M. Werner, declared that the North Atlantic alliance had no intentions of disbanding.

In anticipation of Russia's opposition to NATO as a military alliance, and in view of a certain reluctance by some European countries to antagonise Russia, NATO introduced the North Atlantic Cooperation Council (NACC) which was to become a consultative body on European security issues. NACC was to be open to all countries including those of Eastern Europe. Its role and objectives were, however, not well defined. In the words of a Russian analyst 'the West faces a situation when it has to decide whether it needs an all-embracing strategy in relation to Russia, and if it does what it should consist of' (Kosolapov, 1993, p. 18).

In response to the statements in March 1993 by the then German foreign and defence ministers, Klaus Kinkel and Volker Ruhe suggesting NATO's extension to the East, the so-called Visegrad group of states, which included Poland, Hungary, the Czech Republic and Slovakia, declared their intention to join NATO and the European Union. After extensive discussion between the allies and candidate countries and members of Congress, and within the Administration itself, the American President decided that the United States would support Poland, Hungary, and the Czech Republic for the first round of invitations.

The United states as the initiator and main proponent of NATO's expansion, presented its case for NATO's expansion to the East as a matter of European security. The United States' main argument consisted of reassuring Russia of NATO's peaceful objectives rather than presenting its case in support of the expansion, let alone existence. The American argument ran along two rational, but not quite coordinated lines. On the one hand, the need for a military alliance was based on the concept of European security for the existing members of the alliance. On the other hand, it was claimed that NATO must respond to the need for security of the new members and must therefore expand. Spokesmen for NATO and the leaders of the alliance have all along been careful not to invoke a military threat from Russia. The Yugoslav conflict provided NATO with another argument in favour of expansion despite the fact that NATO did not materially contribute to the solution of the conflict. An additional point was the fear of a collapse of the Russian Federation following the Chechnya conflict.

An opposing view was presented by Yevgenii Primakov who at the time was the head of the Russian Intelligence Service. In November 1993 he declared at a press conference that 'this organisation would bring the biggest military grouping in the world, with its huge offensive potential, directly to the borders of Russia. If this happens, the need would arise for a fundamental reappraisal of all defence concepts on our side, a redeployment of armed forces and changes in operational plans.'

NATO members were well aware of Russia's concern, and continuously uttered reassurances. President Clinton's September 1996 call for NATO enlargement tried to put Russia at ease: 'We are intensifying our efforts to build a strong partnership between NATO and Russia' (Oznobishchev, 1997). Secretary of State Christopher elaborated: 'I want to say this to the Russian people: we welcome you as our full partners in building a new Europe that is free of tyranny, division and war. We want to work with you to bring Russia into the family of market democracies. We want you to have a stake and a role in the institutions of European security and economic cooperation. That is why we seek a fundamentally new relationship between Russia and the new NATO' (ibid.).

During 1996, Russia and NATO succeeded in reaching agreement on the necessity of beginning consultations on the question of mutual relations. Primakov accepted the suggestion, but affirmed at the same time Moscow's negative attitude toward NATO's expansion to the East. In order to establish a basis for the new relationship, NATO suggested a Charter that envisaged a mechanism of regular consultations on the question of European security. The US has also declared its intention not to deploy nuclear weapons on the territory of new member states. These proposals were not so much a matter of compensating Russia for the expansion, but an agreement that would assure Russia's participation in European affairs – an agreement that would exclude the possibility of her military and political isolation in Europe. The general opinion in the West, particularly in the US, was that Boris Yeltsin opposed NATO's expansion because of domestic politics – that is, not to provide the opposition with an excuse to accuse him of betraying Russia's national interests. However, neither President Clinton nor his Secretary of State Christopher have put forward a plausible case for the retention or expansion of NATO. The speech by the new American Secretary of State, Madeleine Albright at the Senate Armed Services Committee hearing on 23 April 1997, although quite elaborate, also failed to clarify the reasons for NATO's expansion to the East (Albright, 1997).

On the crucial question of why NATO is being enlarged, Albright offered four main reasons. First, to protect Europe against the next war. Since the United States has important security interests in central and eastern Europe, and if there were a major threat to the peace and security of this region or if there were a high likelihood of a military conflict, the US would have to decide to act regardless of whether NATO enlarges or not. According to Albright, 'the reason for NATO's enlargement is to deter such a threat from ever arising. Enlarging NATO will help protect Europe against future wars, defend Europe's gains towards democracy, peace and integration, and right the wrongs of the past'. Enlarging NATO will not create new lines of division, Albright claimed, because membership will be open to other countries. Albright clearly chose to ignore the conflict in Bosnia, which the US and its NATO allies failed to prevent and the simmering conflict between Greece and Turkey, both members of NATO. The second reason was to defend Europe's gains in the area of democracy, peace and integration. 'Old disputes between Poland and Lithuania, Poland and Ukraine, Hungary and Romania, Italy and Slovenia, Germany and the Czech Republic are melting away as nations align themselves with NATO', Albright asserted.

The third reason was to right the wrongs of the past. If the US did not enlarge NATO, it would be validating the dividing line

Stalin imposed in 1945 and that two generations of Americans and Europeans fought to overcome. The last reason for enlargement was that it will strengthen NATO by adding new allies. 'In the new Europe', according to Albright, 'the United States and Western Europe have a chance to gain new allies and partners who can and will contribute to our common security.' This last reason appears to be the most plausible one, but at the same time the most controversial when seen from the Russian side. In relation to Russia, Albright emphasised that NATO enlargement 'is not a zero sum game, in which Russia must lose if central Europe gains, and central Europe must lose if Russia gains'. A NATO–Russia Charter, she noted, would give Russia a chance to work in partnership with NATO. Such an agreement would enable NATO to act together with Russia to fight nuclear proliferation, to keep nuclear arsenals safe and to respond to threats to peace.

Every NATO ally and every central European democracy agrees that the US cannot build a free Europe until a democratic Russia is a full participant in Europe, Albright said. 'This means that we must appreciate the remarkable distance that Russia has travelled since it rejected communism. It is also in our own interest to see Russia play an important role in Europe – as a great power, but no longer an imperial power.'

At the same time, NATO has been discussing the terms of a charter that would institutionalise its practical cooperation with Russia. At the Helsinki summit, Presidents Clinton and Yeltsin outlined the possibilities of such a partnership. A joint NATO–Russia Council would give Russia a voice, but not a veto, and a chance to work in partnership with NATO, not within NATO. Both sides are to retain complete freedom of action when they cannot agree.

Regarding deployment of nuclear weapons on the territory of the new members, Albright did not offer a clear commitment. 'Russia', Albright said, 'would also like us to make absolute commitments in the charter about the deployment of nuclear and conventional forces on the territory of new members. But we will not compromise on this issue.' All the US was prepared to do was to restate unilaterally existing NATO policy '. . . that in the current and foreseeable security environment, we have no plan, no need, and no intention to station nuclear weapons in the new member countries, nor do we contemplate permanently stationing substantial combat forces' (ibid). The binding limits on conventional forces in Europe will be set as the US adapts the CFE (Conventional Forces in

Europe) Treaty with Central European countries and all the other signatories at the table. Albright stressed again that the US does not need Russia to agree to enlargement.

In response to Albright's statements, Russia confirmed its opposition to NATO's plans of expansion of its alliance – particularly against the possibility of shifting its military infrastructure to the East. Russia's main concern was that the expansion of NATO may lead to the division of Europe.

## THE RUSSIA–NATO FOUNDING ACT

The NATO–Russia Act setting out a special relationship between NATO and Russia has been considered as an element of lessening the strategic risk accompanying NATO enlargement to central Europe. The deal was not, as Russia wanted, in treaty form – the Act is not even legally binding. As one Western commentator said: 'Yeltsin needs more than a piece of paper to convince Russians that NATO has not stabbed them in the back' (*The Age*, 16 May 1997).

The NATO–Russia Act was supposed to provide Russia with full consultation rights with NATO through a NATO–Russia Council. From the outset, however, Washington insisted that while the Act allowed for the maximum possible consultation and joint decision-taking, it is 'a voice, not a veto'. The defence of the territory of the alliance will continue to be a matter for the NATO Council, but the NATO machine will be more open than it is now. The deal also imposes obligations on Russia – 'just as NATO will be obliged to tell Russia of any major deployment, so will Russia'.

In a ceremony that its participants hailed as marking the definite end of the Cold War, Russian President Boris Yeltsin joined the leaders of NATO's 16 member states in Paris on 27 May 1997 for the signing of a political agreement between Moscow and the Western military alliance – the Russia–NATO Founding Act. The agreement, which followed four months of intense formal negotiations between Russian Foreign Minister Yevgenii Primakov and NATO Secretary General Xavier Solana, and several years of more general political discussions between the two sides, cleared the way for NATO to begin the process of admitting new members at the alliance's July meeting in Madrid. It also signified, symbolically at least, Moscow's acquiescence to the enlargement process and its decision, only grudgingly arrived at, to maintain formal and friendly relations with the alliance despite Moscow's often fierce opposition to NATO's enlargement plans (Prism, 1997).

With regard to nuclear forces, the document restates NATO's often-voiced pledge that it has 'no intention, no plan, and no reason to deploy nuclear weapons on the territory of new members'. Within the context, the document states that NATO is entitled to ensure the security of newly admitted member-states through 'the necessary inter-operability, integration, and capability for reinforcement rather than by additional permanent stationing of substantial combat forces' – a formulation designed to give the alliance flexibility in working with new members while assuring Moscow that 'substantial' conventional forces will not be deployed on their territory.

Yeltsin who was reported to be favourable to the agreement, despite a brief reference to Moscow's continued opposition to expansion, described the Founding Act as 'a historic agreement and our mutual achievement'. He surprised those present when he announced that Russia would disarm all its nuclear missiles targeted at NATO states. Kremlin sources scrambled to clarify that Yeltsin meant only that Moscow would take those missiles off the combat alert and would have their targeting programmes erased. At the same time, Russian leaders continued to warn that Moscow would rethink its relations with NATO should the West decide to grant NATO membership to any of the former Soviet republics, particularly to the Baltic states.

For all the goodwill on display in Paris it seems likely that tensions between NATO and Moscow will continue to boil, and periodically erupt, according to a vast majority of Russian analysts.

## THE VIEW FROM MOSCOW

Russia's resistance to the continuation of NATO's existence as a military bloc after the collapse of the Warsaw Pact has, for a short time, been somehow subdued. Russia apparently accepted the fact that it could not have a decisive voice on political decisions taken outside its area of influence. But when NATO changed its political direction from retaining NATO in its earlier form to expanding to the East with the intention of accepting the membership of former Soviet allies and even republics, Russia began to voice its strong opposition. It had powerful arguments against the enlargement of

NATO since the Soviet threat had disappeared and there were no conceivable reasons for Russia to threaten the West.

Russia's foreign policy at the time seemed to have been in disarray. President Yeltsin during his visit to Warsaw in summer 1993, did not express any opposition to Poland joining NATO. A joint declaration spoke of Poland's membership in NATO as not going 'against the interests of other states, including the interests of Russia' (*Moscow News*, 3 September 1993, p. 3). Under domestic pressure, Yeltsin subsequently modified his position by saying that Russia would accept East European states' membership of NATO if it too became a member.

In order to overcome Russia's opposition to NATO's expansion, President Clinton put forward the Partnership For Peace (PFP) proposal in January 1994. The Partnership For Peace, a 43-member organisation, was not an alliance although it has a military character. PFP was launched as a non-hostile alternative to NATO. Russia, Ukraine, Belarus, and most of the rest of the former Soviet states were participants, as were the members of the former Warsaw Pact and other European countries that wanted admission to NATO. But just as the partners in Central Europe felt that PFP was not sufficient to assure their security and ties to the West, so did Russia believe that PFP was a subterfuge to paper over the dividing line between East and West (Oznobishchev, 1997).

There were many voices in Russia opposing Russia's participation in PFP. The state Duma in particular attempted to prevent Russia's membership, calling it a betrayal. In connection with NATO's plans of expansion the Duma issued an appeal in October 1996 in which it expressed its firm opposition not only to NATO's expansion but to American policy towards Russia. An appeal by the Duma published in the Russian press, speaks of the end of the bipolar world in which two camps confronted each other. 'Today one must abandon the usage of stereotypes of the Cold War period, change the meaning and the character of patterns, which were created on a confrontational basis in that period' (*Rossiiskaya gazeta*, 12 November 1996). The appeal spoke of attempts to replace the process of development of European cooperation with a process of expansion of NATO to the East. 'The activities of NATO cannot be considered as the only determining factor within the system of European security.' The expansion of NATO, according to the Duma, will lead to a geopolitical partition of Europe. It represents the threat of a first serious crisis in Europe after the end of the Cold War.

According to the appeal, in the context of its military programme, the combat potential of the unified military forces of NATO will increase. The acceptance into NATO of even one country of Central or Eastern Europe, will raise significantly the level of NATO's armaments in Europe. Military-political organs of NATO will have to work out a new nuclear policy and a new concept of utilisation of nuclear weapons for the protection of new members of NATO. Consequently, the Treaty on the limitation and control of weapons will be undermined.

Russia's foreign policy came under a great deal of criticism from various other quarters, especially after NATO announced its intention to expand to the East. Russian commentators saw Russia's constantly changing policy regarding the expansion of NATO as an indication that those who determined Russia's foreign and defence strategies over the last few years, had little understanding of Russia's place in the world (Grigoriev, 1996). Most articles in the Russian press express an almost universal agreement that the expansion of NATO is against Russia's national security interests. To reinforce the argument against NATO's expansion, the Russian press quite often quotes opinions of Western analysts who see the expansion of NATO as a harbinger of future conflict in Europe.

The well-known American politician, Stroub Talbott, in an article published in a leading Russian newspaper, draws attention to Russia's lack of confidence in Western intentions. 'Many Russians do not conceal their belief that America's real strategic objective is to weaken Russia or even bring about its disintegration,' according to Talbott. America, Talbott said, must find a way of overcoming Russian suspicions and its tendency to see a conspiracy everywhere (Talbott, 1996). A concern, which Talbott expresses, is that if too many Russians should persist in their suspicion that America wants to lower Russia's status, then concepts such as 'partnership' and 'cooperation' would signify 'policy of pacification' and 'servility', that is, the humiliation of Russia (ibid.). Russia's suspicions regarding America's intentions, says Talbott, is a mirror image of prejudices that still exist in America regarding Russia's future policies. According to this view, Russia represents a toppled Soviet Union which is striving to return to the old ways and habits.

Aleksei Pushkov, a member of the Russian Council on Foreign and Defence Policies, quotes Thomas Friedman, the commentator of the *New York Times*, as saying that the expansion of NATO is the worst thought-out programme since the Cold War period. If the expansion of NATO could achieve mutual understanding with Russia, then Europe would be assured of real security; if, however, there is lack of understanding, then the expansion could lead to European instability (Pushkov, 1996). Pushkov quotes Roderick Brewent, former British ambassador to Moscow, as saying that 'the West must find a way to introduce Russia into the new Europe as a reassured country interested in the status quo'. He also cites François Heisburg, of the International Institute for Strategic Studies in London, who said that 'while achieving rapid expansion of NATO into Central Europe, the Atlantic Alliance is on the threshold of committing the first tremendous mistake in relation to Russia after the collapse of the USSR' (ibid.). Despite the dissenting voices in the West, the North Atlantic alliance was apparently sticking to its strategy of persuading Russia to accept unlimited expansion offering in exchange assurances of non-deployment of nuclear weapons and large military detachments on the territory of new members (Pushkov, 1997).

What were the precise conditions that Russia demanded at the time? According to Pushkov, it referred in the first place to nuclear weapons. It is true, Pushkov said, that NATO does not have at present any nuclear weapons in Europe (except a few hundred bombs stored in Belgium) and does not intend to deploy any for the time being, Brussels and Washington qualify this by claiming the right of unilateral actions. The Americans refuse to undertake an obligation not to deploy nuclear weapons in the future, while Russia would be ready to take an obligation not to deploy its nuclear tactical warheads on the territory of Belarus.

The second condition is the non-deployment of military detachments of the alliance on the territory of new member states and the undertaking not to make any provisions for such a deployment. Finally, as a third condition is the mechanism of cooperation between Russia and NATO; Russia demands its participation in decision-making. Here, it must be said, NATO faced a serious problem – how to provide Russia with the right to share in decision-making without providing her at the same time with the right to veto decisions taken by the alliance.

A special problem was the geographical aspect of the expansion. On the one hand, NATO could not formally undertake an obligation to limit the expansion to three or four new members and to include this in the Charter. This would be tantamount to Russia having the right of veto. On the other hand, could Russia rely on the verbal assurances of its Western partners? – especially in view of the fact that she was promised, after the dissolution of the Warsaw Pact, that NATO would not shift to the East. Furthermore, NATO's expansion to countries with no common borders with Russia is one thing, but accepting Baltic states and Ukraine which have direct borders with Russia is another question altogether. Should this happen, Russia would consider such a step as undermining the basis for confidence. Should Latvia, Lithuania and Estonia join NATO, it would transform the Kaliningrad province into a completely surrounded part of Russian territory, Pushkov concluded.

Some Russian political analysts saw the expansion of NATO as being in the interest of the American military establishment and industrialists. After the collapse of the communist block and the Soviet superpower, the reason for maintaining the military machine and the organisational structure of NATO became questionable – at least for Western taxpayers and politicians, but not for the military (*Finansovye izvestia*, 6 February 1997). The only justification for the maintenance of the military block of NATO after the disappearance of the enemy, was the inertia of endless development. The military acted in the same manner as do international financial bureaucrats. They wished to retain their position.

According to another Russian analyst, Western industrialists saw an opportunity to enter new markets. The acceptance of only three countries – Hungary, Poland and the Czech Republic – signified an additional expenditure of 15–20 billion dollars over the first one or two years. The subsequent change of the technical base and infrastructure would require at least three times as much money. All this meant a gain for Western industrialists and a loss for the Russian military-industrial complex, a traditional supplier of armaments to its satellites. As early as December 1993, NATO generals unambiguously declared that when it comes to Western interests, Russia's opinion will not be considered. Three years later, the absence of Russia's reaction to the planned expansion of NATO was considered as a sign of agreement.

Some Russian analysts adopted, what is viewed in Russia, a defeatist opinion that the West had won the Cold War and had therefore, as the victor, the right to impose its will. By encouraging the splitting up of the former USSR and downgrading it to the status of a third world country, the US was only pursuing its own interests. A view expressed by a number of Russian observers in the autumn of 1993, was that 'Russia was naive' in its expectations of a Western positive attitude (Kosovalov, 1994, p. 5). There was agreement on one point: Western strategy in relation to Russia was predominantly American and was put into practice directly by the United States through NATO.

Some Russians accept, albeit reluctantly, the enlargement of NATO. They claim that if Russia did not reach an agreement with NATO she would 'miss the last train going to the West' and would remain isolated. They claim that Russia does not want to be cut off from important decision-making in Europe, and even without an agreement with NATO, Russia would still remain an important factor in European politics.

There can be little doubt that the widespread criticism of Yeltsin's foreign policy, particularly of his apparent weak posture toward the US, forced him to change direction. The decisive factor in this change was the nationalistic ('patriotic') element in Russian public opinion expressed during the debates in the Duma and in many public polls. The removal of Kozyrev and the appointment of Evgenii Primakov satisfied, to a certain extent, the demands of the opposition in the Duma and also of the national press. Subsequently, Russia's foreign policy became more assertive. By the end of 1996, Primakov was able to define in more precise terms its direction and objectives.

Primakov's first commentaries after his appointment, indicated a predictable sharp turn in Russia's foreign policy, such as 'strengthening of imperial ambitions' and a deterioration in Moscow's relations with the West (Gornostaev, 1997). Signs of rejection of Moscow's love affair with the West, immediately emerged on the diplomatic arena. First to be visited by the new appointee were the CIS republics, while his negotiations with US State Secretary, Warren Christopher, took place later – in February 1996. Russia's position has hardened and on a number of issues has become what may be considered uncompromising. At the same time, Primakov keeps on insisting that Russia does not want to return to the confrontation of the Cold War.

Primakov saw the new international situation as a continuation of the former conflict between the USSR and the West although in a much less confrontational form. The end of the US–USSR clash, despite its historical significance, did not automatically lead to the triumph of democratic principles in international relations, according to Primakov, and the end of the ideological and military confrontation proved to be insufficient to neutralise dangers and risks (Primakov, 1996). Expressing his opposition to NATO's expansion, Primakov underlined the dangers that the expansion would present for Russia if the Baltic states were included. From the Russian point of view the inclusion of the Baltic states into NATO was not only a threat to her security, but also involved the fate of the sizeable Russian minorities residing in these countries. In the case of the Baltic states he invoked the question of human rights. In many regions of the world, Primakov said, there is an urgent need to protect human rights of national minorities. The situation is complex because of the imperative of combining the protection of human rights with the territorial integrity of various countries. This is particularly relevant in the Baltic states. While recognising their territorial integrity, Russia cannot remain indifferent to the discriminatory practices against the Russian-speaking population in Estonia and Latvia.

A further elaboration of the Russian stand regarding the expansion of NATO was an article by Primakov published in October 1996. New divisive lines to replace the old fronts of conflicts must not be allowed, said Primakov. This most important objective of Russia's foreign policy is determining its negative attitude toward the expansion of NATO on the former Warsaw Pact area. But Russia is far from thinking that the expansion of NATO is aimed at a strike against Russia. However, 'intentions and politics are subject to change while the potential for change is ever existent'.

In 1989–1990, Primakov asserted, Western countries gave unambiguous assurances to the Soviet Union that if Germany became united, NATO would not widen the sphere of its activities to the East. He also quoted France's President Mitterrand as saying in the course of his meeting with Gorbachev on 6 May 1991: 'if each of the countries mentioned by me (Poland, Czechoslovakia and Hungary) will assure its security through the conclusion of separate agreements with NATO, it will strengthen the perception by the Soviet Union of isolation and even encirclement. I am convinced that this is not the correct course for Europe' (Primakov, 1996).

Assurances that NATO had no plans to incorporate the East and Central European countries into the North Atlantic Pact, had been given in one form or another in 1990–91 by the US Secretary of State James Baker, the British Foreign Secretary George Herd and a number of other heads of governments, member-states of the block. 'We are far from claiming the right to veto the joining of NATO by any country, but we feel that the proximity of NATO's military structures to Russia's territory, will without doubt, complicate

Russia's geopolitical position, including in its purely military aspect', Primakov said. Russia's approach to NATO, according to Primakov, is determined by two conditions: first, that this organisation had been created during the Cold War for the purpose of global confrontation with the USSR. It was orientated from the very beginning towards a military confrontation, and after the end of the Cold War is far from having been transformed. Second, Moscow understands that NATO represents real power, but sees emerging conditions calling for a change in the character of the alliance. Consequently, Russia does not adhere to its extreme negative position regarding the expansion of NATO, but is ready for a constructive dialogue with member countries regarding the direction and limits of Russia's participation in the military infrastructure of the alliance.

Further clarification of Russia's position came in November 1996 when Chernomyrdin addressed the Lisbon forum where he argued Russia's case against the expansion of NATO (*Nezavisimaya gazeta*, 3 December 1996). Russian diplomacy, said Chernomyrdin, considers as its major objective the prevention of the unconditional approval of the increase in the number of members of NATO by the acceptance of Central and East European countries, but Russian diplomacy continues its attempts to transform the Organisation of Security and Cooperation in Europe (OSCE) into an all-European organisation with an independent legal status. 'Conditions are ripe for NATO's military forces to abandon its preparations for a confrontation along the borders with Russia, and to enter into a process of peaceful solutions under the auspices of the United Nations and the Organisation of Security and Cooperation in Europe', Chernomyrdin said. One of the most important factors in European security is the increased role of the UN and OSCE. Such an objective can be attained by the creation of an European Security Charter, which would correspond to the closing act of the Meeting on Security and Cooperation in Europe signed in Helsinki on 1 August 1975 (ibid.).

Regarding the latter, Russia received the support of France, which agreed to present to the Lisbon meeting a mandate for the establishment of an all-European Security Charter. Germany supported the view that the creation of a legal basis for OSCE would be beneficial for the operation of this organisation. Britain and particularly the US were from the beginning against this position. American concerns were apparently linked to the view that such a step could be seen as a movement towards the realisation of Russia's diplomatic dream – to endow OSCE with a status equal to that of NATO.

A pervasive and detailed analysis of Russia's international position, particularly her relations with the US, was presented by the former Soviet president Mikhail Gorbachev in an article published in November 1996 (Gorbachev, 1996). The American and Russian sides, said Gorbachev, both address each other in terms which sound respectful rather than antagonistic, but in fact they do not act in this way. The expectations that followed the end of the Cold War are in tatters. As a result, the anti-American sentiments in Russia have penetrated even those circles that were considered pro-Western. American attitudes towards Russia have also changed for the worse. This was due to the fact that following the end of the confrontation, one side [the US] behaved as if it had won the Cold War, while the other side was overcome with euphoria. Both sides failed to work out a new model of mutual relations. Little thought has been devoted to the significance of the transformation from enemies to partners. Both sides continued to improvise, but for the US the main problem was how to adapt to a situation in which there is no Cold War.

According to Gorbachev, the internal situation in Russia provides an excuse for America and the West to consider Russia as a foreign body within the group of official democracies. Statements by US and other NATO leaders indicate a concern about Russia's democracy (ibid.). A situation has arisen where any mention of the situation in the CIS and of the need for Russia's integration with other post-Soviet countries, is thought to be suspicious and dangerous. The anti-Russian mood and activities in the Ukraine are being encouraged by the US, and advances with anti-Russian overtones are being made to the President of Uzbekistan. The question of Caspian oil is being resolved in a way that leaves Russia out of the negotiations. The Americans ought to understand, Gorbachev asserted, that any contemptuous or insulting step toward Russia, will be picked up and exploited by the opponents of normal US–Russian relations. It would be a powerful argument for those in Russia (including members of parliament) who feel that the US and its allies have already chosen to exploit Russia's weaknesses in order to isolate her (ibid.).

In October 1996, Aleksandr Lebed, the former Russian military leader and a potential presidential candidate, while addressing the North Atlantic alliance in Brussels, expressed his views on Russia's

international position in almost the same terms as Gorbachev
(*Nezavisimaya gazeta*, 16 October 1996). Europe, he said, is in a
state of confusion. The old system of European security is non-
existent and a new one has not yet been created. Russia, being
part of Europe, must determine her basic interests in the area of
national security on its western borders. From the point of view of
national security, Russia is vitally interested in a peaceful and stable
Europe. In this respect, it is only a unified security space which
would include the entire EU region and in which the security and
interests of each participant are not restricted, that would make
Europe stable. Lebed was convinced that the strengthening and
expansion of military-political coalitions (which as a rule function
at the expense of the interests and security of other countries) would
lead to the appearance of confrontational trends.

Lebed enumerated some of Russia's fears and concerns in the
area of security. Its main concern is the misconceived plan of expansion of NATO – a plan that ignores its negative consequences.
Russia does not believe that by accepting new members, NATO
will immediately move some of its forces in order to conquer Russian wide spaces, but it is clear that the combined military power
of NATO will significantly increase, and will be stationed in direct
proximity to the Russian borders. It means that the acceptance of
only two to three candidate countries would lead to an increase in
NATO's ground forces from 48 to 62 divisions, from 101 to 145
brigades, and an average increase of 15 per cent of combat aircraft
and helicopters. There would also be a real rise in the number of
warships (on account of Poland) and patrolling aircraft.

The next question raised by Lebed was: why is NATO ready for
considerable sacrifices when accepting into its ranks countries with
weak economies, with armies that do not conform to Western standards, and weak democracies? They are not quite ready to become
part of the European Union, but the door is open for them to join
a military alliance.

Lebed discarded NATO's assurances that the expansion does not
threaten anyone. This may be true, says Lebed, as long as Russia
behaves 'properly'. However, the criteria for 'proper' behaviour are
not determined by Russia but by NATO. Russia will in fact be
deprived of the ability to defend its interests if they should cut
across NATO's interests.

Finally, Lebed referred to the old theme of Russia being a different
civilisation. There is a real danger, said Lebed, of the new situa-

tion assuming not only military and political features, but a split in Europe along the lines of civilisations; NATO will strive for a division of Europe into 'pure Europeans' and 'semi-Asian Russians'. Today's expansion of NATO to the East could create a 'cold peace' for a long time to come.

The last point in Lebed's argument, and to some extent in Gorbachev's reference to 'any contemptuous or insulting step toward Russia', expresses the ongoing debate about the significance of the historical and cultural differences between the East and the West. Such contention is being exploited by Russian nationalists and former communists who see any move by the US as directed toward the denigration of Russia's position as a world power and as an equal among equals.

THE DAWN OF A 'COLD PEACE'?

Sergei Rogov, Director of the prestigious Institute of United States and Canada of the Russian Academy of Sciences, sees the new situation as greatly restricting Russia's room for manoeuvre. Since it is assumed that it was the Soviet Union that lost the Cold War, the consequences of this defeat put a heavy burden on the Russian leadership – a fundamental task to move to a market economy and to establish a democratic state system (Rogov, 1996).

Previously, Soviet–US relations were central to the Cold War. It was based on the perception of a balance of power in which Russia was militarily equal to the United States. Today, however, economically Russia is no first-rate partner for the US. An economically weak Moscow can neither dictate its conditions to the US or other developed countries nor even win recognition as an equal partner. Initially, Russia was apparently prepared to accept US leadership without qualification. Russian diplomacy expected Washington would reciprocate by doing its best to ensure that Russia integrated into the Western community as soon and as painlessly as possible. In September 1994, a statement on the principles and aims of promoting trade, economic and investment cooperation – Partnership for Economic Progress – was signed in Washington. However, a refusal to accept Russia as a member of the Western community, coupled with an early enlargement of NATO by admitting ex-allies of Moscow to it coupled with hindrance to all reintegration trends on the territory of the former USSR, could result in the dangerous international isolation of Russia, according to Rogov. Washington seems to be conceiving a new geopolitical strategy whose top priority is the preservation of the system of military-political alliances set up by the US during the Cold War (ibid.).

Throughout the Cold War, avoidance of war had been a paramount policy objective of Western European nations and one of America's fundamental interests. The North Atlantic Treaty Organisation, led by the US, was the means adopted in 1949 to preserve peace in the face of the military might of the Soviets. After the 1955 inclusion of West Germany into NATO the US reassured the rest of Europe that Germany would be restrained 'by a net of mutual obligations'. This objective was accomplished and NATO fulfilled its mission. Logically NATO should have been dissolved as an anachronism, but it has survived.

Today Europe is more secure and less tense. Nevertheless, despite Russia's markedly diminished military capability, countries in central Europe want to join NATO. Poland, Hungary, and the Czech Republic feel the need for membership in a security organisation and want economic ties to the West. Their fears have little factual basis today. The geopolitical position of Poland, for example, is undisputed for the first time in centuries. Nor are the eight other candidates for NATO membership under any direct or indirect threat.

The former Polish Prime Minister Cimoszewicz has aptly summarised the Russian position on NATO expansion (although he believed it unwarranted):

> The Russian government openly and steadfastly opposes expansion of NATO eastward and this view, it should be noted, is shared by the leaders of major opposition parties. According to their line of reasoning, the enlargement of the Alliance would be no more than another Cold War arrangement. The admission of new members in Central Eastern Europe would only mean that the dividing line would be drawn closer to Russia (Oznobishchev, 1997).

The Russians feel that this 'defensive' alliance is directed against them. NATO was created to fight the USSR and now, the Russians are convinced, it intends to serve as a new enlarged anti-Russian alliance. Indeed, the announcement of plans to enlarge NATO has accomplished the virtually impossible – it has unified what were fragmented and conflict-ridden Russian political factions opposing the Western move.

In one respect, however, Russia still holds an important card. While Russia can no longer compete with NATO's huge conventional forces, its nuclear weapons are relatively inexpensive to maintain. Aware that their conventional military forces are not entirely reliable, the Russians place more dependence on their nuclear weapons. Russia's former Defence Minister Pavel Grachev warned that if NATO expands toward his country, Russia's short-range nuclear weapons would be made operational again and the implementation of arms control treaties would be suspended, and any chance of Russian ratification of the START II treaty would evaporate. From the point of view of the majority of Russians, the retention of a sphere of influence within the parameters of the borders of the Russian Federation is seen above all through the prism of 'defence' – as a guarantee against the possibility of further disintegration of the country. The blows to the Russian mind of the past five years in connection with the loss of what had been considered for centuries as the territory of historical Russia are too heavy to consider such reactions as baseless (Bogaturov, 1996). Although Russia does not appear to be reverting to isolationism, she is not ready to cooperate with the West at any price they demand. 'After a number of years of futile, Kozyrevian badly thought out expectations that the West would voluntarily put a limit to its demands on Moscow, it has become clear that the West will never stop there. It is time for Russia to attempt to determine the limits' (ibid.).

The events of the end of 1996 and beginning of 1997, indicate that the possibility of a Cold Peace are becoming a reality. Dmitrii Gornostaev, a Russian analyst, saw the endorsement by the American Congress of Madeleine Albright as the Secretary of State, as the final act which will make this trend irreversible. 'A situation is arising when the leading positions in foreign policy ministries in the US and Russia will be occupied by proponents of a firm line in diplomacy [Albright v. Primakov] (Gornostaev, 1997). According to Igor Maksimychev, another Russian analyst, by acting that way, the West, who always declared that it was defending itself from aggressive communism, is going into an offensive at a time when communism no longer exists, when the USSR is no more, but there is Russia. It is Russia that is presented as a bogy threatening Europe, the defence against whom NATO offers Europe (Maksimychev, 1996).

CONCLUSION

The question of who determines Russia's foreign policy is more relevant today than it has ever been. Traditionally, the former Soviet foreign policy had been determined and put into practice by the higher echelon of the Party and government, and the subsequent strategy by the Politburo of the CPSU. In contemporary Russia, however, the formulation of foreign policy is becoming increasingly subject to the influence of the parliament, political groups, political science centres and the press (Popov, 1994, p. 52). Consequently, the direction of Russia's foreign policy has changed under the pressure of various political forces. Foreign policy is also subject to public opinion. Public opinion is mainly expressed through the forum of the Russian press. What is written and published today is no longer the view of the government or the voice of a single political movement; it is a more reliable source and indicator of the mood of the Russian people.

The Russian nation is not holding a unified position in its attitude toward the government's conduct of foreign policy, but it is united in its views on Russia's place in the world, particularly in its relations to the West. The fundamental question the Russians are asking is: what should be Russia's role, place and influence in the contemporary world situation? The answer to this question, it is thought, would determine Russia's foreign policy objectives, Russia's attitude to world problems, and her relations with other countries. The overwhelming majority of the Russian population is in favour of Russia's resistance to the expansion of NATO and more specifically to the loss of Russia's international standing – that is her retention or reassertion of the status of a superpower. Russia's international prestige has always appeared as an important rallying factor in Russia, and national pride has always been and still is a significant element in Russia's psyche.

An opinion poll conducted in 1996, indicated that a majority of those polled (57 per cent) declared their support for the idea of Russia as a great power – not so much in a military sense, but in its influence in world affairs. Thirty-six per cent expressed the willingness to accept Russia's place in the world as equal amongst equals. Only 4 per cent were in favour of Russia regaining her status of military superpower equal to that of the United States.

A general hypothesis put forward in Russia is that there are basically two opposing views regarding Russia's path of development and its relations with the West. One is the 'pro-Western' path, the other is of 'Russia's unique path' (ibid., p. 53). The debate between the 'Westernisers' and 'Slavophiles' has again emerged with increased vigour during the transitional period of changes in the political system and radical reforms in Russia and particularly in connection with the realisation that Russia lost the Cold War.

Recent opinion polls indicate that public opinion in Russia is almost equally divided. Fifty-two per cent of those polled were for the 'Western' path of development, that is for Russia to absorb Western experiences and achievements of Western civilisation. Forty-five per cent assume that 'Russia's history and geography being located between Europe and Asia should follow its unique Russian path.' These questions are currently being debated not as a matter of foreign policy alone, but specifically as an issue of Russian national identity. It is now being discussed under the concept of a new Russian idea.

# 9 The Russian Idea – Toward a Civic Society

## IDEOLOGY IN RUSSIAN HISTORY

From an historical perspective it is evident that Russia has always lived a life that was to a large extent determined by her past. Due to a number of historical factors (geographical location, climatic conditions, invasions, distance from major sources of world civilisation) Russia found herself on the periphery of Europe. She therefore faced the dilemma of finding her place either in the West or in the East. The problem of choice of Russia's place between East and West existed throughout her history (Sakharov, 1996). The Russian philosopher P. I. Chadaev in his 'Philosophical Letters' said: '. . . we live without a past or future amidst dead stagnation. Russia has made no contribution to the fund of human civilisation and is some sort of blank in the moral order of the world.' This was the beginning of the great debate between Westernisers and Slavophiles that influenced the development of Russian social thought in the nineteenth century.

The Westernisers, who considered Russia as a backward, ignorant and semi-barbaric country, urged rejection of the notion of being part of Asia, to adopt instead Western ideas and to draw closer to Europe thus becoming part of a cultural family of mankind. The Westernisers were opposed by the so-called Slavophiles who did not accept the proposition of a single European civilisation. They asserted that each nation lives and acts according to its own independent 'national spirit' – the 'Russian spirit' being fundamentally different and unique. Thus, Western values and forms of organisation were not suitable for Russia.

The controversy between Westernisers and Slavophiles did not completely disappear after the victory of the Bolsheviks. The idea of Russia's uniqueness and of the gulf dividing Russia from European culture was emphasised by Alexander Solzhenitsyn who claimed that 'Western thinking always committed that mistake of denying Russia its peculiar character'. It was, according to Solzhenitsyn, a grave mistake to measure the Soviet Union with a Western yardstick:

Should I be asked, . . . whether I would propose the West, as it is today, as a model for my country, I would frankly have to answer in the negative. No, I could not recommend your society as an ideal for the transformation of ours . . .' (Solzhenitsyn, 1978, p. 33).

Russia's transition to the modern age has been different from the European experience in one important aspect – a historical drift of her political system toward authoritarian rule. Russia's historical development indicates a constant presence of authoritarian and strong state power. Under such rule, human values which are at the basis of Western culture, were replaced by an ideology of class values which have deformed the Russian cultural organism (Levit, 1990, p. 6). Ignorance, a relatively low cultural level of the population coupled with a mass media monopoly, difficulties and shortages in everyday life became fertile soil for the idea that there is someone up there who can make no mistakes and knows the correct way (ibid., p. 73). The image of a leader who knows and takes care of everything was received with a sigh of relief by the population.

Freedom and the question of a civic society had not been an issue. Most were trying to liberate themselves from a burden of responsibility and to charge the leader or a collective leadership with the task of problem-solving. According to one Russian analyst, the Russian people were actually much happier when they were deprived of liberty. Andrei Sakharov in a conversation with a French writer expressed his view on the subject of freedom in Russia in the following terms: 'Democracy is like an orange – a person who has never tasted it will never ask for it' (*Nezavisimaya gazeta*, 9 July 1997).

Coercion by the all-powerful state became the basis of government policies, an object of mystical, religious admiration which took the place of the displaced Russian religious tradition (Levit, 1990, p. 155). The destruction of the intelligentsia, the carrier of ethical principles and ethical thinking had been devastating in its consequences. The eradication of such carriers of culture as was the intelligentsia also affected its composition and created a spiritual vacuum. The vacuum which emerged as a result of the destruction of Russian traditional culture, had been replaced by the 'cult of the leader' and a castrated type of Marxism which acquired religious connotations.

*Perestroika* and *glasnost* were supposed to correct past mistakes by filling that vacuum and by putting Russian society on the path of democracy and genuine freedom. That path proved to be filled with obstacles caused by the distorted perception of freedom ingrained in the Russian mind. Under the Bolsheviks, the social equality of misery and poverty was a powerful moral support for the undeveloped, illiterate and uncultured Russian individual. It is this circumstance which, despite all the excesses of the totalitarian regime, has attracted and still attracts millions of the lower strata of the Russian society. The Russians of today are shocked by the imperatives of new principles based on personal abilities and initiatives.

According to Mark Rats of the independent *Nezavisimaya gazeta*, except for a small number of more enlightened individuals, the masses have not fully grasped the opportunities which the new freedoms offer. It became, therefore, the task of the government to impose the new rules upon the population without adequate consultation. The paradox of today's Russia is that while under the communists the society attempted to establish a new social order from the 'top', now when these attempts have failed, the Russians are forced once more to introduce the project of a civic society also from the 'top' (Rats, 1996).

No matter how many economic and political reforms are introduced, there cannot be an open society until Russia rids itself of thinking along Marxist dogmas, according to Rats. A civic society cannot be created by laws and decrees, but a government policy can contribute to its emergence, and a legitimate government is only possible in conjunction with a civic society, preferably on the Western model.

The well-known economist, Milton Friedman, published a paper devoted to Russia entitled 'Four steps towards freedom', in which he discusses the reasons for the failure of reforms in Russia. He suggests that the failure is due mainly to economic causes, but, Friedman says, it is futile to apply to Russia the neo-liberal economic and political models operating in the West (Fedotova, 1997).

Some Russian commentators, although agreeing that it is useless to apply Western patterns to the Russian economy, saw the failures as due to non-economic factors – the deterioration of moral values and culture. The main difference between Russia and the West, according to Valentina Fedotova, a Russian analyst, is the role of the government in the process of modernisation. In Russia, it was always the government rather than the masses that was instrumental in advancing modernisation. However, regardless of the way in which modernisation took place, it had always been advanced by a spiritual mobilisation, that is by an ideology which formed values that were of national significance. The post-Soviet period saw the beginning of change in those values. Everything that was considered as spiritually valuable – enthusiasm, readiness for sacrifice, loyalty to the government, patriotism – has become subject to severe criticism. The general atmosphere of 'rejection' is accompanied by the rejection of past experiences, including the rejection of not only socialist ideology, but ideology in general, not only of socialist values but of all values (ibid.). The process of reform resulted in a large volume of literature about the autonomy and responsibility of the individual which, it was expected, would emerge, and about Protestant work ethics, which is proving difficult to inculcate. Many social scientists in Russia concluded that Western institutions and principles, which the government attempted to introduce, have been transformed into substitutions. This, they assert, has occurred because Russian reality has so far successfully resisted the introduction of any 'perfect' model.

Russia has no possibility of forming instantaneously of all the structures and institutions of a civic society, something that gradually evolved in the West. Russia must be able to do it over time. All attempts at creating a civic society through laws and decrees are doomed to failure (Rats, 1990). This is why despite the new freedoms and a new constitution, a crisis has been slowly building up.

## TOWARD A CIVIC SOCIETY

The crisis in the constitutional system of the Russian Federation that has finally emerged in 1993 has been caused by the failure of the transition toward a new form of management – a transition from a Soviet republic to what resembles a presidential republic, according to Oleg Rumyantsev, executive secretary of the Constitution Commission (Rumyantsev, 1993). The weakness of the Constitution was reflected in the conflict which emerged between the President and legislature in 1992–93. It was mainly evident in a struggle for supremacy between the presidency and legislature. It caused the so-called 'war of laws' (Gill, 1996).

In September 1993 Yeltsin dissolved the legislature and called an election and plebiscite for a new constitution in December of that year. The new constitution strengthened the office of the president at the expense of the legislature, but it resulted in the emergence of a permanent breeding ground for tension between the institutions of power – the Duma and the president (Rumyantsev, 1993).

The second cause of tension was a conflict of ideologies between the liberal reformists of Western inclination and the traditionalist patriots. The earlier stage of 'multipartyism' with its conflict between the communists and the democrats, has been replaced by the eternal Russian quarrel between Westernisers and nationalists – a quarrel complemented by the differences between radicals and opportunists, between the new and the old establishment.

The third cause was the collapse of the Soviet Union. The signing and subsequent ratification of the Belovezh agreement on the dissolution of the USSR and its transformation into CIS contained a number of serious flaws. The will of the people concerning the retention of the Union expressed in the all-Union referendum in March 1991 was rejected, thereby violating the Union and the Russian constitutions.

The fourth cause was the introduction of radical economic reforms. The shock methods of transition to a market economy, the speedy 'capitalism-isation' of economic structures and the demand for additional authority for executive power have led to widespread extremism. The legal system has been destroyed by the action of the decrees and orders emanating from the government itself (ibid.)

The fifth cause lies in the exaggerated role of the subjective, personal influence on Russia's politics by people who lack the necessary art of managing a large continent such as Russia. The Bolshevik syndrome of excessive self-confidence, the messianic complex and unhealthy ambition have left their imprint on the acts of many members of the ruling circles.

Some Russian analysts see these difficulties as a result of the collapse of the power of the state, which led to chaos rather than to an orderly and democratic system. While it is true that Russia began moving toward democracy as evidenced by the elections, elections *per se* are not synonymous with democratisation of society. The fault for this state of affairs is attributed to Gorbachev who instead of democratising the state apparatus and the Communist Party, began by democratising the entire society, in which he did not succeed, and it is for this reason that the state apparatus continued functioning along the old lines (Onikov, 1996).

An assorted collection of political groupings has emerged in Russia, but with the exception of the Communist Party which retained some of the infrastructure and part of the membership of the former ruling CPSU, these remain mostly concentrated in the cities, especially Moscow and St Petersburg. Their leaders see the party organisation as a platform for their personal ambitions. Thus while there appear to be a number of parties, they cannot be considered as an effectively functioning democratic party system.

The 1995 election to the Duma provided the first crucial test of democracy in Russia. The Communists who fought the elections promised to change government policy. Boris Yeltsin, on the other hand, asserted that a communist victory would halt the reform process. The clear winner in the December 1995 Duma election was the Communist Party. It received 22.3 per cent of the vote in the party list election as compared with 11.2 per cent for the Liberal Democrats of Vladimir Zhirinovskii, 10.1 per cent for the government party of Premier Viktor Chernomyrdin, and 6.9 per cent for the radical alternative, Yabloko. The Communist faction in the Duma consists of 149 deputies, while other factions closely allied with it have 72. This gives the communist party 49 per cent of the seats in the Duma (Hough, 1996).

The victory of the left confirmed the existence of a political split into two 'parties of power' – the executive and the legislative. The successes of the opposition in the regional elections indicated a breach of the delicate balance between the president, the government and the leftist Duma. Russia does not have, for the time being, national political parties with a long history of old traditions. It is for this reason that their role is fulfilled by the executive and the parliament. The uniqueness of the Russian situation consists in the fact that the division of two branches of power (executive and legislative) corresponds with the division of political power based on ideological orientations and world views (Koshkareva, 1996). The ideological conflict between the Duma and the executive power does, to a certain degree, restore the divisions in old Russia of the Westernisers and Slavophiles. The government and the president's administration actually embody the liberal-market atmosphere of Moscow and St Petersburg, while the Duma embodies the 'traditional' (not to say socialist) values of the regions (ibid.).

The left-wing victory in the 1995 Duma election was not especially significant because it did not provide the Duma with a decisive voice in state matters. President Boris Yeltsin held the supreme power which he often used, sometimes in an unconstitutional manner.

The power of the Duma was further eroded by the presidential election held on 16 June 1996, in which Yeltsin was re-elected.

A significant factor in all elections since 1989 is that large cities in Russia provided the strongest support for economic reform and democracy and for Boris Yeltsin and his government, while the villages, towns, and smaller cities were the primary base of the opposition. The disparity in political attitudes between the cities and the countryside makes an objective evaluation of the mood in the country as a whole extremely unreliable. Most opinion polls in Russia are conducted in large cities. However, as the bulk of the population (some 80 per cent) live outside the large centres, the conducting of a universal opinion poll becomes an impossible task. Nevertheless, conducting opinion polls is a significant indicator of the emerging democratic process in Russia.

## IN SEARCH OF A RUSSIAN IDEA

More than five years have past since the collapse of communism, but Russia does not seem to be moving along the Western path. Although, the reforms were initiated under the banners of liberalism and democracy, six years on, this liberalism has resulted in the monopoly of a bureaucratised economy, while democracy found its expression in a Constitution which endowed the president with supreme power, in an ineffective parliament, amid court intrigues and with political leaders who dictate their will to ministers and parliamentarians (Kagarlitskii, 1997). Over this period, the mood of Russian society has changed several times. At first it was a mixture of capitalist and communist attitudes, but the speed of the changes led to confusion. The liberal section of the nomenklatura was prepared for a lengthy process of reform. Their leading ideology was social democracy – sufficiently 'socialist' to be accepted by the conservative masses, and sufficiently capitalist so as not to prevent the distribution of property.

Many Western analysts are inclined to attribute the lack of progress to the remnants of the old order and are also inclined to blame the Russian leadership, whether it was Gorbachev or now Yeltsin, for the failure of the reform, which they say prevented the formation of a new type of society in Russia. Few try to analyse the nature of Russian society as a factor which contributed, and still does, to the retention of some of the features of the former system. The dramatic events in Russia of the last decade, which were hailed in the West as a democratic revolution, have been met by the majority of the population of Russia with utter indifference. Except for the shortlived attempted coup when thousands of ordinary people gathered in front of the White House to express their opposition to the perceived return to dictatorship, most of the time there reigned a sense of fatality and apathy born out of hopelessness, which is so characteristic of the Russian national character (McDaniel, 1996).

The mood of despair was most prevalent among the older generation of Russians. They began to perceive the communist period as a failure and the sacrifices that the Russian people made during this period, especially during the Great Patriotic War, as a wasted effort. This does not imply that the pre-*perestroika* Russians were convinced communists. It was, rather, a belief in the leadership with their promises of a better future. This belief was historically ingrained in the Russian psyche – a belief in the supreme Russian authority be it in the person of the tsar or the post-revolutionary dictator. The population was inclined to believe in Stalin's motto 'life became better, life became more joyous', and if the reality had not been in accordance with that statement, there was always hope and the expectation that one day it would.

Some Russian analysts assert that the uneasy fusion of modernisation and the traditional elements of Russian culture, which embodied a fundamental contradiction between ideas and practice, was one of the causes of the system's collapse. After the collapse of the system that made great promises, the country found itself in an ideological vacuum. It could not see its future in capitalist values neither could it see a return to the old system.

The new generation of young Russian intelligentsia, those that were born after the war and who experienced the new trend toward more freedom, began to search for an answer to the question: 'Where is Russia heading?' It is not a new question. The question of Russia's historic destiny 'as a nation among all other peoples and nations' has been a central preoccupation of Russian thought for the last two centuries (ibid., p. 10). It is called the Russian idea – a notion closely connected with the concept of an ideology, or to be more precise, a national ideology. A national ideology in Russia is, strictly speaking, a non-state ideology because according to the Russian Constitution 'no ideology can be established as state ideology'. It is for this reason that the twice

elected President as the guardian of the Constitution, has instructed
Russian intellectuals to work out not a state, but a general national ideology. Is there a difference? asks Evgenii Sagalovskii, a
Russian analyst. State ideology in the full meaning of the term,
assumes the obligation of all citizens to accept it, and this in itself
is pure totalitarianism. National ideology, on the other hand, is
consciously and voluntarily accepted by the citizens and consequently
represents something more acceptable (Sagalovskii, 1996). Sagalovskii
asserts that any national ideology, excluding the idea of national
independence and security, is unsound because it is based on a
dangerous fallacy of national exclusivity or superiority of one religion
over another, for example. National ideology in its open or concealed form includes the Russian idea of messianism and is consequently aggressive by its very nature. It is true that a state ideology
existed in the former USSR, but apart from the four years of war
with Germany when Russian patriotism united the nation, there
was no common national ideology. Everybody conformed to the
state ideology but few believed in it. As President Yeltsin once
said: 'it is necessary to invent a national ideology in order to unite
all Russians'.

Not surprisingly, the subject of the Russian idea surfaced as soon
as communism was perceived as obsolete. Something more akin to
the Russian identity had to be found. The search for a Russian
idea has become an almost universal task. The search has taken
on different forms. Some see the Russian idea in the communist
past, but most Russian intellectuals are trying to find a compromise between the old concept of Slavophiles and Westernisers. The
discussions that took place in the nineteenth century have surfaced
with increased intensity. The present debate expresses the meaning of 'the Russian idea' in the conviction that Russia has its own
independent and distinguished cultural and historical tradition that
sets it apart from the West (McDaniel, 1996, p. 11).

Sakharov, a contemporary Russian social scientist, (Sakharov, 1996)
claims that Russia is a particular civilisation, unlike any other in
Europe, but he asserts at the same time, that Russia must travel,
although much later, through the same stages of civilisation as did
other civilised countries. In other words it is a society in transition. Russia is a special civilisation which absorbed in the course
of many centuries much of Western as well as Eastern traits which
she melted down into something unique (Zagorodnikov, 1996).

According to those who support the new approach to ideology, the constant and lengthy process of taking advantage of freedoms should have as its final objective the creation of a Russia as 'a unique civilisation', which would disclose its potentials and all its power to the world, and which would finally channel the course of its history into the evolutionary stream. This peculiar path assumes that the stages of civilisation through which the West passed, that is, the transition to democracy, to a civic society and legitimate government, will acquire in Russia distinct differences from foreign models. According to Yakov Plyais, a social scientist, one of the most important features of Russian civilisation is the special relationship between the material and spiritual aspects of society. While it is true that today the material factor is gaining predominance, the role of spirituality in Russia is being maintained. A Russian by his very nature 'is obliged to be on a high spiritual and humane level'. Due to various reasons, mainly linked to Russia's past (especially the Soviet past), one must take into consideration the claim of Russia's 'longing for an ideological narcotic' (Plyais, 1997). This means that Russian society and the government need an ideology. Apart from national values, above all Russian patriotism, the ideology must also include other qualities created by Russian society such as religious orthodoxy, which have become part of the Russian mentality. It must also include some socialist principles (particularly those that are linked with the social protection of citizens).

National ideology should not be confused with party ideology, particularly with the ideology of a ruling party. It was the 'the leader of all times and nations', who understood that in a society on a generally low political culture level it would be possible to successfully apply an ideological drug and through it to attain certain objectives. The importance of the ideological narcotic during the first decade of Soviet power cannot be underestimated. Consequently, under certain historical conditions, an ideological narcotic is indispensable and plays a positive role (ibid.).

Khrushchev tried to introduce a more materialistic element into the ideology. Since the new programme of the CPSU, the masses saw in communism an image of a consumer's paradise. After years of hardship and sacrifice, communism was supposed to become at last not only an idea of brotherhood and mutual support, but also a gigantic supermarket, where everybody would be able to obtain whatever they needed without queuing up and free of charge. A change in this objective occurred almost unnoticed because in any political system an objective is no more than a way of justifying means. The Soviet system, however, had not succeeded in its objective of creating a consumer society. The system failed in its competition with capitalism. Communism was rejected not by the awakening of the society, but by a revolt of disappointed consumers and the leaders of this revolt was the ruling elite itself.

The new Russian man, without even realising it, created a kind of 'communist idea', but only privately and for himself through the redistribution of wealth, particularly property. Distribution of property was a very attractive idea, but did not allow for a transitional period. Social democracy could not achieve it and was replaced by liberalism. According to Boris Kagarlitskii, contemporary Russian liberalism has its peculiar features – it is a bourgeois ideology without a bourgeoisie (Kagarlitskii, 1997). Instead of a bourgeoisie there are nomenklatura cadres, functionaries and black marketeers who are dreaming of becoming bourgeois. The image of capitalism, which existed only in Soviet political economy text-books, suddenly began to materialise. Former researchers in capitalist horrors have become its practitioners, while intellectuals who dreamt of a capitalism with a human face have become disappointed.

Nationalism was another alternative idea. In a classless society in which class solidarity seems an abstract slogan and 'high ideas' ridiculous, it is the 'voice of blood' that is supposed to unite the people. Politicians with various points of view, from Lebed to Zyuganov and from Zhirinovskii to Yeltsin, began to turn toward national values and traditions. But the 'national idea' has not become linked to a tangible socio-economic path. According to one Russian analyst, 'without a synthesis of ideas with economic progress, no ideology is able to penetrate the consciousness of the masses, but without a national idea the citizens and the government cannot see an objective to which they should strive in the course of their activities' (*Nezavisimaya gazeta*, 30 June 1996).

Andrei Zagornikov, in an article entitled 'A national idea or an idea of a nation' (Zagorodnikov, 1996), asserts that Russia must be different from other countries by its kind of democracy, by its spirituality and high degree of civilised relations between the people. A 'national idea' according to the author, is an interconnected totality of ideas (including national ideas) of values which reflect the peculiarity of the existing political order and the national specificity of the country. The Russian government's 'national idea' reflects the political ideology of the people in power but not the expectations of the ordinary man. As a result of its penetration, the entire social system may become politicised, which may restrict the sphere of activities if not bring about the complete oblivion of civic society. In the final analysis it can lead to the restoration of the totalitarian past. The author sees a 'national idea' as being offered according to Mussolini's formula, 'one nation – one government' – a formula that leads to the minimisation of the sphere of free activities of men. The term 'national idea' should be replaced by an 'idea of a nation', according to the author. The 'idea of a nation' encompasses the answer to the question 'how and what is the nation thinking of itself?' It is a question of national identity.

Another Russian intellectual, Sergei Mitrofanov, rejects the romantic theory that the Russian idea is supposed to consist of a combination of Western liberalism and internally institutionalised humanism of the Russian East. The author compares Russia with the United States where, as he says, American identity is expressed not only through its brain power but through universal credit cards and MacDonalds that have spread all around the world. In Russian history by contrast, there was nothing but slavery and humiliation (Mitrofanov, 1996). The question of national identification in Russia reached a level of acuity unparalleled elsewhere. Contemporary politics in Russia are defined to a large extent by the answers to the question of what place the 'New Russia' should strive to occupy in the history of the Russian state (Shenfeld, 1994, p. 6). There are two basic criteria which the Russian people apply today. Some see Russia as a continuation of the Soviet empire, in which Russia played a predominant role. Despite the dramatic changes that have taken place, the Soviet period retains significant weight in the Russian consciousness. Others see Russia's future in a return to the old tsarist Russian empire with its Orthodox religion and old values. Tsarist Russia remains a powerful historical embodiment of the Russian state (ibid., p. 12).

Everybody in Russia understands that the ruling ideology is in crisis, that something has to change. However, this does not mean that a new ideology will triumph. Although the principles of liberalism and democracy are incorporated in the Russian Constitution, in government programmes and in the obligations to the International Monetary Fund, they are of little use. What is needed are concrete decisions dictated by pragmatism rather than ideology, according to Boris Kagarlitskii. But the government needs an ideology. As one Russian commentator expressed it succinctly: 'The search for ideology will continue until the government is ready to change its present ideology or society changes the government' (Kagarlitskii, 1997).


RUSSIAN SOCIETY TODAY

The claim that Russia needs an all-embracing national ideology which would unite Russian society is increasingly being heard in political circles. However, none of the proposed ideas about government and society is capable of becoming an all-embracing ideology because of the lack of agreement on the kind of society Russia needs (Kutkovets, 1997). The Institute of Sociological Analysis began conducting a large-scale survey in May 1996 as part of a research project on the subject 'Russia's peculiar path – what is it?' It attempted to clarify the attitude of Russian society to the various ideas circulating in political circles, on the desirable form of government for Russia, and on its relation with society and the individual. Those surveyed were presented with a number of ideas from which they had to choose the three most acceptable to them.

Following the survey, the Institute divided those polled into several distinct political groupings according to their perception of Russia as a country and of its social and political system. In the first group were those who believe that Russia should be a country of the Russian people. Those choosing this definition are called for convenience 'Russian Nationalists'. The second group consisted of those who assert that Russia should be a militarily strong country ('state power'). Next were the so-called 'internationalists' who believe that Russia should be a multinational state of many ethnic peoples with equal rights. Another important group included those who claim that Russia must return to a socialist system (called here 'Restorers of socialism'). The so-called 'Unifiers' propose a Russia around which would be created a new, voluntary union of former Soviet republics. Among other groups were proponents of a restored Russia as a strong military empire within the borders of the former Soviet Union ('Imperialists'); Russia as a country the power and strength of which will be secured by the improving welfare of its citizens ('Post-Soviet individualists'); Russia as a country with a market economy, democratic freedoms and observance of human rights ('Democratic Westernisers'); and finally, Russia as an Orthodox Christian country ('Orthodox Christians').

The survey indicated that in today's Russia the most popular idea is that of Post-Soviet Individualism (52 per cent), followed by Democratic-Westernisers (41 per cent) and Internationalists (35 per cent). There was also a strong representation for State Power (21 per cent), Unifiers (19 per cent) and Russian Nationalists (16 per cent). Among the minor groups were the Orthodox Christians (13 per cent), Restorers of Socialism (12 per cent) and Imperialists (7 per cent).

### 'Democratic Westernisers'

This group includes the largest number of people with higher education (22 per cent), the highest number of people up to 25 years of age (17 per cent) the highest number of residents of large and medium-size towns (50 per cent), and the greatest number of high earners (40 per cent). It differs from the others in its critical attitude toward the Soviet period. Almost two-thirds consider that after 1917 the country went on a path that was contrary to its national and traditional way of development – it views communism as a break with Russian history. On the other hand, 80 per cent of people in this group admit that collectivism under Soviet rule was more inherent in the consciousness of the Russian people than it is today. They also claim that collectivism was of more benefit to the government than it was to the people.

They are less inclined to see the West as a real or potential danger for Russia. Their attitude is also characterised by the watered down concept of 'defence consciousness', which was predominant during the Soviet rule in the form of the 'besieged fortress' mentality. Nine out of ten prefer a Western political and economic system, but while suggesting that Russia become part of the Western world, the democrats consider that Russia would prosper only thanks to its own distinctly original path unlike the Western one. The image of Russia as a great military power is superimposed in their mind with an image of Russia's economic backwardness, which creates an inferiority complex. In particular, many democrats (over 40 per cent) consider that Russia is being reduced to the role of a supplier of raw material to the developed countries. They also complain of the 'flight of brain power' from Russia.

As for electoral preferences, the vast majority would vote for the reformist politicians.

**'Restorers of socialism'**

This group consists mainly of people with only primary education (40 per cent), people over 50 years of age, inhabitants of villages (40 per cent) and the greatest percentage of the relatively poor (57 per cent). In contrast to the first group, the majority of Socialist restorers (54 per cent) are inclined to believe that after 1917 Russia's development followed its traditions and its national peculiarities. In other words, the communist idea is considered as a predetermined part of Russia's history. Such a perception is interesting because it runs counter to the Soviet view of the October Revolution as a break with the pre-revolutionary past. Over 80 per cent of this group are convinced that during the Soviet period, there were better opportunities for the individual to find a suitable position in life than today. An overwhelming majority (78 per cent) believe that during the Soviet period there was a higher degree of observance of human rights.

Socialists are convinced anti-Westerners. The majority (70 per cent) reject Western standards of consumption and are inclined to be satisfied with the level of material security of the Brezhnev era. Fifty-six per cent of 'Restorers of Socialism' prefer the Soviet path of development. Many of them (at least the largest percentage) see the West as enemy number one, and believe that the external threat to Russia emanates, above all, from the US and West European countries.

The Socialists hope that law and order, and other attributes that can serve as an example to the world, can be achieved through a socialist society based on the Soviet model. Like the democrats, Socialists believe that Russia can prosper only thanks to its own distinctly original path. The most important factor for the Socialists is state control over the economy. The belief that the Russian people possess a higher level of spirituality than their Western counterparts is held by most people in that group.

In the 1995 elections, the vast majority of Socialists (67 per cent) voted for the communists or their closest political allies. In the presidential elections they were inclined to vote for Zyuganov.

The above survey indicates that Russian society is searching for an ideology that would rally the people and provide them with a sense of unity. The most attractive ideology is not the one that determines the type of government in power but rather the mutual relations between society and the individual. The post-Soviet man is an individualist rather than a collectivist. The rejection of the Soviet system is interwoven today in the mass consciousness with an affection for Soviet orderliness, which even in the eyes of many anti-communists looks more attractive than today's reality. This explains to a large extent the fact that many of those who are aware of the excesses of the Soviet system are still voting for the communist party and its leaders.

The attitude towards the past is one of the main political problems in any country, and, like all political questions, it cannot be solved either by a complete negation of the past or by its apologists. The negators and apologists can only compete during the short period of revolutionary break with the past and change of regimes. This is precisely the period into which Russia has entered. In the ideological sphere, an important feature of this period is the simultaneous opposition to socialism and capitalism, from which grew – with modifications – an idea of a special 'third' way for Russia, which has a nationalistic (not to be confused with a patriotic) touch (Rats, 1996).

## IDEOLOGY AND THE ECONOMY

The recent discussion on national ideology in the Russian press, consciously or unconsciously avoids the economic question. The economic crisis, which has already lasted for a number of years, also contains, among other elements, an ideological cause – a crisis in the philosophy of economic liberalism that relates to Russia's historical conditions, according to Russian analysts. Any national ideology, openly or secretly, strives toward the achievement of economic welfare. This objective can be attained through individual success and private business – a factor of the 'American dream' which is based on Protestant ethics and historical experience under conditions of an absence of government support (Filatov, 1997).

There are two peculiarities in the Russian national psychology which have developed under the influence of historical circumstances – the suppressed feelings of personal responsibility and a perception of social justice, which is in contrast with the European and North American concepts. The absence of political freedom and possibility of influencing the elite through representative democracy has revived the Russian traditional form of protest – 'shutting oneself in' from a critical appraisal of reality. The tragedy of Russian reality is that in the 1980s the ruling elite did not succeed in modernising the country. The failure of the Gorbachevian *'uskorenie'* – acceleration – has underlined the fruitless attempts. Gorbachev's failure was determined by the fact that it did not base itself on sufficient economic responsibility and interest in the economic chain. Instead of a system of measures aimed at strengthening the economic responsibility of enterprises, it went on the path of redistribution, which led to a legalised 'new wave' of transforming 'power into property' (ibid.). This has become a belief in the effectiveness of private property, in the simplicity of transforming property relations and creating an efficient market economy. However, such transformation was only in a legal sense, that is, in the form of property deeds, but not in a sense of motivation and responsibility for the results – not about business ethics.

The adoption of a legal framework regarding property did not take into account several important factors. Property relations cannot be established within a precisely determined time-span, but must come as a result of a natural evolution of society. Private property can only be exploited efficiently when it has a solid economic base in the form of private investment undertaken with full knowledge of the risks involved. Property obtained 'by coincidence' is as a rule wasted, that is, it has a tendency to be converted for the benefit of current non-productive consumption.

According to published data, the efficiency of the Russian economy in 1996 was worse than the inefficient economy of twenty years earlier. The privatisation by decree under the Russian circumstances is not leading Russia to a reformed economy but to its collapse. There are increasing signs of feudalisation rather than capitalism-isation of social relations in Russia.

The period of the initial accumulation of capital in Europe ended a few centuries ago, after the Revolution and other social upheavals. The situation in Russia is radically different. Here, the formation of legitimate property relations is inhibited by the following factors:

- by a mentality, which is based on other than European historical experience;
- by an imperfect legal basis, arbitrariness and breaches of the privatisation procedures;
- by the direct participation in privatisation of criminal and sub-criminal elements;

 • by the absence of confidence in the legitimacy of their rights within a significant section of 'owners' themselves.

Because of its institutional nature, so-called private property retains its instability, it moves towards an oligarchic monopoly and, at the same time, continues to derive the means of its development from the resources of the state. As a result, the Russian economy has acquired its own peculiar features – market economic in form, and non-market uncompetitive in content.

## CULTURE AND POLITICS IN RUSSIA

In May 1989, George Bush outlined his new attitudes towards the USSR. He asserted that it was the US that prevailed in the struggle between 'democracy and freedom', between 'tyranny and conflict'. He suggested the integration of the Soviet Union into the community of nations (*The New York Times*, 13 May 1989). His statement was received in Moscow with a degree of scepticism. One Soviet commentator accused Bush of persisting in 'old clichés' and 'stereotypes' (*Pravda*, 14 May 1989). What Bush undoubtedly meant was that Russia was on the way to becoming a society with similar values and objectives to the West. The general perception in the West, at least among the politicians, was that once the reforms were introduced and put into effect, the kind of society that would emerge in Russia would acquire common features with the West and similar values.

Few Western analysts and commentators have taken into consideration the ideological factor which always had great influence over the life of Russian society and consequently on Russia's attitude to the outside world. There is one main reason for this state of affairs. The West with its set of societal values and a tradition of democracy, which it displays as an example to be followed by every other society in the world, does not find it necessary, at least at present, to search for new ideas especially after the collapse of communism and the bankruptcy of Marxism as a social theory. It, therefore, applies its own criteria to Russia.

The basic principle guiding this kind of reasoning is that in the present world order, commonality of purpose, culture and civilisation will promote goodwill among nations and will be conducive to peace in Europe. This may have been a correct assumption when applied to West European nations, but has already proven to be wrong in relation to Russia for one simple reason – Western politicians have only a vague idea of the problems besetting Russia today. They look mainly at the economic and political aspects of the reforms, but this does not go far enough to understand, let alone to act in accordance with, Russian reality.

According to one Russian commentator the West should change its perception of Russia as a country that will shortly join the family of Western liberal states and adopt their system of values in the foreign policy context. This perception is the result of a belief that for Russia liberal democratic government should be an example and a desirable objective because the Western model is the only one that is functioning well and is the best of any alternative. Now that the Bolshevik system has collapsed, the way to Western democracy is open for Russia. Such preconceived ideas, as well as the thesis of the 'end of history in Russia', are not only questionable but can also be dangerous. A speedy transition of Russia to Western democracy would create more problems than it would solve. A transition would be realised at the expense of suppressing important distinctively Russian tendencies in Russia and may provoke a backlash.

Russia, by rejecting communism as a unifying ideology (imposed by indoctrination), found itself in an ideological vacuum, which it is still attempting to fill. Russia is in the process of searching for its own path within its internal discordances and contradictions. Russian minds have always had the ability to place Russia and the Russian people within a system of particularly Russian social values. Theories such as 'Moscow the Third Rome', 'the Orthodox Church', 'Holy Russia', 'Party, Ideology and Nationalism' (Soviet era), and finally 'The New Thinking' (Gorbachev), have been the product of Russian ideologues. When the latest ideological scheme collapsed together with the totalitarian regime, it became obvious that the people are no longer protected from their misfortunes by a utopia. The Russian people painfully perceive an ideological vacuum. The Russians have difficulties in living in such a vacuum – they need an ideological narcotic. Today many Russians grieve over the loss of an all-embracing ideology. This is understandable because Russia has always been a country in which the ideological determination of her historical path played an important role (Kosolapov, 1993).

An expression of the present trends in Russian thinking can be found in the Political Resolution of the IV All-Russian Congress of the movement 'Our Home – Russia'. The Congress took place in April 1997. It espoused an assumption that Russia is an open democratic country on the way toward a political and economic renewal. Russian society has already adopted democratic and free-market values – respect for diversity of opinions, freedom of conscience, freedom of economic activities and of private enterprise.

An important point in the Resolution was the question of Russia's national security. In this respect the Movement does not differ much from the position adopted by other political groupings. Russia's stability and security cannot be guaranteed without the general support of its armed forces. It speaks about raising the prestige of the 'defenders of the Fatherland' (*Nezavisimaya gazeta*, 19 April 1997). According to the Resolution, the movement 'Our Home – Russia' is a right-of-centre movement based on liberal values and national traditions. That is – the uniqueness and continuity of Russia's history, commitment to the idea of the organic unity of the Russian nation, while maintaining her ethnic diversity, and to the idea of Russian patriotism and social justice.

The Congress expressed its support for Russia's role as a leading world power and for her increased prestige on the international arena as one of the guarantors of world stability and security. It also expressed support for the reintegration of the CIS.

In some way it adopted a position similar to those who claim that the West should meet the situation in Russia with understanding. 'The mistake that the West is committing in its approach to the new Russia is that it applies the same yardstick to the Russian state as it would to any other country.' The movement 'Our Home – Russia' clearly tries to synthesise the conflicting ideas of Westernisers and Slavophiles, whatever their motives may be. The debate between the 'Westernisers' and 'Slavophiles' that has emerged with increased vigour during the period of changes in Russia's political system, points to a division in Russian society. Recent opinion polls indicate that public opinion in Russia is almost equally divided. Fifty-two per cent of those polled were in favour of the 'Western' path of development, that is for Russia to absorb Western experiences and achievements of Western civilisation, while 45 per cent assume that 'Russia's history and geography being located between Europe and Asia should follow its unique Russian path' (Popov, 1994). Many Russian social scientists assert that culture has always been essential for the development of Russian society (Levit, 1990,

p. 21). According to this view, the present situation in Russia is due mainly to a cultural crisis, especially to the low level of political culture. Nonetheless, the cultural or spiritual element, of which Russian intellectuals and even politicians speak, is ever present in all discussions about Russia's future. There is almost general agreement about the appropriate degree of influence Russia should have in world affairs; that is the question of its retention or reassertion of superpower status. The majority supports the idea of Russia as a great power – not only in a military sense, but in its influence in world affairs.

# 10 Toward a Cold War or a Cold Peace?

## POST-SOVIET RUSSIA

*Perestroika* has been a programme of political and economic liberalisation that was supposed to modernise the Soviet Union; President Gorbachev wanted to end stagnation, which he inherited from the Brezhnev era. He thought that by giving the Soviet people an increased role in setting policy and increased freedom of expression, he would generate more energy and commitment to strengthen the Soviet state. However, those liberated forces moved the Soviet Union and its society (or rather those politically mature) in unforeseen directions. Within a relatively short time-span, communism as a state ideology, and all that it stood for, had collapsed. With the disintegration of the Soviet Union, its replacement by Russia and the emergence of Yeltsin as President, it seemed as if Russia's path should lead to the West – toward a system of liberal government. Indeed, Russia's foreign policy under Yeltsin initially indicated a trend toward joining the industrially developed countries and a definite break with the messianic ideas of the former Soviet Union (Timmerman, 1994). It looked as if Russia despite the internal political disagreements had found its basic direction.

Soon, however, it became clear that the road toward democracy and a free market economy was much more difficult than anticipated. The legacy of 70 years of authoritarian rule and of a centrally managed economy could not be discarded by new laws and presidential decrees. The Russian government under Yeltsin's leadership did not succeed in formulating an appropriate economic policy that would stabilise the situation in the country. It had to resort to improvisations rather than a sequential, well-thought-out order of reforms. It had no choice, because the process of transition from a command system to a free-market economy, from a totalitarian regime to a democratic system in which Russia had little experience, was unprecedented in world history. There was no example to follow.

Russia could boast of some achievements in the democratisation process. The freedoms now available to the Russian population, the existence of various political movements, and the more open society, are claimed to be evidence of the break with the past. Not everyone in Russia agrees. Many Russians assert that democracy without tangible evidence of improvement in the economic condition of the individual is meaningless. Some claim that life under communist rule was much better. Most analysts agree that Russian society is going through a transitional process and that it is too early to make a final judgment as to the final form the society will acquire. Democratisation through free elections resulted in the emergence of various political movements claiming to be political parties, but in fact representing sectional interests. The irony of the present situation is that the Russian parliament, the Duma, is composed of a majority consisting of former communists and nationalists.

Economic reforms face other difficulties. Attempts at reforming the economy through the encouragement of private enterprise and privatisation, brought about a situation in which the government was steadily losing control over the activities of the emerging class of new capitalists. Under the threat of social upheavals by the impoverished strata of the population, it had to tread a narrow path between liberalising the economy and controlling it. As one Russian commentator noted, the 'shock therapy' introduced by Gaidar was imposed on an indifferent, apathetic and disintegrating society. This in turn led to unprecedented economic crisis and administrative and social chaos (Arbatov, 1994).

## FAILURE OF REFORMS

Ten years after the collapse of communism and the disintegration of the Soviet Union, and six years after the beginning of reforms, Russia's international position has markedly deteriorated and there is no significant improvement in the domestic situation. Many Russian analysts are asking a simple question: how is it possible that a country rich in resources and with a large number of professional people is unable to solve its economic problems? Sergei Rogov, the director of the US–Canada Institute, approached this question by superimposing the American economic and political model on the Russian economy. He claims that the establishment of an American capitalist system would be the only way to solving Russia's economic problems.

Vadim Belotserkovskii, a prominent Russian analyst, disagrees and attempts to find an answer to a more basic question: is capitalism appropriate for Russia? He maintains that the main difficulty in introducing reforms was caused by the enormous industrial potential built during the Communist period, which proved to be most difficult to privatise. There simply wasn't sufficient private capital available, and capitalism without private enterprise cannot function properly. Belotserkovskii concludes that all present difficulties, all failures of reforms are a result of the incompatibility of Russia with capitalism and capitalism with Russia. He quotes Boris Nemtsov as speaking of the possibility of establishing in Russia a 'national capitalism with a human face' (Belotserkovskii, 1997).

Vladimir Popov, another Russian analyst, attributes the failure of the reforms to the lack of mental identity of the Russian population, which he defines as the degree of compatibility of the reforms with the mentality of the Russian people. He is supported in this assertion by Professor Pavel Gurevitch who points out that while social innovations are being undertaken, 'psychological confusion' is not taken into account (Popov, 1997).

Some Russian academics affirm that the Russian mentality has already undergone a significant change under the influence of the reforms. Others assert that mentality does not play any role. Finally there are those who claim that the reforms have broken the back of the Russian mentality and that this in turn will lead to a psychological and spiritual degeneration of the society. In the West, according to Popov, economic reforms have created a middle class and a civic government, while in Russia they have resulted in a stratification of the population into a rich minority and a poor majority.

However, the real cause of the increasingly intense internal conflict lies much deeper; it lies within the disagreements on the question of Russia's national identity (Timmerman, 1994, p. 17). Other former Soviet republics, following the collapse of the Soviet empire, have acquired a national identity, while Russia has lost her own. For the average Russian, the difference between a Soviet and a Russian man is still not clear. Russian identity has previously been connected with the notion of a vast Soviet Russian empire, but from a geopolitical point of view, Russia finds itself today in the territorial situation of three hundred years ago. Russia's historical legacy has produced strong state power and a traditionally weak civic society. This is the main reason why the reforms began from the 'top'. Russian society, according to Popov, needs an ideal, a universal national idea, which will give the people spiritual strength and an ideological support for the reforms (Popov, 1997).

It is not only the people that seek self-identification, but the government is also seeking a means of rallying the masses. It is trying to formulate foreign policy that would express the mood of the population and would be in accord with their self-awareness. The composition of the Duma does not make the task of formulating a foreign policy any easier. The conservative forces represented by the communists and the nationalists are clamouring for a more assertive Russian foreign policy.

In one respect, however, there is a consensus of opinion among all political leanings: Russia must remain in the future a great and influential power. The differences are in the form that this power ought to take. Initially, Yeltsin and the former Russian foreign minister Kozyrev, were supporters of a European-Atlantic direction. This was to include democratisation based on a Western model, de-ideologisation and demilitarisation – a policy that would link Russia with the West as an equal partner. In this respect it resembled the ideas of the traditional Westernisers in tsarist Russia. Subsequently, under pressure from conservative forces, this attitude has undergone a subtle transformation. It began to express the ideas of the former Slavophiles with their belief in Russia's mission and her place in the world. In fact it now embodies the struggle between two opposing ideologies.

## THE QUESTION OF IDENTITY

A survey of the history of the period of communist rule and of the Soviet Union's foreign policy clearly points to a process of erosion of communist ideology which had been taking place since the consolidation of Bolshevik power. Initially, ideology became a means for rationalisation and legitimation of the regime, and this was reflected in policies which indicated an accommodation of theory with a given situation. But erosion had been imposed upon the Soviet regime by the forces of international politics and by changes in the structure of the Soviet state and society. The Soviet Union saw its national interests within the context of the security of the USSR and, as a corollary, the stability of the regime. It perceived the Western capitalist world, especially the United States, as basically hostile to it. The existence of foreign danger, real or imaginary, and the resulting siege mentality had been seen as a fixed principle in the thinking of the Soviet government (Ulan, 1976, p. 284).

Another principle was the apparent irreversibility of Stalin's model of socialism. It was thought that once socialism had triumphed it could not be eliminated. Slowly, the thesis of irreversibility began to undergo a subtle modification. It was brought about by a need to adopt a new understanding of the essence of socialism, its aims and, consequently, new practice. *Perestroika* was the answer to this need (Kosolapov, 1993, p. 39).

One of the tasks of *perestroika* was the resurrection of a genuine Russian culture. It was a task of dehumanising of the people. The process of dehumanisation of Russian society was enhanced by the fact that there were always two contrasting elements: an element of serfdom and an element of resistance based on personal responsibility. It is this latter, although hidden but latent, strata of society that made *glasnost* possible. Even the most radical totalitarian system cannot entirely rule over the inner world of every individual. It is impossible to prohibit thought and moods, which carry the potential, if not of open resistance in the present, at least of future resurrection of what was suppressed yesterday (Olshanskii, 1989, p. 102).

The next stage in this process was the collapse of the socialist experiment, of the Soviet Union and Russia's defeat in the Cold War. As a result, some Russian analysts say, it became necessary to reject the last 70 years of Russia's Soviet and socialist history, to revert to the past and to begin anew. Today, Russia conducts a spiritual search for its past (Kosolapov, 1993, p. 40). It is a search for a Russian identity, which was destroyed by the seven decades of communism and replaced by an amalgamation of Soviet and Russian nationalism.

Nationalism, one of the momentous movements of the nineteenth and twentieth centuries in much of the rest of the world, has followed a somewhat different course in the Soviet Union. Russian nationalism existed for some time, but had been harnessed to serve the ends of Soviet communism. Soviet nationalism, although it had many links with Russia's past, was not a purely 'Russian' product; it also represented the ideology of the new regime. The leaders needed Russian nationalism to fill the void left by the destruction of beliefs and customs capable of satisfying the Russians (Barghoorn, 1956, p. 260). Russian nationalism became equated with Soviet patriotism, and the supremacy of everything that was Russian with the superiority of the Soviet system (Cooper, 1989, p. 32).

At present, there are indications that communist ideology is being replaced by a renewal of the Great Power chauvinism and nationalistic ideas, which are being embraced by a significant part of the establishment and political elite (Arbatov, 1994, p. 8). Supporters of the Great Russian empire idea, strive to regain Russia's lost status as a world power. They take as a point of departure the spiritual basis of the 'Russian idea', which imposes on the country a specific 'mission' in relation to other nations. Among the supporters of this idea are the former communists and the nationalists. Both rely on an ideology which subordinates the right of the individual to the interests of the collective, class or nation.

Many Russian analysts see the emerging Russian Empire idea in the context of the search for a Russian identity. The search is, above all, psychological and intellectual compensation for the absence of society's self-awareness of the new, sovereign Russia. It is, at the same time, one of the most important elements and stages in the formation of such self-awareness. And this in turn makes it necessary to examine the mutual links between the emerging self-awareness of Russian society and the foreign policy of its government.

Within the search into the past, it was inevitable that the old intellectual heated dispute between the Westernisers and Slavophiles would surface once more – the former advocating a move closer to the West, including a possible merge and adoption of its values, the latter emphasising Russia's uniqueness. According to one Russian intellectual, the dispute between the Westernisers and Slavophiles has been transformed into one of the major obstacles on the way to Russia's advancement. He is critical of those who attempt to transform Russia and the Russian civilisation into a kind of a 'New West' or 'New East'. This, he says, is impossible and even dangerous.

The popular notion of 'reintegrating Russia within the family of industrial democracies' is illusory because Russia was never part of this family. The idea of making out of Russia a 'New West' is unrealistic and potentially destructive. It would reinforce in the Russian conscience the 'complex of historical failure', which has already acquired an almost chronic state. However, by admitting its differences from the West, Russia must not counterpoise itself as an example; Russia must learn to be itself. Russia's real choice cannot be boiled down to a dichotomy – toward the West and then progress, or rejection of the West and then 'a black hole' (Kosolapov, 1993, p. 48).

Russia's failures are basically self-inflicted, according to the well-known figure Aleksei Arbatov. But instead of admitting its own responsibility for the failures, and analysing its causes, a large part of Russian society submits itself to the political indoctrination on Russia's unique path, that Russia does not need freedom, and that her mission in the world is her greatness. According to this view, Russia is destined for a 'unique role' because of her size, strategic and political interests stretching outside her territory, and other factors of historical importance that make her superior to other smaller countries. Such ideas, according to Arbatov, will in the end frighten the outside world and instil new fears of Russia as an enemy of the West (Arbatov, 1994, p. 10). Such attitudes may become counter-productive and lead to the unification of forces of the former Soviet republics being directed against Russia. They may even obtain aid from the West, South or East, accompanied by political and economic sanctions, and a renewal of the Cold War (ibid.).

The sources of such ideas, according to one prominent Russian analyst, can be found in the beginning of the 1990s, in the Russian masochistic 'complex of historical failure'. Within the ideological context, in contrast to citizens of other countries, the majority of Russians feel historically defeated. This complex was not so much a reaction to the communist ideology, as to the advancement and pursuit of former illusory, unrealistic, utopian objectives, and to the alienation of foreign policy from the interest and concerns of the average Russian.

Russia today, as perceived by a large part of the population, lacks a national identity and finds itself thrown back to the Russian identity of the tsarist times. The choice Russia faces today is either, despite the international environment, to fulfil its specific 'mission' of restoring the empire, or to gain an understanding of its new role as a normal nation, and as a great power pursue a pragmatic policy that will combine national interests with cooperation with the outside world (Timmerman, 1994, p. 18).

## NATIONAL INTEREST AND NATIONAL SECURITY

The swift collapse of communism and the disintegration of the Soviet Union had only been foreseen by a handful of Western analysts. Nevertheless, a claim that the potential for a conflict between East (Russia) and West (United States) has disappeared with the demise of communism would be rather simplistic. The question of insecurity and siege mentality goes much deeper and, as an analysis of contemporary Russian politics indicates, still persists today – long after the collapse of communism in Russia. It is closely linked with the concept and definition of Russia's national interests and national security.

The concept of national interests is not new, it has often been debated during the Soviet period. Despite the apparent ideological motivation of Soviet foreign and domestic policies, the decisive factor was national interest. It had been quoted on numerous occasions when pragmatic considerations acquired priority in the formulations of policies. A similar situation is arising in the new Russia. Simultaneously with the attempts at creating a new 'Russian idea', a discussion is taking place on what constitutes Russia's national interests. As a result of the attempts by supporters of various trends to separate national interests from domestic policy and to make them a central theme of Russia's international activities, it created more conflicts, each group claiming its specific interests as the interests of the government. It is for this reason that Russia's foreign policy has become less predictable.

A seminar, in the course of which professional diplomats attempted to define the national interests of the former USSR, took place in early 1991. The consensus of opinion was that after 1917, Moscow's policies were mainly ideologically motivated. Although, at present ideology takes second place, a contemporary concept of national interests has not yet been determined. E. Bazhanov the author of an article on the subject of national interest, analysed the theoretical principles of the concept (Bazhanov, 1991). There are three major objectives of any government, according to the author. These are, security from external threats, the satisfaction of the material and spiritual needs of its citizens, and defence of its political and economic position on the world arena, that is, strengthening its influence. Failure to achieve the first two objectives can only lead to the collapse of the regime either from foreign enemies or from within (ibid.).

Analysing the above from a historical perspective, it is clear that pure ideology never fully determined Soviet foreign policy. In the post-revolutionary period, messianic motives and the desire to exploit the existing opportunities in the outside world in order to develop the Soviet economy, were the prime movers. In the 1940s, during the Great Patriotic war, the question of survival overshadowed any of the other considerations. After the end of the war,

Stalin established on the periphery of the USSR a number of regimes on the Soviet model. He thought that the presence of communist governments would assure the security of the Soviet Union
and would also enhance its economic interests. He also had 'great
power' aspirations, that is, to acquire influence over countries which
were once in the sphere of influence of the Russian Empire. In
the 1950 to 1970s, the 'great power' syndrome took over all other
foreign policy considerations and a struggle with the US for world
hegemony had been waged at the expense of the needs of the people
and solidarity with communist movements (friendship with anti-
American Arab states who were at the same time fierce opponents
of communist ideology). The ambitions of the men in the Kremlin,
says the author, had caused them to neglect the real needs of security.

Despite the huge defence expenditure and superhuman efforts,
the vision of a peaceful world remained unattainable. On the contrary, the greater the number of Soviet missiles installed, the denser
became the circle of enemy rockets around Soviet borders. Under
these circumstances it became impossible to realise the second
objective – that of satisfying the needs of the population. It is not
surprising, therefore, that *perestroika* had to come. Within a short
time, the Soviet Union managed to make peace with the thought
that a third world war was not around the corner, to reduce defence expenditure and to acquire more prestige in the world. The
reduction in defence expenditure and the quest for increased prestige in the world, have not been translated into internal popularity
for the government. Many critical voices blaming the government
for the loss of its East European allies and for allowing the US to
rule over the whole world could be heard. There were also claims
that Russia had lost its superpower status.

A special meeting devoted to Russia's economic security was
convened on 27 January 1997. The question under discussion was:
what are the major criteria that determine the economic security
of a country? (Illarionov, 1997). During the discussions it was stressed
that a link exists between economic security and economic growth.
Anything that contributes to economic growth also contributes to
economic security and meets national interests. Conversely, anything that prevents economic growth undermines economic security and is not in the national interest. There was general agreement
that the main threat to Russia's economic security springs from
the government, at least from today's government.

Another threat to Russia's security was seen in the apparent division of the society – not in the sense of a division into social strata – but in the diversity of opinions voiced by Russian intellectuals (Arbatov, 1994). Such diversity applies not only in matters of domestic policies, but more importantly about Russia's destiny in the post-communist era. Despite the sharp disagreements regarding domestic and foreign policies, there appears to be a consensus of opinion in relation to the strategic objective of national security. For Russia, such an objective is to remain a leading world power in the full meaning of the word, not only as a member of the Security Council with the power of veto. What most Russians would like to see is a country economically, militarily and politically strong enough to be capable of imposing its authority in world affairs as well as able to withstand any outside pressures. With few exceptions, all political movements and parties in Russia agree that this ought to be the main national priority. However, even in this respect there are serious disagreements as to what constitutes national security. For some people in Russia it means a heavy burden while for others it is a noble mission (ibid., p. 5).

In April 1996, President Boris Yeltsin, issued a decree 'On government strategy for economic security of the Russian Federation'. The presidential press-service commented on the decree saying that the government strategy in the area of economic security is an integral part of the concept of Russia's national security. The 'Basic Principles' of the decree contain three major factors: the aspect of internal and external threats to economic security, the criteria of Russia's national interests in the economic area, and the mechanism of economic policy (*Ekonomika i zhizn*, no. 21, May 1996). Among the major threats to Russia's economic security is the high level of impoverishment of the population and the increasing differentiation, deformed structure of the economy, excessive reliance on the fuel-energy sector of the economy, non-competitiveness of many domestic enterprises, decline of production in important branches of the economy, the forcing out of domestically produced goods from the domestic market by imported goods, the increasing socio-economic development gap between various regions and the criminalisation of society and the economy.

Further discussion on the subject of Russia's national interests is contained in a thesis about the future of the post-Soviet political space published by the Council on Foreign and Defence Policy (SVOP). It offers a number of suggestions of what constitutes Russia's national interests (Tezisy, 1996). Among Russia's vital interests is securing freedoms, raising the wellbeing of the population, and the territorial integrity and independence of Russia. Closely linked to the latter is the prevention of domination of foreign powers, especially military and political powers, within the territory of the former USSR, as well as prevention of the formation anywhere in the world of a coalition hostile to Russia while strengthening political, economic and military union with Belarus, Kazakhstan and Kirgizia.

In the economic sphere, Russia's vital interests lie in unhindered access to strategically important resources including transport routes and seaports of former Soviet republics, the consolidation of the position of the Russian national currency on the territory of the former USSR, and reinforcement of the Russian position as an economic and technological leader of the CIS.

Among important national interests, mentioned in the Thesis, is the prevention of breaches of human rights of national minorities, above all Russian minorities in former Union republics, and the retention and enhancing of the position of the Russian language and Russian culture in former republics.

Yeltsin's decree and the Thesis of the Council, both seem to point to a hardening of Russia's attitude toward the outside world. Both place a major emphasis on the retention of Russia's former position as a leader of the former republics. They also indicate the existence of old suspicions about an international conspiracy aimed at weakening Russia's international position. The perception of the outside world as being basically hostile, is connected with the changes that have occurred in the world after the collapse of the Soviet Union. The concept of the new world order, so much promoted by the American president, is seen by the Russians as a move towards a unipolar world instead of the multipolar world order which Russia expected and is still promoting. The new international situation is understood in Russia in terms of the end of the bipolar world – a world in which international politics were determined by the East–West conflict. But, according to many Russians, it would be wrong to assume that with the end of the bipolar world order, the peace process has already been accomplished, and that the world is entering an era of international cooperation. The main difficulty, according to Russian commentators, lies in the fact that the United States is not ready yet to surrender its role as a supreme world leader. The United States has not changed its military doctrine and policy.

Looking at the American perception of the new world order it becomes clear that it is based on the retention and strengthening of the US leading role on the international arena. The objective of US military policy in the 90s is to build up its military power and its military-economic potential, in accordance with a policy which envisages the application of force for the protection of its interests in any region of the world. It is clear that the American approach to international politics is leading to a weakening of Russia's international position and a decline in Russia's world influence' (Politsyn, 1991).

Both questions – Russia's integration in the world economy and her place and role in international affairs – are as relevant as ever. With the demise of a bipolar world order and the emergence of a multipolar world, the question of Russia's place in that new order has assumed increased importance. Most Russian analysts are basically in favour of a multipolar world in which, they assert, America's role as the policeman of the world would be diminished and replaced by the United Nations (Kazennov, 1997).

Surprisingly, some Russian commentators while admitting Russia's diminished role as a world power, advocate the support of a unipolar world under the leadership of the United States. They argue that under such a world order, Russia as America's major partner, would be able to maintain its role in decision-making on the international arena. It is beyond doubt, according to this view, that Russia has a vital interest in a multipolar world, but from a realistic point of view, Russia cannot claim her rightful place because of the growing number of other countries, like China, whose influence in world affairs is increasing at the expense of Russia's. In such a situation, Russia's may become the balancing force between the US and other emerging powers (ibid.).


HOW RUSSIA PERCEIVES THE WEST

In the final analysis, the newly emerging East–West conflict is no longer an ideological confrontation, but a question of mutual perceptions. On the American side, there is a growing impression that Russia's imperial aspirations have not disappeared despite the end of the Cold War. Those promoting this point of view could be justified by referring to Russia's present search for an idea that would unite the nation. The suggestion of a new Russian idea invariably includes Russia's retention of her place in world affairs, and this already indicates a confrontational attitude toward the outside world.

Such perceptions are mirrored in Russia in relation to the West in general and the United States in particular. Indicative of the Russian attitude is a draft of a paper entitled 'The perception abroad of Russia and of Russian business' proposed for the Programme of the Council on Foreign and Defence Policy – 'Russia and the World' – and published in a Moscow daily. The final version of the paper will be distributed in Russia and abroad, especially among foreign business circles and the mass media (*Nezavisimaya gazeta*, 3 July 1997).

The paper points to the emergence of a number of difficulties in the relations between Russia and the West despite significant progress in the economic and other areas, especially since the end of 1994. 'It was a normal process of transition from romantic illusions, linked to the end of the Cold War, to cooperation based on pragmatism' (ibid.). The difficulties in mutual relations are connected with the normalisation of the situation in Russia. This has brought out the question of Russia's national interests that conflict with those of the West. Another reason for the difficulties is the retention in both societies of ideological stereotypes and views whose sources can be found in the Cold War. Russia's integration into the world community of nations, therefore, is dependent on the overcoming of mutual misunderstandings between Russia and the West. According to the paper, today as in the past, Russia's image in the Western mass media is generally negative. Russia is perceived as a challenge or even a threat to stability in Europe and in the world. The main criticism of Russia in the Western press is that Russia's democracy does not conform to Western standards. Russia is still far from being a Western-type model of a market economy with appropriate legislation, an attractive taxation system, and developed infrastructure. A further criticism of Russia is the integrationist trend which the West considers as a renewal of Russia's imperial ambitions (ibid.). The emergence of old stereotypes of Russia as a threat to the West, is gaining increased credence in the West. The stereotype of a 'military threat of a new kind' is also gaining recognition. Although, President Clinton has never named Russia as the possible threat to US national security, his foreign policy toward Russia has some features of the earlier conflict during the Cold War.

An additional threat to European security is the perceived danger of the disintegration of Russia, similar to what occurred in Yugoslavia. The announcement of the latter danger, according to the paper, is to make public opinion in the West used to the idea that in case of such an event, the West would be justified in protecting its interests in Russia by any available means. Such a perception smacks of the kind of intervention the West applied following the Bolshevik revolution.

Russia is characterised in the West as a corrupt society ruled by crime. According to this perception it is assumed that crime will be exported from Russia and that in Russia itself this process is enhanced by individuals placed at the Russian government level. At the same time, however, Western criminal elements are penetrating Russia and the West does nothing to prevent it.

Another argument against Russian integration is that Russia is unable to implement reforms without Western assistance, which imposes on the West the obligation of controlling the activities of the Russian administration. This is particularly noticeable in the stance of the IMF, which demands the implementation of a number of IMF rules.

The worst feature of the Western attitude toward Russia is that some elements in the West are exploiting these arguments in an attempt to change the political balance of internal forces in Russia. In this respect they have the support of some Russian politicians. The paper does not suggest that the 'information offensive' on Russia is caused by the activities of some ill-intentioned forces. It is a logical result of Western financial and economic business interests acting within the context of world competition. In the near future, such an 'information offensive' will become stronger as the political and economic situation in Russia stabilises, a situation which will directly conflict with the interests of her foreign partners who see Russia as a potential competitor (ibid.)

The paper recognises Russia's partial responsibility for this state of affairs. Among the contributing factors are political instability, the impoverishment of a large segment of the population, which prevents the implementation of reforms, and the low level of commercial culture among Russian businessmen. In conclusion, it suggests that Russia is making a serious effort to improve its image in the world. 'Russia must not close its eyes to the fact that a campaign aimed at discrediting Russian business and Russia in general is being waged in the West' (ibid.).

## COLD PEACE OR COLD WAR?

A close scrutiny of the various political ideas being advanced in Russia today indicates a divergence of views about the solutions to Russia's economic difficulties and political problems. The pressures being exercised upon the Russian President to force him to implement further economic reforms are counterbalanced by former communists who would like a return to the old system. The way the government responds to such pressures is also clear evidence of the confusion and uncertainty which pervades the Russian leadership, including Boris Yeltsin. There is one area, however, in which there appears to be almost a consensus of opinion – that is, the role and place of Russia on the international arena. In this respect, Yeltsin seems to be determined to meet the demands of the Russian majority for a more resolute Russian foreign policy. It was the United States that provided Yeltsin with an issue on which he could count on general support – NATO's expansion to the East.

The question of Russia's place in world politics assumed increased importance in connection with NATO's plans. After four years of debate and consultations the Madrid summit has finally decided on NATO's expansion. This decision has shifted the relationship between Russia and NATO onto a different level in the form of Russia–NATO Council. According to one Russian commentator, the Russia–NATO Council, which began functioning after the Madrid summit, may be considered as an embryo of a peaceful European order, and it is up to Russia to exploit this instrument with its huge possibilities. The Russia–NATO Council offers Russia for the first time the possibility to exert its influence in its relations with the alliance. The normalisation of mutual relations between Russia and NATO will provide the possibility of concentrating on the main problem of Russia's foreign policy – Russia in Europe (Maksimychev, 1997).

A contrasting view was presented by Aleksei Pushkov, a member of the Russian Council on Foreign and Defence Policy. He criticised some American circles that are attempting to transform the Council into an ineffectual organ that will not be able to solve any serious problems (Pushkov, 1997). For the time being, the alliance in Brussels adopted an ambiguous position, according to Pushkov. On the one hand it underlined the importance of Russia's participation in the activities of the alliance, on the other, it insisted on restricting the competence of the Council. On the question that directly affects Russia's security – the acceptance into NATO of the Baltic states – it maintains that it is beyond the scope of mutual consultations. In this way, according to Pushkov, Russia begins its cooperation with NATO under restricted possibilities of participation in European affairs.

There is a widespread perception in Russia that the West is applying Western concepts for transforming Russia. Added to this view is a realisation of the ineffectiveness of Western material support of economic reforms, as well as the clash with Western competition on international export markets. It was these factors that made Yeltsin and Kozyrev vulnerable to criticism by those who were against Russia's reliance on Western models and considered the policy historically naive.

The revision of Russia's foreign policy is still an ongoing process and depends to a great degree on the response of the outside world to the changes taking place in Russia. Some Russians define the present situation by the old name of Cold War or by a more benign definition of 'Cold Peace'. Seen from the Russian perspective, the United States is pursuing a policy geared at the denigration of Russia's image and the domination of the United States in the political, economic and military areas. This was clearly expressed by the Russian foreign minister Primakov, when he said that 'the inertia of former political thinking is still in evidence. The stereotypes that became entrenched during the 40 years of the Cold War in the minds of Western political leaders have not yet disappeared despite the dismantling of strategic missiles and the destruction of thousands of tanks' (Primakov, 1996).

Primakov saw the new world order as being composed of 'leaders' and those that are 'led'. This mentality, he said, is being fed by the illusion that in the Cold War some countries have been victorious while others have been defeated. Such a mentality indirectly encourages a trend to create a 'unipolar world' (ibid., p. 3). Primakov accused the United states of exploiting its economic and military power to attain its political objectives. As an example he quoted the Helms–Berton law which punishes those who economically cooperate with Cuba. Similar pressure against Iran's and Libya's trading partners resulted in attempts to continue intensification of the economic blockade. Since the end of the Cold War, some of the discriminatory trade restrictions are still in force and Russia is still included among developing countries. Under the pretext of 'non-market status' of the Russian economy, the West is applying anti-dumping measures to Russian exports (ibid., p. 5).

## CONCLUSION

Russia's view of the outside world and consequently her foreign policy, is still influenced by the old debate about Russia's place on the world stage. But Russia's foreign policy, in contrast to the communist period, is subject to a multitude of internal and external forces which exert pressures upon the government and are also influencing public opinion.

On the domestic front the most important determining factor is the economic situation which forces the government to undertake various measures – mainly by decree – to alleviate the present difficulties. The government in its attempts to reform the economy is under pressure from various groups that are trying to protect their interests. Among such groups are the military establishment, which puts claims on resources, the industrial lobby demanding protection from imports, trading organisations lobbying for reduced tariffs, and various financial interests lobbying for liberalisation or restrictions of foreign financial relation rules.

Another factor in the formulation of Russia's foreign policy is the Russian parliament – the Duma – which is composed of various political groups, but is dominated by former communists and their allies the extreme nationalists. Their influence upon Russia's policy is also indirectly connected with public opinion through which they try to exert pressure on the government to adopt a more radical position on the question of Russia's national security.

This latter question is of particular importance because of the prevailing belief in Russia's role as a world power. An important factor in that regard, one that has always played a significant role in Russia's attitudes to the outside world, is the mistrust shown it and a perception of aggressive intentions toward it. Such a perception which was a feature in Russia's foreign policy under the tsars and later under the communist rule, is still discernible in present-day Russia.

This perception takes the form of objections to the policies of international financial organisations. Such institutions as the World Bank, International Monetary Fund and the European Bank for Reconstruction and Development, are perceived as applying pressure on Russia to adopt economic policies that would conform to the rules established by them, but which are perceived as being against Russia's national interests.

Such perceptions have implications for US foreign policy. The

United States needs to maintain an approach that can adjust to important problems raised by a major nation in transition. As an outsider viewing this process, said one American analyst, the United States should be careful not to examine the situation in Russia through the prism of Western conceptions.

Russia's relation with the world is conditioned not only by what is happening outside her borders, but to a large extent by the attitude of Russian society on the question of Russian identity and Russia's role on the world stage. By contrast, America's attitude toward Russia is determined to a large degree by what is happening in Russia. American politicians look upon Russia from mostly economic and political perspectives. The important question of the state of Russian society and its perception of Russia's destiny as a factor of Russia's attitude to the world is largely overlooked. The question 'quo vadis Russia?' can only be answered if the West takes into consideration the entire complex of internal factors, including the peculiarity of the Russian character and the strong influence of Russia's past.

NATO's expansion to the East seems to point to the contrary. The United States' insistence on the expansion without offering a valid reason for it, is perceived in Russia as a threat to its security and reinforces the old beliefs. Reading the Russian press one cannot fail to notice that the opposition to NATO's expansion is almost universal. It is seen in Russia not only as a factor that may affect Russia's national security, but as a more fundamental question which often arises in Russian foreign policy debates of whether Russia needs a unique path of development and consequently a special role in the world, or by adopting internationally accepted (Western) values, should join the world community of nations and follow the path of development of Western countries. This question revolves around the traditional debate which has lasted for almost two centuries – is Russia predominantly part of the European culture, or being a Euro-Asian country, should she lean toward the East, Asia, or perhaps become a blend of European and Asian cultures and traditions (Popov, 1994). The outcome of this debate may determine the state of international relations and the stability of the European continent.

# References

Aboltin, V. (1968) *Sotsialisticheskaya revolutsia i sovremennyi kapitalism* (Moscow).

Aeab-Ogly, E. (1988) 'Realnost novogo myshlenia', *Kommunist*, no. 2 (January).

Aksenov, A. (1993) 'Reformy ili anty-reformy?' *Ekonomika i zhizn*, no. 10 (March).

Albright, M. (1997) 'Albright on NATO at Senate Armed Services Committee', US Information Service (23 April).

Aleksin, V. and E. Sheveliev (1996) 'VMF v obespechenii natsionalnoi bezopasnosti Rossii', *Nezavisimaya gazeta* (24 October).

Arbatov, A. (1994) 'Rossiya: natsionalnaya bezopasnost v 90-e gody', *Mirovaya ekonomika i mezhdunarodnye otnosheniya*, No. 7.

Arbatov, G. (1973) *The War of Ideas in Contemporary International Relations* (Moscow: Progress Publishers).

Backgrounder (1990) 'U.S.–Soviet relations', United States Information Service (9 April).

Backgrounder (1991) 'U.S.–Soviet Relations Experiencing a Difficult Period', United States Information Service (5 March).

Barghoorn, F. C. (1956) *Soviet Russian Nationalism* (New York: Oxford University Press).

Bazhanov, E. (1991) 'V chem zhe nashi gosudarstvennyie interesy', *Izvestia* (12 April).

Belotserkovskii, V. (1997) 'Sovmestimaya Rossiya s kapitalizmom?', *Nezavisimaya gazeta* (14 August).

Berdyayev, N. (1948) *The Origin of Russian Communism* (London: Geoffrey Bles).

Berdyayev, N. (1946) *Russkaya ideia* (Paris: YMCA Press).

Blinov, N., Kokarev, M. and Krashennikov, V. (1996) 'Ob obespechenii ekonomicheskoi bezopasnosti Rossii', *Ekonomist*, no. 4 (March).

Bogaturov, A. D. and V. A. Kremenyuk, V. A. (1996) 'Tekushchie otnosheniya i perspektivy vzaimodeistviya Rossii i SShA', *Nezavisimaya gazeta* (29 June).

Bovin, A. (1991) 'Posle krizisa', *Izvestia* (12 March).

Bovin, A. (1991) 'Dumat' o svoikh interesakh', *Izvestia* (2 October).

Brzezinski, Z. K. (1967) *Ideology and Power in Soviet Politics* (New York: Frederick A. Praeger).

Brzezinski, Z. K. (1973) *Between Two Ages: America's Role in the Technotronic Era* (New York: The Viking Press).

Bykov, O. (1990) 'Kontseptsiya mirnogo sushchestvovaniya v svete novogo myshleniya', *Mirovaya ekonomika i mezhdunarodnye otnosheniya*, no. 2.

Caldwell, D. (1985) 'U.S.–Soviet Political Relations: A Regional Assessment, *AEI Foreign Policy and Defence Review*.

Carrère d'Encausse, H. (1990) *La gloire des nations ou la fin de l'Empire soviétique* (Paris: Fayard).

Chistyakov, A. (1994) 'Changes in the Middle East and the Outside World', *International Affairs*, no. 5 (Moscow).

Claudin, F. (1975) *The Communist Movement, from Comintern to Cominform* (London: Penguin Books).

Codevilla, A. M. (1988) 'Is There Still a Soviet Threat?', *Commentary* (November).

Cohen, A. (1997) 'A New Paradigm for U.S.–Russia Relations: Facing the Post-Cold War Reality', The Heritage Foundation (Washington, DC) Backgrounder No. 1105 (6 March).

Cooper, Leo (1989) *The Political Economy of Soviet Military Power* (London: Macmillan).

Dallin, A. and G. W. Lapidus, (eds) (1995) *The Soviet System: From Crisis to Collapse* (Boulder: Westview Press).

Degras, J. (ed.) *Soviet Documents on Foreign Policy* (Oxford: Royal Institute of International Affairs).

Degras, J. (1971) *The Communist International, 1919–1943 Documents* (London: Frank Cass & Co.).

Evstafiev, D. (1996) *Nezavisimaya gazeta* (14 November)

Fedotova, V. (1997) 'Vozmozhna li modernizatsiya bez rusofobii?', *Nezavisimaya gazeta* (16 January).

Filatov, V. and Fateev, S. (1997) 'Mify liberalnoi ekonomiki', *Nezavisimaya gazeta* (16 January).

Galbraith, J. K. (1990) 'Which Capitalism for Eastern Europe?', *Harper's Magazine* (April).

Georgiev, V. (1997) 'Finansovyi krizis v armii', *Nezavisimaya gazeta* (31 January).

Gill, G. (1996) 'Whither Russian Democracy?' in *In Search of Identity – Five Years since the Fall of the Soviet Union* (Melbourne: Centre for Russian and Euro-Asian Studies, University of Melbourne).

Gizatov K. (1989) 'Protivorechiya i ikh proyavlenie v natsionalnoi psikhologii', *Kommunist*, no. 11 (July).

Gorbachev, M. S. (1987) *October and Perestroika: the Revolution Continues* (Moscow: Novosti Press Agency).

Gorbachev, M. S. (1988) *Perestroika i novoe myshlenie* (Moscow: Politizdat).

Gorbachev, M. (1996) 'Slova i dela', *Nezavisimaya gazeta* (23 November).

Gornostaev, D. (1997) 'Poyavilas li u Rossii novaya vneshnaya politika', *Nezavisimaya gazeta* (9 January).

Gornostaev, D. (1997) 'Moskva i Vashington pered novym krizisom', *Nezavisimaya gazeta* (15 January).

Graebner, N. A., (ed.) (1963) *The Cold War: Ideological Conflict or Power Struggle?* (Lexington, MA: D.C. Heath & Co.).

Grigoriev, S. (1996) 'Novyi strategicheskii kurs Rossii na zapadnom napravlenii', *Nezavisimaya gazeta* (13 January).

Gruber, H. (1974) *Soviet Russia Masters the Comintern* (New York: Anchor Press).

Gudkov, E. (1991) 'Te li garantii?', *Krasnaya zvezda* (20 February).

Gundarov, I. (1996) 'Uspekhy razvitiya feodalizma v Rossii', *Nezavisimaya gazeta* (22 November).

Gwertzman, B. (1980) 'Reagan Favours Linking Arms Talks to Soviet Behaviour around the World', *New York Times*, 7 November.

Hill, C. (1972) *Lenin and the Russian Revolution* (London: The English University Press).

Hodnett, G. (ed.) (1974) *Resolutions and Decisions of the Communist Party of the Soviet Union* (Toronto: University of Toronto Press).

Holloway, D. (1990) 'State, Society, and the Military under Gorbachev', *International Security*, Vol. 14, no. 3.

Horelick, A. L. (1990) 'U.S.–Soviet Relations: Threshold of a New Era', *Foreign Affairs*, Vol. 69, no. 1.

Hough, J. F., Evelyn Davidheiser, E. and Goodrich Lehmann, S. (1996) *The 1996 Russian Presidential Election* (Washington, DC: Brookings Institution Press).

Ikhlov, E. (1996) 'Pobedit li islamski mir?', *Nezavisimaya gazeta* (14 November).

Illarionov, A. (1997) 'Ekonomicheskaya bezopasnost i natsionalnye interesy', *Izvestia* (22 January).

ITAR-TASS (1997) 'God Evgeniya Primakova', *Rossiiskaya gazeta* (10 January).

Kagarlitskii, B. (1997) 'Pyat let v poiskakh rukovodyashchei idei', *Nezavisimaya gazeta* (29 January).

Kampelman, M. M. (1985) 'Can the US and the Soviet Union Coexist?' *USA Today* (March).

Karpov, M. (1996) 'Chernomyrdin addresses the Lisbon Forum', *Nezavisimaya gazeta* (3 December).

Kasaev, A. (1996) 'Rossiya povorachivaetsya litsom k vostoku', *Nezavisimaya gazeta* (31 January).

Kazennov, S. and Kumachev, V. (1997) 'Epokha razrusheniya bipolarnogo miroustroistva', *Nezavisimaya gazeta* (10 July).

Kennedy, F. J. (1969) 'Inaugural Address', US Government Printing Office, Washington, DC.

Khrushchev, N. S. (1959) 'On Peaceful Coexistence', *Foreign Affairs* (October).

Kolchin, S. (1995) 'Rossiya–blizhnee zarubezhe: vzaimootnosheniya, interesy, tseli politiki', *Mirovaya ekonomika i mezhdunarodnye otnosheniya*, no. 4 (April).

*Kommunisticheskaya Partia Sovetskovo Soyuza v rezolutsiyakh i resheniyakh* (1953) (Moscow).

Kondrashev, S. (1996) 'Otnosheniya s Kitaem – srednesrochnyi optimizm', *Izvestia* (22 November).

Korolev, S. (1991) 'Potoropilis' bombovym udarom', *Rabochaya tribuna* (29 January).

Korotchenko, I. (1996) 'Protses voennoi integratsii v SNG nabirayet silu', *Nezavisimaya gazeta, independent military review* (13 January).

Korotchenko, I. (1996) 'Igor Rodionov vystupil za sozdanie oboronnogo soyuza', *Nezavisimaya gazeta* (26 December).

Kortunov, S. (1990) *Kommunist*, no. 12 (August)

Koshkareva, T. (1996) 'Vlast sformirovala dvukhpartyinuyu sistemu', *Nezavisimaya gazeta* (28 November).

Kosolapov, N. (1993) 'Rossiya: samosoznanie obshchestva i vneshnaya politika', *Mirovaya ekonomika i mezhdunarodnyie otnosheniya*, no. 5.

Kosovalov, N. (1994) *Mirovaya ekonomika i mezhdunarodnye otnosheniya*, no. 1.

Kramer, M. (1989) 'Soviet Military Policy', *Current History* (October).

Kubalkova, V. and A. A. Cruickshank, (1980) 'Detente: not with Hindsight', *Australian Outlook*, Vol. 34 no. 2 (August).

Kulagin, V. (1996) 'The Eastern Sector of Russia's Foreign Policy', *International Affairs*, no. 7.

Kulikov, V. G. (1990) 'Organizatsiya Varshavskogo Dogovora: proshloe, nastoyashchee, budushchee', *Mirovaya ekonomika i mezhdunarodnyie otnosheniya*, no. 3.

Kulski, W. W. (1973) *The Soviet Union in World Affairs* (Syracuse, NY: Syracuse University Press).

Kutkovets, T. and Igor Klyamkin, I. (1997) 'Russkie idei', *Nezavisimaya gazeta* (16 January).

Kuzmichev, V. and Narzikulov, R. (1997) Vneshnetorgovoi oborot Rossii vnov uvelichilsya', *Nezavisimaya gazeta* (14 January).

Lazarev, A. (1991) 'SSSR–Yaponiya: vremya novykh podkhodov', *Krasnaya zvezda* (2 April).

Lebed, A. (1996) 'Address to the North Atlantic Alliance in Brussels on 7 October 1996', *Nezavisimaya gazeta* (16 October).

Lebedev, N. I. (1978) *A New Stage in International Relations* (Oxford: Pergamon Press).

Lenin, V. I. *What is to be Done?* (Moscow).

Lenin, V. I. (1965) *Collected Works*, Vol. 28 (Moscow).

Levit, S. Ya. (1990) *Ekologiya kultury* (Moscow: Akademia nauk SSSR).

Lynch, A. (1990) 'Does Gorbachev Matter Anymore?', *Foreign Affairs*, Vol. 69, no. 3.

Maksimova, M. (1992) 'Ot imperskovo soyuza k sodruzhestvu nezavisimykh gosudarstv', *Mirovaya ekonomika i mezhdunarodnye otnosheniya*, no. 4 (April).

Maksimychev, I. (1996) 'Sovmestima li "bolshaya NATO" s bolshoi Evropoi?', *Nezavisimaya gazeta* (15 October).

Maksimychev, I. (1997) 'Bolshaya Evropa dolzhna stat' konkretnoi tselyu', *Nezavisimaya gazeta* (31 July).

McDaniel, T. (1996) *The Agony of the Russian Idea* (Princeton, NJ: Princeton University Press).

Miko, F. T. (1990) 'The New Eastern Europe and U.S. Policy', *CRS Review* (March–April).

Mirskii, G. (1996) 'Who destroyed the USSR?' *Nezavisimaya gazeta* (23 November).

Mitrofanov, S. (1996) 'Nuzhna li nam russkaya ideya?', *Nezavisimaya gazeta* (18 October).

Morgentau, H. J. (1973) *Politics among Nations* (New York: Knopf).

Narzikulov, R. (1996) '1996: Smutnoe vremiya v ekonomike', *Nezavisimaya gazeta* (31 December).

Neverov, V. and Igolkin, A. (1992) 'Russkaya neft i mirovaya politika', *Ekonomika i zhizn*, no. 41 (October).

Ogarkov, N. (1981) 'Na strazhe mirnogo truda', *Kommunist*, no. 10 (July).

Ogarkov, N. (1985) *History Teaches Vigilance* (Moscow).

Olshanskii, D., (1989) *Voprosy filosofii*, no. 8.

Onikov, L. (1996) 'Gosudarstvu nuzhna vnutriapparatnaya demokratiya', *Nezavisimaya gazeta* (26 November).

Orlov, S. and M. Kolpakov (1990) 'Po-prezhnemu zapugivayut', *Krasnaya zvezda* (1 March).

Osipov, G. *et al.* (1996) *Reformirovanie Rossii: mify i realnost'* (Moscow).

Oznobishchev, S. (1997) 'Russia and NATO: the Coming of a Previously-announced Crisis', *Prism*, Vol III, The Jamestown Foundation (February).

Patersen, P. A. and N. Trulock III (1988) 'A "New" Soviet Military Doctrine: Origins and Implications', *Strategic Review* (Summer).

Pechenev, V. (1996) 'Rossiiskaya vneshnaya politika po otnosheniyu k stranam SNG i Baltii', *Nezavisimaya gazeta* (22 November).

Pentony, E (ed.) (1962) *Soviet Behaviour in World Affairs* (San Francisco: Chandler Publishing Co.).

Petrov, V. (1997) 'Stanet li realnostyu voennaya reforma?', *Nezavisimaya gazeta* (3 September).

Pinder, J. and Pinder, P. (1976) 'West European Economic Relations with the Soviet Union', in Pipes, R. (ed.), *Soviet Strategy in Europe* (New York: Crane, Cussack).

Pipes, R. (1981) *U.S.–Soviet Relations in the Era of Detente* (Boulder, CO: Westview Press).

Pipes, R. (1984) 'Can the Soviet Union Reform?', *Foreign Affairs* (Fall).

Pisar, S. (1970) *Coexistence and Commerce* (New York: McGraw-Hill).

Pismennaya, E. (1997) 'Dostizhenie ustoichivogo rosta ekonomiki zaplanirovano na konets stoletiya', *Finansovye izvestia* (23 January).

Ploss, S. I. (1986) 'A New Soviet Era?', *Foreign Policy* (Spring).

Plyais, Y. (1997) 'U kazhdoi tsivilizatsii – svoi put' razvitiya', *Nezavisimaya gazeta* (16 November).

Pogorelyi, M. (1991) 'Chto pokazala voina', *Krasnaya zvezda* (8 March).

Politsyn, A. and Linkevich, V. (1991) 'Novyi mirovoi poryadok', *Krasnaya zvezda* (18 June).

Popov, N. (1994) 'Vneshnaya politika Rossii', *Mezhdunarodnaya ekonomika i mezhdunarodnye otnosheniya*, no. 3.

Popov, V. (1997) 'Zakon mentalnoi identichnosti – pochemu reformy v Rossii terpyat porazhenie?', *Nezavisimaya gazeta* (14 August).

Portanskii, A. (1997) 'Zapad obespokoen sostoyaniem rossiiskikh reform', *Finansovye izvestia* (29 April).

Potapov, V. (1990) 'Kak sokhranit' Soyuz?', *Ekonomika i zhizn*, no. 47 (November).

Primakov, Y. (1996) 'Mezhdunarodnye otnosheniya nakanune XXI veka: problemy, perspektivy', *Mezhdunarodnaya zhizn*, no. 10 (October).

Prism, (1997) Vol. III, no. 8, The Jamestown Foundation (30 May).

Pugachev, B. (1990) 'Rossiya-tsentr: vozmozhen li "brak po lyubvi"?', *Izvestia* (4 December).

Pushkov, A. (1996) 'Virus porazhenstva i evropeiskaya politika Rossii', *Nezavisimaya gazeta* (10 December).

Pushkov, A. (1997) 'Ni mira ni voiny v otnosheniyakh s alyansom', *Nezavisimaya gazeta* (17 January).

Pushkov, A. (1997) 'Rossiya–NATO: Sovet, no poka ne lyubov', *Rossiiskaya gazeta* (13 August).

Rats, M. (1996) 'Belye i Krasnye', *Nezavisimaya gazeta* (8 October).
Reshetar, J.S. Jr. (1974) *The Soviet Polity* (New York: Dodd, Mead & Co.).
Rodionov, I. (1997) 'Prezident podpisyvaet vse novye ukazy po voennoi reforme', *Nezavisimaya gazeta* (18 July).
Rogov, S. (1996) 'Russia and the U.S.: A Partnership or Another Disengagement', *International Affairs*, no. 7 (Moscow).
Rostow, W. W. (1967) *The Dynamics of Soviet Society* (New York: W. W. Norton).
Rumyantsev, O. (1993) 'Demokratizatsiya i vnutrennaya politika', *Rossiiskaya gazeta* (13 March).
Rybakov, O. (1996) 'Pervoe pyatiletie SNG', *Mezhdunarodnaya zhizn*, no. 9 (September).
Rybkin, I. (1995) 'The State Duma and Russia's External Interests', *International Affairs*, nos. 11–12 (Moscow).
Sagalovskii, Y. (1996) 'Bolshe khramov, khoroshikh i raznykh', *Nezavisimaya gazeta* (19 November).
Sakharov, A. N. (1996) 'Rossiiskoe gosudarstvo i zakony historii', *Nezavisimaya gazeta* (11 June).
Sergeev, I. (1997) 'Voennykh ugroz dlya Rossii ne prosmatrivaetsya', *Rossiiskaya gazeta* (12 August).
Shapoval, S. (1996) 'Sovetskii Soyuz byl ubit informatsionnym virusom anti-SSSR', *Nezavisimaya gazeta* (10 December).
Shenfeld, S. D. (1994) 'Post-Soviet Russia in Search of Identity' in Blum, D.W., *Russia's Future – Consolidation or Disintegration?* (Boulder, CO: Westview Press).
Shokhin, A. (1996) 'Rossiya priznatelna Zapadu za podderzhku reform', *Finansovye izvestiya* (5 November).
Sloan, S. R., (1990) 'NATO and the Warsaw Pact: Do They Have a Future?', *CRS Review* (March–April).
Sokolovskii, V. D. (ed.) (1963) *Military Strategy, Soviet Doctrine and Concepts* (New York: Praeger).
Soloviev, V. (1996) 'Vtoraya voennaya doktrina', *Nezavisimaya gazeta* (6 November).
Solzhenitsyn, A. I. (1978) *A World Split Apart* (New York: Harper & Row).
Stalin, J. V. (1967) *Sochinenia*, Vol. XV (Stanford: Hoover Institution).
Szamuely, T. (1974) *The Russian Tradition* (London: Secker & Warburg).
Talbott, S. (1996) 'Amerika i Rossiya v menyayushchimsya mire', *Nezavisimaya gazeta* (27 November).
TASS, (1986), 'Podkhlestyvaya gonku vooruzhenii', *Pravda* (28 February).
TASS (1991) 'Speech by Gorbachev on the First All-Army Party Conference', *Izvestia* (1 April).
Tezisy Sovieta po vneshnei i oboronnoi politike (1996) 'Budushchee postsovetskogo prostranstva, vozroditsiya li Soyuz?', *Nezavisimaya gazeta* (23 May).
Timmerman, Ch. (1994) 'Vneshnaya politika Rossii: poiski novoi identichnosti', *Mirovaya ekonomika i mezhdunarodnye otnosheniya*, no. 2 (February).
Trofimenko, G. (1990) 'Soedinionnyie Shtaty i my', *Kommunist*, no. 18 (December).

Ulan, A. B. (1976) *Ideologies and Illusions* (Cambridge: Harvard University Press).

Vartanyan, A. (1996) 'Rossiya, SShA i printsipy politicheskogo realizma', *Nezavisimaya gazeta* (9 July).

Vasilchuk, E. (1996) 'Prizraki "kholodnovo mira" vnov poyavlyayutsiya na gorizonte', *Finansovye izvestia* (4 May).

Vasilchuk, E. (1997) 'Ekonomika zabludilas v poiskach dukha soglasiya', *Finansovye izvestia* (18 February).

Vasiliev, A. (1991) 'Kem i kak opredelyalas' pozitsiya Sovetskogo Soyuza v konflikte mezhdu Irakom i Kuveitom', *Komsomolskaya pravda* (16 February).

Vasiliev, G. (1989) 'Pochemu oni pritormazhivayut', *Pravda* (9 September), p. 4.

Vasiliev, G. (1990) 'Ruka, szhataya v kulak', *Krasnaya zvezda* (28 March), p. 3.

Vorobev, P. (1991) 'Poprobuem razobratsya', *Trud* (11 April).

'Z' (1990) 'To the Stalin Mausoleum', *Daedalus* (Winter).

Zagorodnikov, A. (1996) 'Natsionalnaya ideya ili ideya natsii?', *Nezavisimaya gazeta* (19 October).

Zamyatin, L. M. (1985) *Ideologischeskaya borba i voprosy mira* (Moscow: Novosti).

Zheglov, M. (1991) 'Varshavskii Dogovor i bezopasnost Evropy', *Krasnaya zvezda* (22 February).

# Index